PROVENWIVES™

Devotional
A Roadmap to Restoration

Foreword by: Shaunti Feldhahn

Brianna Edwards

TABLE OF CONTENTS

T hank you for picking up this study! It is a labor of love that we are confident will direct you to the heart of God as He heals and revives the things in your life that are broken and dead. When exploring artwork for the cover, we were inspired by how perfectly the flowering cactus represents our hope for our readers. The cactus survives, even thrives, in the desert where many other plants do not. Its flower is a beautifully delicate representation of its potential and its spikes stand in stark contrast with the fierce capacity to preserve and protect. We are praying for every set of hands that picks up this book—may Jesus use it to ignite great purpose to preserve and protect your marriage and teach you that it is more than possible for you to thrive and produce beauty even in the desert.

FOREWORD

"Love is the greatest gift each of us can offer." (page 79)

His struggles become ours, don't they? We love the man in our life so much—and yet our heart may be deeply bruised or broken; collateral damage in his battle with sexual temptation. Or we watch our husband tearfully wrestling to overcome a visual pattern that began in middle school, and we feel compassion even as we feel confused about why the struggle even *exists*. Or maybe we deal with intense anger or betrayal after uncovering an addiction he had hidden for years.

Does any of this sound like your story? If so, there is hope.

Mother Teresa once said, "We can do no great things; only small things with great love." And by picking up this book and study, you are taking the first step on a journey to showing your husband—and yourself—great love and healing.

Some of you simply want to know how you can support a man who struggles occasionally. Others need a life-line for a last-gasp effort to save a marriage ripped apart by sexual addiction. Most of you will be somewhere in between. Everyone will have questions, fears, and uncertainties. And the one common denominator for all of us is that every day, we will be looking for ways to help our man change.

Yet there's only one person we can change. And it's not the person lying on the other side of the bed.

Thankfully, after fifteen years of interviewing and surveying thousands of women and men who are dealing with these issues, and hearing from hundreds of specialists and therapists, I can assure you of two things:

First, no matter what the future holds, the efforts you make now to work through your own feelings, patterns, and hurts are incredibly important for *you*. This process is just as much about you as it is about your man. It is so crucial that you take the opportunity to address the pain or concern in your heart.

Second, as you take the courageous step to understand your man's struggles, to think through boundaries, and to work on your own thoughts and actions, you are very likely to see a supernatural, transformative impact on the man in your life. In our research, I have heard literally thousands of such examples.

We serve a God who delights in bringing peace and healing to *all* who are hurting—no matter their part in the story. I love the deliverance pictured in the Psalms.

> Some wandered in desert wastes... their soul fainted within them. Then they cried to the Lord in
> their trouble, and he delivered them from their distress.... For he satisfies the longing soul, and the

hungry soul he fills with good things. Some sat in darkness and in the shadow of death, prisoners in affliction and in irons.... Then they cried to the Lord in their trouble, and he delivered them from their distress. He brought them out of darkness and the shadow of death, and burst their bonds apart.... He sent out his word and healed them (Psalm 107:4-20, ESV).

This path to healing takes great courage and work. It takes prayer and faith. As you begin to heal, you will be asked to extend a love, grace and intimacy to your husband—a grace that some of you simply may not want to give. Yet as you do, you are living out an example and a picture of Christ's sacrificial love for us.

And that grace is a part of the story of restoration.

Your guide on this journey, Brianna Edwards, has walked a similar road with her husband—and now with many other wives. She shares your heartache, but also the great hope of having seen so many marriages restored.

More importantly, as you invite Jesus on this journey, He will be with you. He IS hope. Because He is the One who brings the transformation as you enter into this small thing done with great love.

—Shaunti Feldhahn
Shaunti is a groundbreaking social researcher, and best-selling author of *For Women Only*

INTRODUCTION

This study is long overdue. I have sat across from countless women who have been hurt by the revelation that their husband, fiancé or boyfriend is trapped in sexual sin. I have watched the tears fall as they explain the pain and frustration they are experiencing. Every woman's story is unique, but the feelings are so often the same. It's natural to question love, to feel the insecurity, to doubt, and to be angry.

This study was birthed from the angst of the stories I've heard; stories like yours, stories like mine. On a cold Sunday morning, my husband admitted to having a decade-long struggle with pornography. My world was shattered, and I didn't know where to turn. If I confided in a friend, I felt that I would be throwing my husband "under the bus." I certainly couldn't tell my parents. Where could I go to seek relief for my aching heart?

Eventually, I learned the hard way that no one except Jesus Christ would be able to help restore my broken heart and resurrect our marriage. I searched His Word for answers, for His perspective and His heart about my situation. God was gracious in renewing my hope and joy through years of personal Bible study. Through the process I was finally able to say that my husband's admission to his addiction was one of the best things that ever happened to our marriage.

This study is a culmination of the truths God impressed on my heart as I sought Him, as well as wisdom I received from other godly individuals. These godly resources include three different professional counselors, other wives who understood my struggle and pain, pastors, and many books written by godly men and women. Woven in the following pages you will read personal stories of others who have walked through this journey. My deepest gratitude goes out to each one of these individuals. Without them, my marriage would not be where it is today, and this study would never have been written.

The following pages are filled with portions of Scripture, the only truth that transcends time and has the power to heal and restore. It is a companion study to the *Proven Men* study, written by Joel Hesch. Hopefully your husband will be going through the pages of that study while you are going through this one, but if not, don't be discouraged. God is more than able to heal your heart even if your husband is unwilling to pursue wholeness right now.

Please know that you are not alone. I hope that as you read each day you will feel like you are sitting across the table from a dear friend, sipping coffee and sharing stories. I sat down with a wife just days ago, listening to her broken heart as she shared the pain she felt after learning about her husband's long-term addiction to porn and masturbation. As I left the coffee shop, I realized that I had summarized this entire study during our time together. I wish that I could share that same experience with each one of you. Instead of speaking with you, I'll be speaking to Jesus about you, asking that His Spirit will reveal truth to your heart and that you will experience full and abundant life through Him. It's possible, because I have experienced it, other wives have experienced it, and so can you.

"I have come that they may have **life and** have it to the **full**" (John 10:10).

A little bit about the format of this study:

This study is divided into eight chapters, with five lessons for each chapter. Each day should take you about thirty minutes to complete and includes a key verse and thought at the beginning of each lesson. Don't just do homework, but treat it as "heartwork." God wants to speak to you like He spoke to me and other *Proven Wives*. Open your heart to the Lord and connect with other Proven Wives.

If you are unable to finish the material in one day, don't worry... just pick it up the next day. It's more important that you take your time and carefully read through the study, allowing the Holy Spirit to challenge and encourage your heart. Occasionally there will be additional material in an appendix, or a special assignment to complete over the weekend.

Whether you finish a day or not, stick with this devotional. I promise, if you do this study for the eight weeks, Jesus will do incredible things in healing your heart, and in the process, your relationship.

We used the New International Version of the Bible, unless otherwise noted. I also love the New Living Translation. Feel free to use whatever version is most comfortable for you. My prayer is that this study will be transformational for you and your marriage. Most importantly I pray that it draws you closer to Christ and increases your awareness of His deep love for you. May you be even more like Him eight weeks from now.

SPECIAL NOTE

Our supporters made this resource possible. As you begin this journey and start experiencing breakthroughs and victory, we want you to know that the generous support of faithful men and women like you made this study a reality. It is our vision to provide life-transforming resources to every man and woman who wants to experience lasting victory from the strongholds of pornography and sexual addiction by partnering with local churches to offer our curriculum combined with accountability and ongoing discipleship. As a non-profit organization, our work is not possible without donations from like-minded individuals, companies, and foundations. Therefore, if this study proves to be a blessing to you, we ask that you prayerfully consider blessing others by becoming a ministry partner through your financial support. You can learn more and make your gift at our website: *www. ProvenMen.org* or *www.ProvenWomen.org*

WEEK ONE

THE JOURNEY BEGINS

Philippians 1:6 "He who began a good work in you will carry it on to completion until the day of Christ Jesus."

WEEK 1 DAY 1

KEY THOUGHT: God showers us with His grace and love throughout our life's journey.

Many of you are opening this study hoping to get some immediate relief from a very painful situation. My heart aches for you. I've been there. I'll never forget the moment when my husband shared with me that he was struggling with a pornography addiction. My heart was broken, angry, desperate, despairing, and fearful. I felt betrayed, alone and unsure of where to turn next.

This study is a response to those same cries that are pouring out of your heart right now as you read these words. The pain that comes from sexual addiction is far-reaching. You are not alone.

This study will be a journey. There are no easy answers, no quick fixes. The only way to true healing is through daily submission to God and His power to cleanse, regenerate and restore. We must cling to the promise in Philippians 1:6, "He who began a good work in you will carry it on to completion until the day of Christ Jesus." As my mother gently reminds me when I am consumed with the daily frustrations of life, "It's a process." I love and hate that word, process. It means that there will be a constant struggle. It means that there is no clear end in sight while I still have breath in my lungs and blood pulsing through my veins. It means I must submit my flesh to God's Spirit, which is neither fun nor easy.

But there is grace in the word "process." It means that God knows I won't get it all at once and has patience with me while I trip and fall each day. He knows my limitations and won't give up on me. It means that I get to look back, years later down the road, and reflect on all the moments when God showed up and proved His love and faithfulness. It deepens my appreciation for the victories achieved on the backside of the struggles.

Right now, grace is probably the furthest thing from your mind. I know that was the case for me. You may resent the fact that you are even reading these words, thinking, "Why me? Why us? This is all his fault." You think your husband is undeserving of any grace.

Or maybe you think you are the one who is undeserving. You believe you aren't good enough, pretty enough, smart enough to receive genuine love. That there must be some fault on your part to bring this situation into your life. You don't deserve God's grace.

What about you? Is it harder for you to give grace or receive grace? Why?

_____

_____

_____

_____

_____

The truth is that none of us deserves grace. But God lavishes it on us freely, in spite of our sinfulness. It is God's gift through Jesus Christ to all of mankind (Ephesians 2:8-9, Romans 5:1-2, Romans 5:8).

As you pick up this study today and each day, cry out to God to **change** your heart. Ask Him to prepare your heart for the journey, to give you strength to press on. Ask Him to **soften** your heart, to receive His mercy, grace and compassion, and extend it to those who have wounded you. Ask Him to **heal** your heart, to bind up your wounds and renew your hope.

The best way to begin a journey is to find an ideal guide. Someone who knows the path that lies ahead and will lead you safely to your destination. Fortunately, our Guide not only knows the way, He is the Way. And the Truth. And the Life (John 14:6).

Let's start our first day together asking Him to guide us using two different prayers from Scripture. The first is from the book of Ephesians, written by the apostle Paul to a group of fellow believers that he loved dearly. And it is my prayer, as well as all those contributing to this study, for you as we travel this road together.

READ THE BIBLE

Read Ephesians 1:15-20

I pray for you constantly, asking God... to give you **spiritual wisdom and insight** so that you might **grow in your knowledge of God.** I pray that your **heart will be flooded with light** so that you can **understand the confident hope** he has given to those he called—his holy people who are his rich and glorious inheritance.

WEEK 1

WEEK 2 .... WEEK 3 .... WEEK 4 .... WEEK 5 .... WEEK 6 .... WEEK 7 .... WEEK 8

DAY 1

I also pray that you will **understand the incredible greatness of God's power for us who believe Him.** *This is the same mighty power that raised Christ from the dead.*

On the lines below, write out the bolded words. Take a moment to pray that God will give you each one of these things through His mighty power.

_____

_____

_____

_____

_____

_____

If you are a follower of Christ, you can be filled with hope and power, the same power that rose Jesus from the grave! It dwells in you through the Holy Spirit. God, please open our hearts and flood them with light so we can see these truths and walk in them with confidence!

And now another prayer for you, a beautiful psalm of praise written by David. Read through it silently in your mind first, and as you read, circle the things that you are specifically asking God to bring into your life as you draw closer to Him. Then go back a second time and speak it out loud as a prayer, replacing the pronouns "you" and "your" with "my" and "mine" to make it more personal in the first half.

PSALM 103
Praise the Lord; my soul; all my inmost being, praise his holy name.

Praise the Lord, my soul, and forget not all his benefits—who forgives all your sins and heals all your diseases, who redeems your life from the pit and crowns you with love and compassion, who satisfies your desires with good things so that your youth is renewed like the eagle's.

The Lord works righteousness and justice for all the oppressed. The Lord is compassionate and gracious, slow to anger, abounding in love.

He will not always accuse, nor will he harbor his anger forever; he does not treat us as our sins deserve or repay us according to our iniquities.

For as high as the heavens are above the earth, so great is his love for those who fear him; as far as the east is from the west, so far has he removed our transgressions from us.

As a father has compassion on his children, so the Lord has compassion on those who fear him; for he knows how we are formed, he remembers that we are dust. The life of mortals is like grass, they flourish like a flower of the field; the wind blows over it and it is gone, and its place remembers it no more.

But from everlasting to everlasting the Lord's love is with those who fear him, and his righteousness with their children's children—with those who keep his covenant and remember to obey his precepts. The Lord has established his throne in heaven, and his kingdom rules over all.

Praise the Lord, you his angels, you mighty ones who do his bidding, who obey his word. Praise the Lord, all his heavenly hosts, you his servants who do his will. Praise the Lord, all his works everywhere in his dominion. Praise the Lord, my soul.

We are just starting our journey together, but we are closing for today. We've asked God for His wisdom and insight. We've praised His name. Our hearts are in the correct posture, expectant and waiting for God to answer our prayers. We are looking to Him alone to restore and heal.

HEARTWORK

As we come to the end of today's lesson, I want to ask you to pray one more time. This time, pray for your husband. I know it may be difficult to pray for your husband when you are so angry and hurt, but praying for him is the most powerful thing you can do to usher in change and healing. God wants to bring hope and life to you both. Think of two specific ways you will commit to pray for him, write them down, then spend at least five minutes talking to God about these things.

_____

_____

_____

CHARGE

Brokenness is a devastating reality, but Jesus was broken so that I can be whole and free. I will fight for my marriage.

WHERE DOES IT HURT?

John 10:10 "The thief comes only to steal and kill and destroy; I have come that they may have life and have it to the full."

WEEK 1 DAY 2

KEY THOUGHT: Sexual addiction is a cancer that devastates everything in its reach.

I hate going to the doctor. The entire process is frustrating to me. Waiting on hold to get an appointment, trying to find time to actually be seen, sitting in the waiting room for what seems like an eternity… and that's all before you actually get seen by the doctor. Perhaps even more frustrating is the realization that after you've tried to explain your concerns, the doctor has no real answer for you except "take a few of these and see if it helps." Does he really understand my need? Does he really know what it will take to make me feel better? Will this sickness or pain ever end?

Illness stops us in our tracks and forces us to ask some tough questions so we can find our way back to healthy. Our symptoms are indicators of underlying issues that require diligence and intelligence to diagnose and repair. Likewise, pornography addiction is a big red flag that indicates significant dysfunction going on in the heart and mind of the user.

Early on in my marriage, I knew something was wrong but I couldn't quite figure out what. When I finally learned of my husband's pornography addiction, all of the issues I was concerned about started to make sense. For years I had wondered why my husband felt so far away emotionally. I couldn't understand why he spent long nights awake in the basement instead of coming to bed with me. At times I even felt like there was a stranger in the room having sex with me, like my husband was someone that I didn't know. Sex was supposed to make us feel close, but instead it made me feel alone and confused. Our marriage was sick, infected and painful.

You picked up this devotional because you have been deeply wounded by your significant other's addiction to pornography. Instinctually you know that something is wrong. Think of this first week of study as your doctor's appointment. You need to fully understand what is going on internally with your marriage before you can move on to get wholeness and healing. That will require an honest look at the depths of sexual sin—why it is so devastating to the addict and those surrounding him.

WEEK 1 .... WEEK 2 .... WEEK 3 .... WEEK 4 .... WEEK 5 .... WEEK 6 .... WEEK 7 .... WEEK 8

DAY 2

Years ago, our pastor and his wife sat at our kitchen table on a crisp fall afternoon, present with us in one of the most difficult moments of our marriage. My husband had just admitted that he was struggling with a serious pornography addiction—again. I was devastated by his relapse and felt my world spiraling out of control. In that moment, our pastor gave a poignant description of my husband's struggle that has stuck with me to this day. He compared his pornography addiction to cancer. The disease of sin had attacked his soul and left behind devastation and the lingering smell of death. Like cancer, it quietly and secretly spread like wildfire and had destroyed the health and vitality of his soul. And there we were, in a pivotal moment, unsure of how we could ever find the cure.

In order to stop the devastating consequences of sexual sin, both you and your husband must declare war on it. It requires aggressive treatment. You both must be willing to do the hard work, the heart work. You must go after it with a vengeance, seeking out every deadly cancerous cell. It will come with a cost—your time, energy, and convenience. You will have to face things that are difficult to talk about, things that most of us would just like to disregard, things that we hope will go away on their own. A pornography addiction cannot be ignored, or it will continue to grow and spread its poison, just like cancer. Thankfully, there is a Doctor who has the cure, the "Lord who heals you" (Exodus 15:26).

John 10:10 was a verse that they shared with me soon after my husband's relapse, and it spoke to me many times during the healing process. It's our key verse for today. Read it now and write it out below.

_____

_____

_____

_____

God's desire for us is to experience life, but the enemy's plan is to kill. 1 Peter 5:8 says "your enemy the devil prowls around like a roaring lion looking for someone to devour." Ephesians 6:10 says that he schemes against us. On the lines below, take some time to write out how the enemy, through the temptation of sexual sin, has brought death and destruction to your marriage. Think of this journaling as your time with the Great Physician. What do you long for in that relationship that seems impossible now? What hurts? What is broken? What makes you worried? What makes you want to vomit? He already knows your thoughts and feelings, so don't be afraid to get it all out.

_____

_____

_____

_____

WEEK 1 · · · · · · · · · WEEK 2 · · · · · · · · · WEEK 3 · · · · · · · · · WEEK 4 · · · · · · · · · WEEK 5 · · · · · · · · · WEEK 6 · · · · · · · · · WEEK 7 · · · · · · · · · WEEK 8

DAY 2

_____

_____

_____

_____

_____

_____

_____

_____

_____

_____

_____

_____

As painful as it is for you right now, there is a flicker of hope that you may not be able to see quite yet. Whether you stumbled upon your husband's pornography addiction or he confessed, the secret sin is out in the open. You can begin to deal with it rather than wonder about it. You may not see the way out, but God does. He doesn't want you or your husband to linger in the cancerous death grip of sin. The darkness of sin is no match for His resurrection power.

Open your Bible and read John 1:1-5. Fill in the blanks below:
In Him was _____ and that _____ was the _____ of all mankind. The light shines in the darkness, and the darkness _____.

Jesus has come to bring both life and light! Nothing is impossible for Him! He is able to do "immeasurably more than all we ASK OR IMAGINE, according to HIS POWER that is AT WORK WITHIN US" (Ephesians 3:20-21). Jesus wants to meet you where you are, in the midst of your pain and frustration, to bring you hope and healing.

HEARTWORK

End today by meditating again on some of the verses we studied yesterday. Ask God to bring forgiveness, healing, redemption, love, compassion, satisfaction, and renewal to your marriage. Only He can. Imagine what these things would look like in your marriage. Thank God for where each of these elements are existent, even if only a little. Ask God for help where they're not.

Psalm 103:2-5

Praise the Lord, my soul, and forget not all his benefits—
who forgives all your sins and heals all your diseases,
who redeems your life from the pit and crowns you with love and compassion,
who satisfies your desires with good things so that your youth is renewed like the eagle's.

Take a few moments in the presence of your Healer to both ASK for and IMAGINE forgiveness, healing, redemption and satisfaction in your life. Ask Him to reveal His love and compassion to you in a personal way.

EXTRA

Appendix M, included at the end of this study, is a thorough look into the "why" behind the "what." It's a raw and honest look into why pornography is so harmful to relationships. Perhaps your heart is not quite ready yet. That's OK.

CHARGE

Brokenness is a devastating reality, but Jesus was broken so that I can be whole and free. I will fight for my marriage.

FALSE INTIMACY

Romans 1:24-25 "Therefore God gave them over in the sinful desires of their hearts to sexual impurity for the degrading of their bodies with one another. They exchanged the truth about God for a lie and worshiped and served created things rather than the Creator."

WEEK 1 DAY 3

KEY THOUGHT: Sexually addictive behavior thrives on this false notion: To avoid inevitable relational pain, I must force relational satisfaction.

Yesterday we talked about how sexual sin is like a cancer that kills everything in its path. Today we are going to dig deeper to discover the root of the problem. In order to kill a weed, you have to get all the way down to the root system and remove it, so the weed won't grow back and kill the life-giving plants around it. As a wife, understanding the roots of why your husband/fiancé/boyfriend is addicted to pornography will be crucial as you do battle with the cancer of sexual sin.

If you grew up in the church, you may have felt like sex was "dirty" or even a bad word to say. I can just picture my friends and me whispering and spelling it out behind our hand, "You know, S-E-X." The church's main message regarding sex can be summed up in one word—**don't**. Unfortunately, this approach ignores the fact that sex was created to be a beautiful and unifying GIFT from God. Sex is the vessel God created to bring about new human life. And it can and should be a very physically satisfying experience.

No wonder the enemy wants to take the truth and mix it up with a cocktail of lies. John 10:10 comes to mind again—the very thing that God created to bring life, Satan has ambushed to usher in destruction and death. He has stolen God's original design and masterminded a counterfeit: FALSE INTIMACY.

Harry Schaumburg gives an insightful glimpse into this concept in his book, *False Intimacy*, by outlining three different types of intimacy:

Perfect intimacy: This refers to the pre-fallen relationship Adam and Eve shared. Naked and unashamed, they joined sexually and relationally with the fullest of pleasure, without hesitation or a hint of self-doubt.

Read Mark 10:6-9. Write down the phrases that indicate the perfect intimacy Adam and Eve experienced in the Garden of Eden.

_____

_____

_____

_____

_____

_____

Unfortunately, when Adam and Eve sinned, the opportunity for perfect intimacy on earth was lost. The best case scenario for us now is real intimacy.

Real Intimacy: This is the sexual and relational intimacy two spouses share within their committed, loving marriage. Self-doubts exist, but the couple communicates together and enjoys each other relationally and sexually. Given the reality of a world of imperfect relationships, both partners face disappointments. Within the enjoyment of real intimacy, both partners experience fear of being exposed, fear of abandonment, fear of loss of control, and fear of their respective sexual desires. In their sexual expression, both are dependent on and open to what the other spouse will do.

This idea of real intimacy is what many of us long for within marriage. We recognize that there will be struggles along the way due to our sinful nature and life's circumstances, but we dream of a loving emotional and physical connection with our spouse. It's the stuff that draws women to romantic movies… love conquers all. We even make mention of it during our wedding ceremony, vowing to "have and to hold from this day forward, for better for worse, for richer for poorer, in sickness and in health, to love and to cherish, till death (do) us… part." Yes, it takes work, but it's worth it.

When real intimacy becomes difficult, elusive, or painful, many of us try to create what Schaumburg identifies as false intimacy.

False Intimacy: This is NOT an attempt to find real intimacy. In actuality, it's an avoidance of the pain often caused by real intimacy. A sex addict creates a fake relationship to achieve a sense of relational satisfaction with something or someone who can be controlled, such as a picture, an actor on the video screen, or a prostitute. **The primary goal of sexually addictive behavior is to avoid relational pain—essentially, to *control* life.**

Schaumburg goes on to explain that all of us are committed to avoiding relational pain. In the right context, this is actually a healthy response. But, for the sex addict, the desire to **construct** their **own** reality through the **illusion** of false intimacy brings even greater distance from the reality in which God has called him/her to live. The more the addict embraces what is false, the less he/she cares about what is good and loving—and the more they are captive to the desire to create a **sense** of control over our [their] circumstances.[1]

Note the *underlined* words from the reading above. A sex addict is attempting to control life, to be God. Ultimately, God is the only one who has control, and any attempt on our part to manipulate life's circumstances for our selfish desires will lead to sin and shame. The repetitive attempts to be God and control His creation regardless of the consequences are the very definition of an addiction. It's choosing to believe the lie that we can be like God.

This exchange of truth for lies goes all the way back to the original fall of man in the Garden of Eden. Adam and Eve were given all they needed for life and health and happiness, yet they chose to believe Satan's lie that God was withholding something from them.

Satan's trap is illustrated in Genesis 3:

> Did God really say, "You must not eat from any tree in the garden"?
>
> The woman said to the serpent, "We may eat fruit from the trees in the garden, but God did say, 'You must not eat fruit from the tree that is in the middle of the garden, and you must not touch it, or you will die.'"
>
> You will not certainly die," the serpent said to the woman. "For God knows that when you eat from it your eyes will be opened, and you will be like God, knowing good and evil."
>
> When the woman saw that the fruit of the tree was good for food and pleasing to the eye, and also desirable for gaining wisdom, she took some and ate it.

Satan drew Eve's attention away from all the good things God had provided and called her focus onto the one thing that He was seemingly withholding from her. Her lack of trust in her Creator and His good plans for her caused her to disobey, and Adam followed along. Their sin ushered in dysfunctional and painful relationships between mankind and all of creation. And so now we live in a world where perfect intimacy is no longer possible, marred by original sin. Because real intimacy is difficult, many people opt out and escape to their fantasy world where they are god and rejection isn't an option.

Schaumburg states it this way: "A sexual fantasy stems from a desire to gain more in a relationship than is possible. It's an attempt to gorge ourselves with passion and move into a state free of any chance for disappointment. Simply put, we want to enter the Garden of Eden again."[2]

WEEK 1
WEEK 2
WEEK 3
WEEK 4
WEEK 5
WEEK 6
WEEK 7
WEEK 8

DAY 3

Today we explored the three different levels of intimacy. Write down a summary of each below:

PERFECT: _____

REAL: _____

FALSE: _____

HEARTWORK

What would it take for you and your spouse to find real intimacy within your marriage? End today by reading a passage from Scripture that may have been read during your wedding ceremony, 1 Corinthians 13:4-8a. Here we find what it takes to experience this real intimacy, this true love.

List below all the characteristics of love.

_____

_____

_____

_____

_____

Now pray this passage as a prayer, asking God to teach you to truly love your husband. Pray the words out loud, asking Him to make you or help you be each one of those things. Then pray that God will do the same for your husband.

CHARGE

Brokenness is a devastating reality, but Jesus was broken so that I can be whole and free. I will fight for my marriage.

TRUE DESIRES

Psalm 73:25-26 "Whom have I in heaven but you? And earth has nothing I desire besides you. My flesh and my heart may fail, but God is the strength of my heart and my portion forever."

WEEK 1 DAY 4

KEY THOUGHT: Our greatest desire should be for God alone. Our pursuit of anything else will always lead to emptiness and disappointment.

I love chocolate. And bread. And pasta. If there was a diet that revolved around just those three things, I would be set. You could say I crave, want, and desire those foods. And I know I am not the only one.

For most of us, our food cravings are manageable. We understand the dangerous health risks and imbalance that would result from an entirely white flour and sugar-based diet. It's obvious because we are bombarded with advice on what to eat, when to eat it, and how to work off those extra calories if we decide to indulge anyway.

But what happens when desire morphs into something more? When we desire something that God created more than God Himself, we sin. We turn a good thing into a "god thing" (everything God created was good, Genesis 1:31). We place our trust in something that will always fail us and leave us with unmet desires. The tree in the Garden of Eden was good, sex is good, marriage is good... but none of them are God, who alone is worthy of our worship and complete devotion.

Mike Wilkerson expounds upon this idea in his book *Redemption*. Through the story of Exodus, Wilkerson explores the origin of addictions and the slavery we experience when trapped in sin. He explains, "In sin, we worship anything and everything other than God. We tend to exalt a substance, an experience, a person, or a dream to the level of a god. We define life by its attainment, and we feel like dying when it eludes us. It becomes even bigger in our eyes than God himself and takes His place in our lives. The Bible calls this "idolatry." So, addictions, for example, aren't just drug, alcohol, food or pornography problems. They are **worship disorders**. They flow from a heart bent on **worshiping created things rather than the Creator**."[3]

The Bible also talks about this, specifically noting sexual sin, in Romans 1:24-25.

Therefore, God gave them over in the **sinful desires of their hearts** to sexual impurity for the degrading of their bodies with one another. They **exchanged the truth about God for a lie** and **worshiped and served created things rather than the Creator**—who is forever praised.

The people that Paul is writing about in this passage are the victims of false intimacy. Although they knew God, they neither glorified him as God nor gave thanks to him (Romans 1:21). They ignored the truth that God alone is worthy of worship and believed the same lie that Adam and Eve did: "Why should you be satisfied living under God, when you could live as God?" And when we try to live as God, we make a mess out of our lives.

Before you become too judgmental of your husband's worship disorder, take a moment for personal reflection. We as wives are also guilty of idolatry, of worshiping the creation over the Creator, of getting fooled by the lies. We look to our husbands to meet all of our needs, or at least I do. I had a preconceived idea that began in early childhood (I blame kid movies) that "someday my prince will come." Someday, somewhere, somehow, I would meet the perfect guy and then all my dreams would come true and we would live "happily ever after." My trust was in the ideal man. As a matter of fact, the unhealthy desire I had for my husband is one of the consequences of original sin.

Consider this slightly controversial but very insightful commentary on Genesis 3 from Wendy Alsup: "Women's problem is that they worship the men in their lives and look to them for affirmation and provision emotionally and spiritually for things that God alone is supposed to provide. Their problem is IDOLATRY."[4]

My husband is a wonderful man. He's a hard worker, a respected member of our community, an excellent leader, and a loyal friend. He loves me and our children deeply, I don't ever doubt that. He is a blessing in my life. But he is not perfect, which means he is not God and can't be my Savior. We have had many valleys, some major detours down scary paths, and our share of knock-down drag-out fights. And I've been right there with him, contributing to the dysfunction with my own sinful desires, my unfair expectations, and my manipulations. How do you know when a good thing has become a "god thing," or in other words, an idol?

Wilkerson outlines three piercing questions that can indicate when **natural desires** become **lustful ones.**

WHEN ARE YOU ANGRY?

"Anger makes a judgment: this is wrong, unfair, unjust."

"Perceived entitlements can lead to such misguided anger. An entitlement is what you believe is yours by rights. A husband may believe he is entitled to sex from his wife while she believes she is entitled to his affection. If one doesn't give what is owed, the other feels righteous in condemning the failure."[5]

OUCH!!! That hits home. When I don't get what I feel I am owed, I get angry. I am definitely guilty of this one.

WHEN ARE YOU ANXIOUS?

"Anxiety kicks in when life feels a bit out of control or a touch too risky."

"Anxiety replays the conversation you just had, calculating whether you left the right impression. It worries what people think. Anxiety frets that there's never quite enough money, attention, time, affection, leisure, or success. It assumes that the worst case is the most likely."

"Anxiety is a shade of fear, which is the flipside of desire. You want something, and you're afraid you won't get it. Or you have something you're afraid to lose."

That one really hits home too! As a people pleaser and a worrier, I am again guilty of this so often.

WHEN DO YOU WANT TO ESCAPE?

"Escape becomes more enticing as life becomes more difficult. Near the extreme end of the escape spectrum are addictions of all kinds: drugs, alcohol, food, sex. Near the subtle end of the spectrum are constant checking of email, sports scores, or social media, aimlessly watching TV or surfing the web, unnecessary snacking, consuming hobbies, or workaholism. Even religion can be distorted and used as an escape from reality: "God is sovereign, so there's no point to dealing with _____.""

"Some escapes are necessary for a balanced life: a refreshing nap, family vacation, dinner and a movie. In fact, it was for the sake of rest that God provided the Sabbath day. But these healthy escapes aren't designed to take you out of reality but to plug you back into it."

"If you find yourself regularly running, what are you running from? What is difficult, uncomfortable, or painful that you want to avoid?"

Again, guilty. I'm a workaholic. I can't stand to sit still and feel useless when I am not doing something. I can't even watch a movie without doing something else at the same time.

All three of these questions are obvious in correlation with false intimacy—the sex addict is riddled with anger, anxiety and a desire to escape. But what about in your life? Where do these byproducts of false worship surface?

Here are a few examples of things I have seen elevated to God-status in my own life or in the lives of my friends:

Words of praise from others	A close friendship
Being perfect	Being a mom
Position/status at church, school, work	Attention/affection from my husband
Shopping	Money
Food	Marital status
Having the perfect body	Education

The list could go on and on. Take some time to think about the things you have exalted as a god. Write them below.

_____

_____

_____

So how do we stop worshiping these things instead of God? How do we get our husbands to stop worshiping sex instead of God? The answer is so simple, yet so difficult to practice.

SEEK Him first, DESIRE Him most.

> Matthew 6:31-33
> Do not worry, saying, "What shall we eat?" or "What shall we drink?" or "What shall we wear?" For the pagans run after all these things, and your heavenly Father knows that you need them. But seek first his kingdom and his righteousness, and all these things will be given to you as well. Therefore, do not worry about tomorrow, for tomorrow will worry about itself. Each day has enough trouble of its own.

> Psalm 73:25-26
> Whom have I in heaven but you? And earth has nothing I desire besides you. My flesh and my heart may fail, but God is the strength of my heart and my portion forever.

> John 6:68
> Simon Peter answered him, "Lord, to whom shall we go? You have the words of eternal life. We have come to believe and to know that you are the Holy One of God."

Choose one of these verses and write it on a note card. Place it somewhere you will see it daily. Commit to memorizing it this week.

HEARTWORK

Look back over the list you made and confess it to your Heavenly Father. It's important to be introspective and examine our hearts, but I urge you to let *Him* see these parts of you. Tell Him you're ready to trust Him in these areas of your life. Ask Him to give you a heart that desires Him above all else. Take as much time as you need in prayer as you reconcile with Him.

CHARGE

Brokenness is a devastating reality, but Jesus was broken so that I can be whole and free. I will fight for my marriage.

THE WAY, THE TRUTH, THE LIFE

John 14:6 "I am the way and the truth and the life. No one comes to the Father except through me."

WEEK 1 DAY 5

KEY THOUGHT: A relationship with Christ is the starting point on the path to real intimacy.

Over the course of this first week we have looked at sexual addiction through various lenses. We have compared it to cancer, labeled it as idolatry, and defined it as false intimacy. We have recognized that we, too, are guilty of misplaced worship and that Jesus is the only one worthy of our adoration. If we seek Him first and desire Him most, we will have our hearts in the right place.

All of this hinges upon one thing: a relationship with Jesus Christ. It is impossible to experience true transformation personally and within marriage without his life-transforming power. I recognize that many of you reading this may already have made a decision to trust Christ as your Savior, but I would be remiss if I did not address it in this study.

My teenagers are part of our church's local youth group called Collide Student Ministry. Every Wednesday night they participate in live worship, teaching, and small group time. One particular Wednesday, after a long week filled with mom taxi duties, I found myself part of a conversation with my kids that disturbed me. It went something like this:

ME: "What are you guys talking about at Collide this week?"
KIDS: "I dunno." (typical)
ME: "Aren't you guys in the middle of a series about the gospel?"
KIDS: "Oh yeah, that's right. Forgot."
ME: "Well, it's been a long day... I think we can skip tonight. You guys already know about the gospel and don't need to be there for the lesson."

As soon as those words left my mouth I felt a deep conviction from the Holy Spirit. You don't need to be there? You already know enough about the gospel?

WEEK 1

WEEK 2 .... WEEK 3 .... WEEK 4 .... WEEK 5 .... WEEK 6 .... WEEK 7 .... WEEK 8

DAY 5

We should always want to hear the gospel! It is the "power of God for salvation to everyone who believes" (Romans 1:16). It is the only thing that can bring life, hope and healing into our messed-up lives.

Turn to Appendix A and read it as if you are hearing the gospel for the first time. If it is your first time hearing this biblical truth, my prayer is that you will respond to it and be changed forever.

Now that you have read Appendix A, I hope that the truth of the gospel message penetrated your heart. For those receiving the truth of the gospel for the first time, I am thrilled to call you my sister in Christ! This study will be so helpful to you as you take steps forward in your brand-new journey with Him. Reading His Word and spending time in prayer will be like water and sunlight as you grow and transform.

For those of you who already have a relationship with Jesus, I hope that your spirit was encouraged and refreshed. The gospel truly is the starting point and foundation for this study, and without it true life change is impossible. Thanks be to God for His indescribable gift of grace! (2 Corinthians 9:14-15)

Moving forward into the next week of study, you will be challenged to stretch and grow in ways that may seem impossible. Remember, God began a good work in you through salvation and He will be faithful to complete it (Philippians 1:6).

We've tackled some heavy topics this week. Let's end with prayer. I love Philippians 4:6-7; it's a great passage that talks about how to approach God in prayer. On the lines below, write out Philippians 4:6-7.

_____

_____

_____

_____

_____

_____

God does not want you to walk in worry. He wants you to come to Him with your burdens so that He can bring you rest (Matthew 11:28). When you "cast all your cares on Him" you can know that He cares for you (1 Peter 5:7). Giving your burdens to Him in prayer, accompanied by thanksgiving, will lead to a peace that passes human understanding. I know your heart is craving that peace!

WEEK 1 · · · · WEEK 2 · · · · · WEEK 3 · · · · · WEEK 4 · · · · · WEEK 5 · · · · · WEEK 6 · · · · · WEEK 7 · · · · · WEEK 8

DAY 5

HEARTWORK

On the lines below, pour your heart out to God. Are you hopeful, ready to begin a new journey with Him to find healing? Are you hopeless, weary from the weight that sexual addiction has brought into your marriage? Tell God all about it. Lay your burdens at His feet, your desires, your worries. Nothing is too big or too small for Him.

_____

_____

_____

_____

_____

_____

_____

_____

Everyone needs the gospel every day, whether you're a Christian or not. Consider what you wrote in the last lines and talk to God about having intimacy with Him.

WEEKEND HOMEWORK

Memorize Philippians 4:6-7. Write it out on a note card and put it somewhere you can see it every day. Every time you feel anxious, pause and go to God in prayer. Don't forget to also spend time praising Him for His goodness.

CHARGE

Brokenness is a devastating reality, but Jesus was broken so that I can be whole and free. I will fight for my marriage.

TESTIMONY

The Proven Wives study changed the way I see myself, my marriage, my husband and his struggle. For so long I searched for a resource like this to help me navigate through this hardship, but everywhere I looked I found books that only made me feel like a victim. I wanted to be able to do something to help stop this, but the lack of direction on what I could do made me feel helpless, alone, and even hopeless at times. But the call of my heart was echoed when I read through this study. The words I read in each chapter brought life, healing, and purpose to me. It is so much more than an answer to my prayers, it has brought me freedom. I now know that I do have a purpose and a role in this journey, and my husband does not have to fight this alone. I am called to be his ally, helper, and fellow warrior, not just a casualty of his battle. I strongly believe that The Lord will transform lives through this study, because He transformed mine. I am so grateful to all the courageous people who made this a possibility for spouses like me.

Stephanie

Passionate for God,

Repentant in spirit,

Open and honest,

Victorious in living,

Eternal in perspective, and

Networking with other *PROVEN Wives.*

PW

WEEK TWO

THIS IS MY STORY

Psalm 139:16 "Your eyes saw my unformed body; all the days ordained for me were written in your book before one of them came to be."

WEEK **2** DAY 1

KEY THOUGHT: God is not surprised by the details of your story. He is the author, and He knows about every line on every page.

The time has come to share my story. Early on in my journey, when I felt the darkness envelop me and threaten to steal my very life, one of the biggest things that helped me was to hear other women's stories. Stories of hope, redemption and God's grace. When you can't see the way ahead, it helps to know someone else has already traveled before you and made it safely through to the other side. I certainly haven't "arrived" yet, but I pray that my redemption story will impact and encourage your heart as we walk through this together.

STORY: PART 1

I wasn't the boy-crazy type growing up. My time was spent playing sports and getting good grades. I remember having boy crushes in elementary and middle school, but nothing serious.

Sex wasn't talked about in my home; as a matter of fact, I didn't even know the correct term for the female reproductive parts until late into my teenage years (I think it was covered in 5th grade sex education, but I must not have been paying attention). I had questions about my own sexuality, but was unsure about where to ask them.

Home was a safe place filled with love, but definitely not somewhere we talked about sexual intimacy. One of the main reasons it was not discussed was my mom's past. As I got older I heard bits and pieces about the sexual abuse my mom had endured as a child. I know the pain that resulted from her abuse made it difficult for her to talk about sex.

I grew up in the church, but, again, sex was not discussed. And if it was, the only message being broadcast was DON'T have sex. It was sinful and only led to disease or early pregnancy. Avoid it at all costs. And the same message was reiterated at my small Christian high school.

WEEK 1 .... WEEK 2 .... WEEK 3 .... WEEK 4 .... WEEK 5 .... WEEK 6 .... WEEK 7 .... WEEK 8

DAY 1

Still, I had feelings and stirrings inside of me that I didn't understand. I wanted to be kissed, held, touched, loved. Romantic books, TV shows and movies stirred those same desires from within, but I didn't know if it was normal or healthy.

I began dating as a sophomore in high school. Up until that point I had spent all my energy on finding a best friend and had been sincerely disappointed. I was a loyal friend but was a "smotherer" and got jealous very quickly. I was "too much" to handle, or at least I felt that way. When boys started paying attention to me, I found a new sense of value and worth.

Once I started dating I never stopped. I was a "serial dater," always in a relationship, even in my small Christian high school with only twenty-six in the graduating class. Having a boyfriend brought the feelings of approval and acceptance I was searching for. When I broke up with a boy or he broke up with me, I would quickly find someone else to attach myself to.

Each new relationship brought deeper levels of physical intimacy, but I had clear boundaries as far as sex was concerned. Sex was exclusively for when I got married. I even made a covenant with God and my parents to stay pure until my wedding day, and I had a ring on my finger to remind me of the promise I had made. I made it through high school without compromising my values.

Christian high school was followed by Christian college. I went to a very small Bible college far from home. It was strict (like no pants on women, dorms locked at 10:00 p.m., no physical touch between girls and guys strict), but I didn't mind so much. I was a perfectionistic rule-follower and could thrive in this environment. Obey the rules and you will be accepted and achieve success. Easy.

Then I met HIM. My future husband. The first time I saw him I was immediately drawn in by his charisma and his beautiful blue eyes. This guy had the cutest grin that unveiled a bit of a mischievous streak. It didn't take long before we began dating, and we spent every spare moment we had together. He was studying to be a pastor, and I felt God was calling me to be a pastor's wife, so it was literally "a match made in heaven." My heart felt at home knowing I had finally found the one person who would love me unconditionally.

This guy made me feel unlike anyone else ever had. I was captivated by him and couldn't stop thinking about him. He made me feel safe, and his ability to make me laugh had softened my stiff, pessimistic tendencies.

Our physical relationship was the only real struggle we had while dating. We were both very attracted to each other, and the struggle to remain sexually pure was a constant battle. The restrictive dating rules at our college seemed to magnify the sexual tension. I soon found myself saying "yes" to things that I should have been saying "no" to.

I enjoyed our physical relationship and didn't even know if it was OK for a woman, let alone a Christian woman, to feel that way. But the pleasure I experienced every time we crossed a boundary line was immediately clouded

by deep feelings of guilt, remorse and shame. We were doing youth ministry together on the weekends and acting out our sinful desires during the week.

Although we never had physical intercourse, we danced all around the line. There's a passage, 1 Corinthians 7:8-9, that says, "Now to the unmarried and the widows I say: It is good for them to stay unmarried... but if they cannot control themselves, they should marry, for it is better to marry than to burn with passion." That was us, "burning with passion" in our late teenage years and into our early twenties. We knew we had to get married, and so we did on a hot midsummer's day in my hometown. I was ecstatic, thrilled to be spending the rest of my life with my best friend and ready to be rid of the guilt that had plagued me for so long.

What I didn't realize when I said "I do" was that my husband had a secret addiction to pornography that started early on in his teenage years. He never mentioned it once while we were dating or engaged.

More about my story tomorrow. What is important for today is that sharing your story is good. It's necessary for healing. It's part of the journey. But with it brings feelings and memories we don't want to re-live. Writing out my story brings out a flood of emotions. I remember the deep sadness etched on my mother's face when I found her crying all by herself in the laundry room, mourning the pain of her childhood abuse. I remember the guilt I felt growing up, struggling alone to make sense of how I felt about my own sexuality. I can feel the lonely ache of my heart to find someone, anyone, to truly love me for me. My lips curl up at the edges as I recall the first time I saw my husband, the complete giddiness I felt every time he walked into the room.

All of us have a story to share, a story given to us by God. We have all experienced moments of pain, joy, confusion, loneliness, and fear. Our human experience, our search to find approval and love, unites us all.

When I finally realized that my story was not random, that God was in every detail, I began to understand that He alone was the one who could genuinely love me for who I am.

Take some time to read Psalm 139. Read the words out loud.

Now narrow your focus and look again at the verses. On the corresponding lines, choose a phrase from each verse that proves God knows your story, that He knows every detail of your life.

VERSE 1: _____

_____

_____

_____

WEEK 1 .... WEEK 2 .... WEEK 3 .... WEEK 4 .... WEEK 5 .... WEEK 6 .... WEEK 7 .... WEEK 8

DAY 1

VERSE 2: _____

_____

_____

_____

VERSE 3: _____

_____

_____

_____

VERSE 4: _____

_____

_____

_____

VERSE 7: _____

_____

_____

_____

VERSE 13: _____

_____

_____

_____

VERSE 16: _____

_____

WEEK 1 .... WEEK 2 .... WEEK 3 .... WEEK 4 .... WEEK 5 .... WEEK 6 .... WEEK 7 .... WEEK 8

DAY 1

_____

_____

VERSE 17: _____

_____

_____

_____

How does it make you feel as you read these verses about God's continued presence in your life? Do you believe them? Why or why not?

_____

_____

_____

_____

_____

_____

_____

_____

_____

_____

_____

Although these verses are beautiful, to be honest, there are many times when I have felt that God has been missing in the lines of my life's story. Sometimes it seems He has been absent for an entire chapter. For the most part, as I grew up, I believed God loved me and was on my side. It seemed like He had answered all my prayers when I met my husband. All my childhood dreams were coming true. But as life brought with it more disappointments, that trust began to wane, and I seriously doubted His goodness and His presence in my life.

WEEK 1 .... WEEK 2 .... WEEK 3 .... WEEK 4 .... WEEK 5 .... WEEK 6 .... WEEK 7 .... WEEK 8

DAY 1

HEARTWORK

Later on in the week we are going to dive deeper into why it can be so difficult for us to believe that God is actively a part of our story. As we end today, spend some time journaling below about a time when you felt His love in a tangible way. If you can't think of a time, write out a prayer asking God to reveal His very personal love for you this week.

_____

_____

_____

_____

_____

_____

_____

_____

_____

_____

_____

CHARGE

This is not a mistake. I am equipped and accompanied by the One who made the plan.

WHERE ARE YOU NOW THAT I NEED YOU?

Hebrews 4:16 "Let us then approach God's throne of grace with confidence, so that we may receive mercy and find grace to help us in our time of need."

WEEK 2 DAY 2

KEY THOUGHT: God understands our pain and wants us to face it with Him.

Yesterday we talked about how God is intimately involved in every detail of our story. Today we will dive into how we handle the disappointing chapters, when the pages are filled with painful and ugly details and the "happily ever after" seems like an impossibility.

STORY: PART 2

My husband grew up in a very conservative Christian home. When his parents were teenagers, before they committed their lives to Christ, they both made reckless decisions. With good intentions, they tried to safeguard their children from making similar decisions. They were in church every time the doors opened, and my husband was told from a very young age that he was called to be a pastor. While other boys were dreaming of being superheroes, he suppressed those dreams and did what a good Christian boy would do. He was a leader in his church youth group and even went to "preacher boy's club," winning the award at the state level for preaching.

But behind all the good things, he was struggling with the pressure to live up to everyone's standards, coupled with the normal temptations that teenage boys face. Like me, he was longing for acceptance and approval. Combine that with a volatile relationship with his father and you had the breeding grounds for a pornography addiction. My husband accidentally found a pornographic magazine at the age of fourteen, and he was hooked. He struggled all throughout high school to keep his addiction a secret, afraid that the church would make him publicly apologize. His reputation for being the "perfect Christian kid" was one that he had carefully built, and an admission to a pornography addiction would destroy everything. He was terrified.

Jumping forward, we made it through the first few years of marriage relatively unscathed. We had our share of arguments, but for the most part we had a happy marriage. We got pregnant on our honeymoon, and a few weeks after our son was born we blindly moved across the country. We wanted to start a new life away from the legalistic and constricting environment we had endured through college, ready to forge a new path for ourselves and our small family.

WEEK 1 .... WEEK 2 .... WEEK 3 .... WEEK 4 .... WEEK 5 .... WEEK 6 .... WEEK 7 .... WEEK 8

DAY 2

Our move brought some tough financial times. No longer pursuing the ministry, my husband was working as a CNA in a local nursing home. It was hard work with very low pay. We found ourselves on government assistance to get baby formula, giving plasma twice a week to pay for diapers. A man's sense of self-worth is so often tied to his occupation and his ability to provide, and my husband felt like a failure.

Enter the addiction. My husband would come home late at night and go down into our basement where the computer was located. Frequently I was already in bed, exhausted from dealing with a toddler that never slept. Unbeknownst to me, my husband was spending the late-night hours looking at pornography online.

I sensed something was wrong with our relationship, but I didn't know what it was. He always seemed preoccupied and distant. What was once a thriving sexual relationship became routine and cold.

One night I was confiding in a dear friend about some of the unhealthy things I was sensing in our relationship. She suggested that perhaps my husband was looking at pornography. I was dumbfounded. No way, not my husband! We had sex regularly, and I just couldn't imagine him doing that. I eventually got up the nerve to ask him about it, and he denied it adamantly. I never broached the subject again.

September 11, 2001, happened, and my husband joined the Army. He was profoundly impacted by the attack on our country. His entire life, he dreamed of being a soldier, and he couldn't ignore the compelling feeling inside to serve in the military and protect our nation. He came back lean, strong, and invigorated by his newfound success in the Army.

We got pregnant with our second child, and he landed his dream job. Everything seemed to be going well. I still felt some distance between us, but I assumed it was just the norm for a busy young family. At that time, I was journaling almost every day, and I remember very clearly that God was preparing my heart for something. I didn't know what, but my prayer was that I would obey and trust Him completely, no matter what the next chapter was going to bring.

Then I found out what God had been preparing me for. On a cold Sunday morning in the early winter of 2003, my husband went forward at church. He went directly to our pastor and admitted to a pornography addiction that had spanned over a decade. My husband finally caught up with me after the service ended and said, "I need to talk to you." Through tears he confessed his addiction and vowed to do whatever it took to make things right again. My heart broke for him because the Holy Spirit had softened and prepared it. We tearfully embraced, and I reassured him of my love and forgiveness.

I don't remember much changing after that day. Perhaps I thought since his addiction was out in the open it wouldn't be a problem any more. The compassion I felt towards him was obvious when he confessed; certainly he knew I cared, I forgave him, and we could move past this issue.

Life continued on at a hurried pace. I gave birth to our daughter, he graduated from school and began his dream job, and we started looking for our first home together. In November of 2003, we received the phone call that I was dreading: My husband was being called to war, to serve his country through a deployment to Iraq.

He had three days to pack and ship out for his mobilization. At the time, we had a three-year-old and a six-month-old and were about to close on our first house. Just days after he left, the house we were supposed to buy got foreclosed on and destroyed by the owner. In that same week, my baby girl rolled herself off our bed and broke her leg. I had no idea it was broken because she was such a happy baby. I didn't realize she was seriously injured until three days later when she cried as I changed her diaper.

I sat in the hospital room sobbing my eyes out. The hospital staff was asking me tough questions about whether I had abused my baby girl. My world was crashing in around me. I felt all alone as I faced the reality of raising my two young children as a temporarily single mom, finding a new place to live, and dealing with the very present fear that my husband may not come home again.

Oftentimes we don't want to believe God is in our story because of the painful details. How could a good God allow such pain? For me, I was facing some very real fears. The climate during Operation Iraqi Freedom was very tense. America was angry, unsure of why we were even at war. Stories of Americans being beheaded were streaming all over the news. I couldn't watch TV anymore because I would have nightmares that my husband was one of them.

I decided to move in with my parents because I knew I couldn't do it alone. I was jealous of all my friends back home that still had their husbands with them. I was angry that during the most formative years of my children's lives they had to grow up without their daddy. First steps, first words, singing them to sleep every night... he missed all of it.

Open your Bible once again and reread Psalm 139:19-22. When we read these verses yesterday, we focused on how God knows every part of our story. But do you hear the angst in David's voice as he pens this section of the psalm? He knows God cares about him, that He is involved with every detail of his life; but there is still evil in the world. Why doesn't God just destroy the wicked? We face those same thoughts and feelings daily. Why, why must I deal with this evil, this pain in my life?

Mike Wilkerson addresses this internal conflict in his book *Redemption*. He reminds us that not only does God see our pain, He understands it too. Jesus' commitment to sacrifice His life for all of mankind brought extreme pain—true emotional pain as He was betrayed and abandoned by those closest to Him, excruciating physical pain as He was beaten and crucified, and finally deep spiritual and mental anguish as He bore the weight of every sin ever committed.

Wilkerson recounts the pivotal moments before Jesus faced the cross:

> Jesus knows the struggle to accept the Father's wisdom in allowing such pain. He knows what it is to trust a God who could make it stop but doesn't. "Father, if you are willing, remove this cup from me" (Luke 22:42). Jesus desperately wrestled with the Father's plan—and not just once but three times.

> Notice too what Jesus *didn't* do in the garden: ignore the pain of his situation. He didn't drown it out with some addiction. He didn't deny it. And he didn't mask it with a platitude about God's sovereignty, either. He faced it and ran to the Father in his distress.[6]

Jesus knows pain, yet He turned to the Father in his distress and resigned Himself to God's ultimate plan. How often, when we are facing difficult circumstances, do we try to fix them in our own strength? How often do we question His goodness, blame Him for the evil we are facing, assume He has forsaken us?

> The reason many of us have given up hope on seeking our Father's grace and mercy is that, at an emotional level, we sense that he is the very source of our pain; it just hurts too much to draw closer to the one who could stop evil but hasn't.

> The problem isn't that God has abandoned us in our pain, but that sometimes we refuse to face it with Him.[7]

Have you struggled with these feelings? That God is the very source of your pain? That you can't trust a God who could stop or prevent it but doesn't? That He has left you to face it alone?

Take some time to honestly answer each question below.

_____

_____

_____

_____

_____

_____

Jesus can meet you here, my friend. He understands pain, loneliness, and abandonment. Let's look a little deeper at the scene from the Garden.

WEEK 1 .... WEEK 2 .... WEEK 3 .... WEEK 4 .... WEEK 5 .... WEEK 6 .... WEEK 7 .... WEEK 8

DAY 2

Read Mark 14:32-36. Record below the phrases that talk about the pain He was experiencing.

_____

_____

_____

The phrase "My soul is overwhelmed with sorrow to the point of death" strikes me most. I have certainly felt that way. It brings me great comfort to know that Jesus understands that feeling, and even more poignantly than I ever have. And how did He deal with that intense grief?

We find His response in Mark 14:35-36. Jesus prays. He asks God to remove the pain. And He resigns Himself to His Father's will. But not just His Father, His *Abba*. This word reveals Jesus' relationship with God.

> *Abba* was a word heard at home on the lips of a child addressing a father, but it was rarely heard on the lips of a worshiper addressing God in prayer. When Jesus called the Father his *Abba,* he revealed the great depths of intimacy with God that could be known by a son.

> When was such deep intimacy revealed? Amidst Jesus' anguish, he pressed in even closer to the Father. The very experiences that threaten to drive you the farthest from God are the **exact experiences** that bring you into closest possible fellowship with your Savior. As God's adopted children, we have this same amazing privilege as Jesus Himself—to call God *Abba*—and it is often in our worst suffering that we most need to.[8]

Jesus knows our story, understands our story, and wants us to turn to Him when the story seems tragic and all hope is lost. Hear Him calling you to come:

> Hebrews 4:14-16 Therefore, since we have a great high priest who has ascended into heaven, Jesus the Son of God, let us hold firmly to the faith we profess. For we do not have a high priest who is unable to **empathize** with our weaknesses, but we have one who has been tempted in every way, just as we are—yet he did not sin. Let us then approach God's throne of grace with **confidence**, so that we may receive **mercy** and find **grace** to help us in our time of **need.**

Do you believe God not only sees your pain but understands it? Name it here and imagine Him taking it from you.

_____

_____

_____

WEEK 1 .... WEEK 2 .... WEEK 3 .... WEEK 4 .... WEEK 5 .... WEEK 6 .... WEEK 7 .... WEEK 8

DAY 2

HEARTWORK

As we end today, spend some time in prayer.

First, thank Jesus that He chose to walk in our shoes, to understand the struggles of humanity. Thank Him for enduring the cross—the physical, emotional, and spiritual anguish—so that you could experience forgiveness and freedom.

Next, tell God about your needs and your hurts. Come to Him with confidence, knowing that He cares, He is listening and wants to flood your heart with His mercy and grace. Speak the words out loud, don't be afraid to cry to Him and tell Him how your soul is aching.

Finally, ask God to give you eyes to see the hope and power you were called into through the risen Christ (Ephesians 1:18-21).

CHARGE

This is not a mistake. I am equipped and accompanied by the One who made the plan.

THE WAR INSIDE

Psalm 73:26 "My flesh and my heart may fail, but God is the strength of my heart and my portion forever."

WEEK **2** DAY 3

KEY THOUGHT: When we make a good thing into a "god thing," we commit idolatry.

STORY: PART 3

While my husband was fighting a war overseas, what we didn't realize was that we were about to fight the biggest battle our marriage had ever faced. Internally we both had a sinful storm brewing, ready to rear its ugly head and destroy our marriage.

My husband finally came home after a fifteen-month deployment. We plunged forward into the next chapter of our lives—bought our first home, sent our children off to school, and I got a job working from home.

On the surface everything seemed great. We had survived some really lean years financially and made it through the long months apart during his basic training and his military deployment. I thought my husband's admission to a pornography addiction hadn't really impacted our marriage that much, but it had. Deep down I didn't trust him. The rose-colored glasses I wore on my wedding day had morphed into a magnifying lens zoned in on all his flaws. I was harsh, critical, impatient and selfish. Combine that with the long deployment and I had become emotionally detached. I couldn't put all my eggs in that basket anymore. What if he was deployed again? What if he started struggling again? I was emotionally vulnerable and lonely. My heart craved love and acceptance, and I began to search for it somewhere else.

As soon as my husband came back, we submerged ourselves into volunteering at our local church. We led in the children's ministry and small groups. I quickly became close friends with our pastor's wife. She was everything I wanted in a friend: fun, charismatic, strong. She embraced life with fervor and reflected the hope and joy of Christ in her daily life.

Our oldest children were born only days apart, and we began to "do life" together. Weekly trips to the playground, annual trips to the beach as families, celebrating every birthday and holiday together. But what began as a friendship soon became a codependent relationship.

The time I spent with her was never enough, and I had to have her attention every time we were in the same room together. If she spent time with someone else other than me, even her husband and children, I would get jealous. Her opinion mattered more to me than anyone else's. When she didn't respond to my phone calls or texts, I would get angry and obsess over why she didn't reply.

My husband became concerned about the level of attachment I had to my friend and began to mention it. I denied even the possibility of codependency until my unhealthy need for her approval dramatically came to light over an anniversary dinner. My friend recommended a nice restaurant out of town and suggested we share dinner because of the huge portions. For my husband, sharing a meal was the very last thing he wanted to do that evening. For him, sharing meant that he wasn't providing well. He felt good when he could buy us both a nice dinner, even if we had to get a to-go box for leftovers. I repeated her idea to split even after he expressed his desire to buy me a full meal. My behavior revealed that I cared more about her approval than I did about my husband's plan to make the evening a special one. Our casual conversation quickly escalated into World War 3. The only sparks that flew that night were angry words... we argued for hours over something that would have cost us an extra $20. I wish I would have realized that night that my decision to ignore him would eventually cost a lot more than a meal.

In spite of my husband's growing concerns, I continued to pursue my friendship with her. I mean, what's wrong with having a good Christian girlfriend? Especially the pastor's wife? If someone in her position wanted to spend her free time with me, certainly that meant that I had value and worth. She understood me, cared about me, and hadn't broken my heart.

My choice to distance myself emotionally from my husband ate away at his soul. His past addiction began to creep back in. Again, I was oblivious to his struggle. I mentioned the emotional distance in our marriage to my friend. She was the same person with whom I had initially shared my concerns with years ago before I knew he had a sexual addiction. Once again, she suggested that maybe he was struggling with pornography.

She went home and told our pastor, and they wasted no time. They were at our doorstep within moments, and after a few walks around our neighborhood, the boys returned, and I discovered that my suspicions were true. He had been struggling with his pornography addiction for months, and, once again, I was clueless.

———————————————

Looking back, I now realize that the dysfunction in our marriage resulted from the same root issue for both my husband and me. At the core of my codependency and his pornography addiction was the same longing—a desire to be loved and accepted. There is only one person that can truly meet that need, Jesus Christ. But we looked elsewhere and found ourselves in a huge sinful mess. We were worshiping false gods or idols.

For those of us who have read the Bible, the word "idol" makes us think of golden calves or small statues. But an idol is so much more than that.

WEEK 1 .... WEEK 2 .... WEEK 3 .... WEEK 4 .... WEEK 5 .... WEEK 6 .... WEEK 7 .... WEEK 8

DAY 3

Pastor Tim Keller, in his book *Counterfeit Gods*, expounds on the true definition of an idol.

- Anything more important to you than God.

- Anything that absorbs your heart and imagination more than God.

- Anything you seek to give you what only God can give.

- Whatever you look at and say, in your heart of hearts, "If I have that, then I'll feel my life has meaning, then I'll know I have value, then I'll feel significant and secure."

- Anything that becomes more fundamental than God to your happiness, meaning in life, and identity.[9]

The irony of an idol is that it's a twisted, exalted distortion of one of God's blessings. We turn a **good thing** into a "**god thing**," exalt the creation above the Creator. In our marriage, my idol was my best friend, and my husband's idol was sex. Friendship and sex are both good things, but they became "god things" for us.

My friendship was a blessing, a gift. God wants us to have friends and created us for community. But I took that relationship and made it my god, gave it complete power in my life. I spent my time trying to **control**, please and manipulate my friend to contrive a sense of **significance** in my life.

My husband and I were given the gift of sex when we got married. It is a blessing, a gift, the only way to bring new life into the world. But my husband had taken sex and made it his god. He used the images on the screen to make him feel in **control** and **significant.**

The Israelites did the very same thing. God blessed them with the Egyptians' gold and silver as they ran from captivity (Exodus 12:35-36). But they took that gift and turned it into a golden calf, an idol.

Read Exodus 32:1-5.

When they cast the golden calf, Moses had been gone for forty days on the mountain with God. This commentary on the passage you just read sheds some light on the situation:

> The Israelites' only access to God's presence—*ever*—had come through Moses. And up to this point in the story, he had probably never been gone more than a day. So it seems the Israelites panicked because with Moses missing, they had lost all contact with God.[10]

Moses was gone, and perhaps the Israelites assumed God was about to leave them too. Would He abandon them out in the wilderness? Rather than wait for Moses to return with God's instructions, they took matters into their own hands. They created something they could touch and see, something to fill their void immediately. They took a good thing (the jewelry acquired from the Egyptians) and made it a "god thing" (a golden calf). "Israel, this is your god, who brought you up from the land of Egypt!" (Exodus 32:4).

WEEK 1 .... WEEK 2 .... WEEK 3 .... WEEK 4 .... WEEK 5 .... WEEK 6 .... WEEK 7 .... WEEK 8

DAY 3

It seems ridiculous that the Israelites would worship a golden calf, a golden image that couldn't provide for them physically, emotionally or spiritually. But their idol worship was a manifestation of a much deeper issue: They didn't trust God.

Read Acts 7:37-41.

Write out verse 39 below.

_____

_____

_____

What was inside the Israelites' hearts in the wilderness? A longing for Egypt. Rather than remember the oppression and suffering they endured at the hands of slave drivers, they remembered this land as the place where they "sat around pots of meat and ate all the food we wanted" (Exodus 16:3). They wanted to go "home," back to slavery, back to where they had full bellies, back to the only life they knew for four hundred years.

The Israelites felt that God had deserted them. Literally. They were in the desert, and it seemed that God and His appointed leader were missing in action. Rather than rely on Him, they replaced Him. How often, when we feel that God is absent or distant, do we find something else to take His place? My first idol was my husband. I looked to him to meet all my needs. When I felt abandoned emotionally by him, I found a new idol, my friend. Something immediate, something I could see and touch, something to make me feel good in the moment. It was all about me. I couldn't trust God to meet my needs anymore, so I took matters into my own hands.

On the lines below, write out some possible idols in your life. What/who do you go to first when you are in crisis or feel alone? What are you worshipping instead of God? Ask Him to reveal it to you.

_____

_____

_____

Ironically, while the Israelites were creating the golden calf, God wasn't absent. He was very present with Moses giving instructions for the entire nation of Israel. And what were the first two commands He gave to them?

Exodus 20:1-4
I am the Lord your God, who **brought you out of Egypt, out of the land of slavery**. You shall have **no other gods** before me. You shall **not make for yourself an image in the form of anything** in

WEEK 1 .... WEEK 2 .... WEEK 3 .... WEEK 4 .... WEEK 5 .... WEEK 6 .... WEEK 7 .... WEEK 8

DAY 3

heaven above or on the earth beneath or in the waters below. You shall not bow down to them or worship them; for I, the Lord your God, am a jealous God, punishing the children for the sin of the parents to the third and fourth generation of those who hate me, but showing **love** to a **thousand generations** of those who **love me** and **keep my commandments**.

God was carefully crafting guidelines to show the Israelites how to live life to the fullest. The starting point for that kind of life was to put Him first, above all others. He was communicating His care for them, like a loving parent, setting boundaries to avoid pain and conflict. But the Israelites broke the very first law and chose to worship something that didn't have intelligence, the ability to speak, a well thought-out plan, or a deep love for Israel.

Here's the main point: Anything we put in the position of God will fail us. Every time. Pornography can't fulfill. It can't love you back. And neither can food, exercise, or alcohol. And while earthly relationships can reflect God's character, they too will fall short and leave you desiring more. The only thing that will complete our heart's deepest longings to be loved and known is a relationship with our Creator.

HEARTWORK

I love how beautifully these verses express this idea:

> Psalm 73:25-26—Whom have I in heaven but you? And earth has nothing I desire besides you. My flesh and my heart may fail, but God is the strength of my heart and my portion forever.

I truly want that to be my prayer, that I would long for God more than anything else. Spend some time in prayer asking God to give you a desire for Him alone. Ask Him to reveal your idols and give you the strength to get rid of them.

On the lines below, write out what God has revealed to you about your idols. Then pray through Psalm 73:25-26 and write down the cry of your heart.

_____

_____

_____

CHARGE

This is not a mistake. I am equipped and accompanied by the One who made the plan.

YOU'RE MY ONLY HOPE

Psalm 146:5 "Blessed are those whose help is the God of Jacob, whose hope is in the Lord their God."

WEEK 2 DAY 4

KEY THOUGHT: Our hope and help need to come from Christ alone.

STORY: PART 4

The years following my husband's relapse were dark ones. We had seven years of marriage under our belt, almost three of those spent hundreds of miles apart with military deployments, yet this new season felt more distant than all the others. Our sinful addictions brought far-reaching consequences within our marriage, family, and friendships.

At the time when my husband admitted his relapse, he was an elder in our church. They asked him to step down. My close friend and our pastor were the leaders of our small group, and because of my unhealthy relationship with her, they asked us to step away from the group for a time. They lovingly explained that we needed space to become healthy, all of us. It hurt deeply.

Meanwhile I was spiraling into a deep depression. Everything I had known and loved, everything I had carefully put into place to make myself feel safe and secure, was gone in an instant. I felt desperately alone, like I had nowhere to turn.

Just days after I found out my husband was struggling again, we were invited to a friend's wedding. It was so difficult to sit through the ceremony. I remember thinking, "This is a bunch of crap. There's no such thing as real love. You say you love each other now, but just wait. A happy marriage is one big lie."

I think I had a mental breakdown that day. During the reception I locked myself in the bathroom and wept. I started repeatedly scratching the inside of my palms with my fingernails. I had so much anger, so much pain inside my heart. I was broken.

It continued on that way for months, which turned into years. I tried to cope on my own but was failing. Every time I saw my close friend at church, I died inside. I missed her. I would run into the bathroom and cry. I wanted so desperately to have someone to talk to and share my brokenness with. I didn't want to live anymore, and I

WEEK 1 .... WEEK 2 .... WEEK 3 .... WEEK 4 .... WEEK 5 .... WEEK 6 .... WEEK 7 .... WEEK 8

DAY 4

shudder now when I remember the many times that I envisioned myself driving off a bridge or grabbing my husband's gun and pulling the trigger.

I was so angry with my husband, so hurt. How could he do this to me? He knew how insecure his addiction made me feel, how it destroyed trust, how it isolated us from each other. In my mind it was all his fault. If he didn't have a porn problem, I wouldn't have had to look elsewhere to get my emotional needs met. If he hadn't messed up, I would be just fine, and we would still be in group and I wouldn't be crying myself to sleep at night.

And then my husband got deployed... again. This deployment was a huge turning point. I was drowning and lost, and I just stopped caring. I even told him so over the phone that I was done. Done feeling, done caring, done investing emotionally into our marriage. It hurt too much, and I just couldn't do it anymore.

During that time, I began running, hoping that some exercise and healthier eating might pull me up out of the darkness. I'll never forget running on the elliptical in our basement, listening to a worship song. It kept saying, "I am free."

That was my breaking point. I realized that I wasn't free. I had been running in place for years, desperately using all my own energy and strength to get somewhere to no avail, just like I was doing on that elliptical. I began to cry hysterically, begging God to help me. I admitted that I was looking to everyone but Him to fulfill me, and that I was bound up in my anger, bitterness, jealousy, and unforgiveness. I pleaded with Him to change my heart, to heal my marriage, to renew my hope.

Are you doing the blame game in your marriage? What are you blaming your husband and/or God for?

_____

_____

_____

_____

_____

HOPE—that word saved me. Proverbs 13:12 says, "Hope deferred makes the heart sick, but a dream fulfilled is a tree of life." That verse is so true. My hope had been in my marriage, and then in my friendship. I leaned on those two relationships to give me purpose and meaning in life.

WEEK 1 .... WEEK 2 .... WEEK 3 .... WEEK 4 .... WEEK 5 .... WEEK 6 .... WEEK 7 .... WEEK 8

DAY 4

Desperate to climb out of the pit I was in, I decided to do a study on the word "hope" in the Bible. Recently I found the notebook I used for that study. I want to share an entry from it with you. It's a Psalm my dad recommended I read on a cold winter day. Before you read my entry, please open your Bible and **read Psalm 13**.

> January 5, 2007—Psalm 13
>
> This Psalm expresses my thoughts and feelings exactly. "How long?—will you forget me forever?—wrestle with my thoughts—*every day* have sorrow in my heart—give light to my eyes or I will sleep in death." David's resolution to his despair was threefold:
>
> 1. Trust in God's unfailing love
> 2. Rejoice in his salvation
> 3. Sing to the Lord for His goodness
>
> Long before they were issuing pamphlets about depression, a man after God's own heart struggled with what I am feeling. Help me remember the answer to my questions and anxiety—your love, salvation and goodness. I believe in these three evidences of your presence in my life. Thank you for speaking to me. Keep my eyes on you.

Reading through that journal entry for me now is so refreshing. Rewriting this part of my story is painful, but it reminds me of how God has delivered me from the depths of despair and from hopelessness. I was unwilling to tear down the idols in my life, and He loved me enough to take them away from me. He wanted me to trust in Him alone, to seek Him alone. I was clinging to false idols that would never fulfill me.

Another Psalm that really spoke to me during that dark time was Psalm 146. **Open your Bible and read it now.**

There are so many great truths in this Psalm! First, did you notice how many times the psalmist says "praise"? Five times. One of the best ways to take our eyes off of ourselves and our pain is to praise. To remember all that God has truly done for us.

On the lines below, take some time to praise God. To thank Him for all He has done.

_____

_____

_____

_____

WEEK 1 .... WEEK 2 .... WEEK 3 .... WEEK 4 .... WEEK 5 .... WEEK 6 .... WEEK 7 .... WEEK 8

DAY 4

Another truth that stood out to me was found in verses 3-4. It reminded me that I shouldn't put my trust in human beings, for they too are mortal and will one day become dust, just like me. The only one who I can fully trust is God, the one who made me and all of creation (verse 5-6).

The last four verses also reveal a beautiful truth. Take time to reread verses 7-10. On the lines below, write out what the Psalmist says God has done for each group of people.

OPPRESSED: _____

_____

HUNGRY: _____

_____

PRISONERS: _____

_____

BLIND: _____

_____

BOWED (or WEIGHED DOWN): _____

_____

FOREIGNER: _____

_____

FATHERLESS & WIDOW: _____

_____

Do you notice a common thread here? These people are in distress, hopeless and helpless. Their situations are inescapable, and their desperation is palpable. Notice that God sees EVERY need—physical, emotional, spiritual—and gives **help** and **hope** (verse 5). He brings justice, satisfaction, freedom, healing, hope, protection, and provision.

WEEK 1 ..... WEEK 2 ..... WEEK 3 .... WEEK 4 .... WEEK 5 .... WEEK 6 .... WEEK 7 .... WEEK 8

DAY 4

You may not be fatherless or blind, but God knows that your heart feels abandoned, and you can't see the way ahead. He knows your desperation and wants to deliver hope to your soul. **Do you believe it?** I can say with confidence that God brought me His help, His hope, when I stopped trying to let a person meet my needs and started seeking Him first (Matthew 6:33).

I'm reminded of the story in Mark 9, where a father brings his son to Jesus' remaining disciples while He was up on the mountain with Peter, James and John. The boy is possessed by an evil spirit which had left him mute and had made numerous attempts to kill the boy. The disciples unsuccessfully tried to cast it out. This father was desperate. He had sought human help and it didn't work; the only outcome was a large religious debate in the crowd.

We enter the scene at verse 21:

> Jesus asked the boy's father, "How long has he been like this?"
>
> "From childhood," he answered. "It has often thrown him into fire or water to kill him. But if you can do anything, take pity on us and help us."
>
> "'If you can'?" said Jesus. "Everything is possible for one who believes."
>
> Immediately the boy's father exclaimed, "I do believe; help me overcome my unbelief!"
>
> When Jesus saw that a crowd was running to the scene, he rebuked the impure spirit. "You deaf and mute spirit," he said, "I command you, come out of him and never enter him again."
>
> The spirit shrieked, convulsed him violently and came out. The boy looked so much like a corpse that many said, "He's dead." But Jesus took him by the hand and lifted him to his feet, and he stood up.
>
> After Jesus had gone indoors, his disciples asked him privately, "Why couldn't we drive it out?" He replied, "This kind can come out only by prayer."

I love the father's honesty. I can imagine inside his head he is thinking, "Yes, I believe; well, not really, probably not as much as I should. But don't let that get in the way of the healing, please help me!" Jesus knows we are humans and that we struggle to believe sometimes. He knows that we look to others instead of Him for help and end up frustrated. Yet He still has compassion and wants to bring healing. **Some things can only be changed by prayer, by seeking Him first.**

WEEK 1 .... WEEK 2 .... WEEK 3 .... WEEK 4 .... WEEK 5 .... WEEK 6 .... WEEK 7 .... WEEK 8

DAY 4

HEARTWORK

End today with prayer. Confess the things you have made idols in your life. As you pray through them, write them down and imagine yourself holding them in your hands… then imagine yourself handing them to Him. Tell Him about your soul's desperation and ask God to bring hope and help to your soul. Ask Him to heal the brokenness in your home, both yours and your husband's. Everything is possible with Jesus.

CHARGE

This is not a mistake. I am equipped and accompanied by the One who made the plan.

THIS IS MY STORY PART 2

Jeremiah 29:11 "For I know the plans I have for you," declares the Lord, "plans to prosper you and not to harm you, plans to give you hope and a future."

WEEK 2 DAY 5

KEY THOUGHT: God promises to redeem and restore when we seek Him with our whole heart.

STORY: PART 5

That day, running in circles in my basement, I had reached my breaking point. I knew that if I continued on in my own strength, trying to piece together life on my own terms, I would stay depressed. I feared the suicidal thoughts that tormented me, and I hated the way I felt about my husband and marriage. In desperation, I cried out to God to set me free from the self-imposed bondage I had created through idol worship.

I knew I couldn't change my husband's heart, but I could take responsibility for my own. The rhythms of daily life had to change. I joined a Bible study with a group of complete strangers from a different church. I was surrounded by women who loved Jesus and who allowed me to share my story in a safe environment. There, my table leader shared how she had struggled with depression for nineteen years. It gave my heart hope, knowing that she had been delivered from her "evil spirits." Even if it was going to take years, I could see a light at the end of the tunnel. Someone who understood showed me it was there, even though it was way off in the distance.

My husband and I went to marriage counseling. We learned how to communicate better and how to identify the deeper issues that triggered our addictions. Following that I went to multiple other counselors on my own, individuals who loved God and who could speak the truth of the gospel over my aching heart. I read books that gave sound wisdom on my identity through God's eyes. I immersed myself in Scripture and prayer. Restoration came when I sought God with my whole heart.

Gradually, things in our marriage began to change. My heart softened towards my husband, and I was able to love him, "warts and all." Instead of turning to someone else, I learned to turn to God when we got into an argument or he began to struggle again. My husband joined an accountability group and found a good friend who could ask him the tough questions about his sexual purity. We began to face life as "we" instead of "me" and "I."

WEEK 1 .... WEEK 2 .... WEEK 3 .... WEEK 4 .... WEEK 5 .... WEEK 6 .... WEEK 7 .... WEEK 8

DAY 5

On the surface, I know I make it sound so easy. It isn't. The Spirit is willing, but the flesh is weak (Matthew 26:41). For us, there were still many moments of intense fighting and wounding words. There were nights when our bodies lay next to each other in bed, but our hearts and minds were worlds away. There were two whole years when it seemed like everything went wrong and the world was crashing in around us. During that time, we had to get gut-wrenchingly honest about our selfishness and unfaithfulness.

Last night, I asked my husband to pick one word to describe our marriage. He responded without hesitation: "thriving." That word brought me so much joy, because I agreed with him. If you would have asked us years ago to choose a word, we would have picked "dying." We didn't like each other, and our marriage was on the brink of divorce, but God didn't want to leave us there.

At this moment what word would you use to describe your marriage? _____

As we move forward through the next few weeks of study, I'm going to share more detailed, practical stories about how we learned to love one another the way Christ loved us. More importantly, together we will explore the truth of Scripture in depth to see how God can restore what is broken and dying. Don't give up hope. The redemption story is available to all of us who believe in Jesus.

One of the most quoted verses in the Bible about personal thriving is Jeremiah 29:11. It's a pleasant verse, one that has an Oprah-ish quality to it. Let's explore the historical context.

Israel once again found themselves in captivity, this time in Babylon. Their idol worship and immorality led to their demise. They were far from thriving. Let's take a closer look. Open your Bible and read Jeremiah 29:10-14.

Israel had turned from God, looking to their own selfish desires to meet their needs. Their idolatry led them back into slavery, repeating the cycle of bondage experienced by previous generations. The only way they were going to be delivered was a complete change of heart. I love verses 12-13 because God gives them a clear path for restoration. Reread those two verses and write down the action words listed there. You should find four phrases.

_____

_____

_____

_____

WEEK 1 .... WEEK 2 .... WEEK 3 .... WEEK 4 .... WEEK 5 .... WEEK 6 .... WEEK 7 .... WEEK 8

DAY 5

When Israel does these four things, what does God promise in return?

_____

_____

_____

_____

_____

I love that the God we serve isn't aloof or distant. He wants to be found, and He tells us how to do it. Unlike our addictions, His intentions are not to harm us or enslave us, but to bring us hope and a future. He is a personal God that keeps His promises, a God that is faithful to complete the good work He started in us when we first trusted in Him (Philippians 1:6).

Psalm 107 describes God's redemptive power so beautifully. It's the psalm written after God rescued Israel from the Babylonian captivity that we just read about in Jeremiah. It's also the story of our marriage. And it can be your story too.

Psalm 107:1-22
Give thanks to the Lord, for he is good; his love endures forever.

Let the redeemed of the Lord tell their story—those he redeemed from the hand of the foe, those he gathered from the lands, from east and west, from north and south.

Some wandered in desert wastelands, finding no way to a city where they could settle. They were hungry and thirsty, and their lives ebbed away.

Then they cried out to the Lord in their trouble, and he delivered them from their distress. He led them by a straight way to a city where they could settle.

Let them give thanks to the Lord for his unfailing love and his wonderful deeds for mankind, for he satisfies the thirsty and fills the hungry with good things.

Some sat in darkness, in utter darkness, prisoners suffering in iron chains, because they rebelled against God's commands and despised the plans of the Most-High.

So, he subjected them to bitter labor; they stumbled, and there was no one to help. Then they cried to the Lord in their trouble, and he saved them from their distress. He brought them out of darkness, the utter darkness, and broke away their chains. Let them give thanks to the Lord for his unfailing love and his wonderful deeds for mankind, for he breaks down gates of bronze and cuts through bars of iron.

Some became fools through their rebellious ways and suffered affliction because of their iniquities. They loathed all food and drew near the gates of death. Then they cried to the Lord in their trouble, and he saved them from their distress. He sent out his word and healed them; he rescued them from the grave. Let them give thanks to the Lord for his unfailing love and his wonderful deeds for mankind. Let them sacrifice thank offerings and tell of his works with songs of joy.

These verses have so many lines that encompass the story I've shared over this past week. I am the redeemed of the Lord and I am proud to share my story. The Lord delivered me from my distress, from utter darkness where there was no one to help, from my chains, from death. And He did the same for my husband.

HEARTWORK

Take some time for personal reflection as we end today. Which of the verses in Psalm 107 describe your story?

_____

_____

_____

_____

_____

What do you hear God whispering to your heart? How is He calling you to respond to Him? Write it down below. Then spend time talking with Him about what you've written.

_____

_____

WEEK 1 .... WEEK 2 .... WEEK 3 .... WEEK 4 .... WEEK 5 .... WEEK 6 .... WEEK 7 .... WEEK 8

DAY 5

_____

_____

_____

_____

Look up Psalm 51:12, Isiah 57:18, and Jeremiah 30:7. What would it look like to be restored in your marriage or to God?

_____

_____

_____

_____

_____

_____

HOMEWORK

Go to Appendix A. Read the Scripture passages. Talk to God about which passage resonates with the state of your heart right now. Commit to memorizing this verse. Write it on a note card and keep it with you.

Write out your own story. Take time to write out your childhood experiences and think about how they impact your relationship with your husband. How did you find out about his addiction? How did it impact you and your marriage? What do you want the next chapter of your story to look like?

CHARGE

This is not a mistake. I am equipped and accompanied by the One who made the plan.

TESTIMONY

YOU ARE A WARRIOR. I am so proud of you for being on this journey. After eight years post "trauma" I was able to get my hands on this study and even then, it tore down some of my tallest walls and exposed the places of my heart that needed healing. It was a significant reminder that I'm responsible for me and a balm to my soul that reinforced just how much I am loved by my Good Father. It helped me work through bitterness that I had accepted as natural and accepted in my life and marriage. This study will mess you up if you let it—in all the best ways. I'm so thankful for the women and men who saw the need to fill this gap and make a way for healing in marriages. KEEP READING! You will be amazed at the miracles that will happen!

Lauren

Passionate for God,
Repentant in spirit,
Open and honest,
Victorious in living,
Eternal in perspective, and
Networking with other ***PROVEN Wives.***

PW

WEEK THREE

WHO AM I?

Exodus 3:14 "God said to Moses, 'I am who I am.'"

WEEK 3 DAY 1

KEY THOUGHT: Your identity is not defined by your circumstances or mistakes. It is defined by your God.

I'm a Moses. Let me explain. Have you ever read through Scripture and realized that you are just like one of the characters? As far as the Old Testament goes, I identify with Moses. He is a rescuer, ready to jump in when things are unjust, ready to fight for the underdog. He is also exceptionally insecure, a man unsure of his own identity.

We meet Moses in the book of Exodus, born a Jewish slave in the land of Egypt. The head Egyptian ruler, Pharaoh, was afraid of the Jewish people, or Israelites, because they were great in number. He feared them so greatly that he ordered all Jewish baby boys to be executed at birth.

Through the sovereign hand of God, Moses' mother placed him in a papyrus basket and floated him down the Nile, where he was rescued by Pharaoh's daughter. She adopted him and he "was educated in all the wisdom of the Egyptians and was powerful in his speech and actions" (Acts 7:22).

Even though Moses was Egyptian royalty, he was conflicted internally about his nationality and heritage. Outwardly, he was an Egyptian prince, but his true loyalties became apparent when he noticed an Egyptian taskmaster beating a Hebrew slave. Incensed, Moses responded immediately. "Looking all around and seeing no one, he struck the Egyptian dead and hid him in the sand" (Exodus 2:12). When faced with injustice, he jumped into action, using his own strength to solve the problem at hand and deliver his fellow kinsmen.

The murder was discovered and news spreads like wildfire. The very next day, Moses again tried to solve injustice when he tried to break up a fight, this time between two Jewish slaves.

When Moses confronted the aggressor, the Hebrew retorted, "Who made you a leader and judge over us? Are you planning to kill me as you killed the Egyptian?" (Exodus 2:14).

DAY 1

Moses' violence was discovered and the news spreads all the way to the Egyptian palace. Pharaoh's favor quickly turned to anger when he heard about what Moses had done. Once again, just like when he was a baby, Moses had to escape the death threats of an Egyptian leader. Moses fled to Midian, where he again became the hero of the underdog by rescuing seven young ladies from the hands of ill-willed shepherds. One of them, Zipporah, became his wife, and Moses lived with her family as a shepherd for forty years (Acts 7:30).

In just the first two chapters of Exodus, Moses has had so many different titles. In his youth, he holds these conflicting names: Jewish baby boy, orphan, adopted son, prince of Egypt. At the age of forty he is an avenger, murderer, and fugitive. He then becomes his wife's rescuer and husband (Acts 7:23-29).

All this transition from one extreme to the next in his personal life is cause for great internal conflict. Is he Jewish or Egyptian? Prince or shepherd? His confusion over his true identity was evident after the birth of his first child, "whom he named Gershom, for he said, 'I have been a foreigner in a foreign land'" (Exodus 2:22). Moses felt like an outcast, like someone who doesn't belong. A man without a country and lacking a clear sense of his identity.

Take a few moments to think about the labels that you have carried in your own life. Things you have been told or circumstances that you have been in that you feel define who you are.

For example, one of the labels that I carried around in my youth and still wrestle with is "boring." It stems back to high school when one of the more popular guys, mid-conversation with me, said, "You're boring. I am going to go talk to someone who is more fun." In that moment I felt rejected, unacceptable and inadequate. Who I was just wasn't good enough. In order to be accepted, I had to be the fun and flirty type. Studious and serious meant I was boring.

On the lines below, write out some of the labels and lies you carry with you. Feel free to journal about the circumstances surrounding each label.

_____

_____

_____

_____

_____

_____

WEEK 1 .... WEEK 2 .... WEEK 3 .... WEEK 4 .... WEEK 5 .... WEEK 6 .... WEEK 7 .... WEEK 8

DAY 1

Like us, Moses defined himself by his own mistakes, life circumstances and personality. But then Moses encountered the God of Abraham, Isaac and Jacob on an ordinary day while tending his flocks. His identity question was about to be answered once and for all. Take a few moments and read Exodus 3:1-14.

On the lines below, write out verse 11.

_____

_____

Think about what Moses was asking God at that moment. His question, "Who am I?" is a deep one, filled with angst and doubt. I suspect Moses felt guilty and unworthy. He was known as a murderer in Egypt. How would he be received if he went back? I suspect he felt afraid and unprepared. Pharaoh was a powerful man, responsible for the enslavement of generations of Hebrews. Certainly forty years of desert living as a shepherd, father, and husband were not the ideal training grounds to prepare Moses for this kind of mission.

Then God flips Moses' question into one of the most powerful statements in Scripture. Read verse 14 again and write out God's reply below.

_____

_____

Moses' identity didn't matter, God's did. Moses asked, "Who am I?" and God replied with "I AM who I am." Not you, Moses, but me. Not your strength, but mine. In his own strength, Moses was a stuttering murderer (Exodus 4:10). His attempts to deliver his people ended in disaster, and the Israelites didn't even realize that God had called Moses to rescue them (Acts 7:25). But even with all his failures, God wanted to use this sinful and confused man to not only deliver his people from slavery, but also deliver them to their destiny in the Promised Land.

When I was asked to write this study, I was struggling with the same question. "Who am I to write this?" The longer I prayed about it and sought God's direction, the more I realized He had been preparing me for this all along. I was an education major in college, so I love sharing what I've learned with others. My minor was English, and I love the written word. I have always had a heart for women's ministry and have been pursuing it for years in my local church. And I am married to a man, who like so many others, struggles with sexual addiction. God reminded me that the struggles and life experiences that He had allowed in my life were the very things He would use to help me write this study. If I had walked in my self-doubt instead of His strength, I would have missed the opportunity to trust the great I AM to do His work through me.

Take a moment to consider all that had happened in Moses' life up until this point. He was born a Jew. He lived in the Egyptian palace, so he knew the enemy firsthand. He had a passion in his heart to help his countrymen.

WEEK 1 .... WEEK 2 .... WEEK 3 .... WEEK 4 .... WEEK 5 .... WEEK 6 .... WEEK 7 .... WEEK 8

DAY 1

He became a foreigner, just like the Israelites in Egypt. Everything in his past was preparing him to lead the Jews out of slavery. But his identity crisis was standing in the way.

When you are married to someone struggling with a sexual addiction, it's easy to attach your identity to their sin. So many labels and lies get planted into our minds by the enemy. "You're un-wanted. Un-loved. Un-acceptable. Un-desirable." I could continue on, but rather than give credence to the lies, let's explore the truth. The truth is, our identity does not lie in him (our husband), but in HIM (our God)! Your husband's sinful actions and words cannot change who you are in Christ.

So, who are you in Christ?

The book of Ephesians is one of my favorites because it contains so much practical truth, including the truth about who we are in Christ. Read Ephesians 1:3-14. For each verse below, write down what God says about your identity in Him on the corresponding blank. Some verses will have multiple words.

Ephesians 1:3 I am

_____.

Ephesians 1:11 I am

_____.

Ephesians 1:4 I am

_____.

Ephesians 1:13 I am

_____.

Ephesians 1:5 I am

_____.

Ephesians 1:14 I am

_____.

Ephesians 1:7 I am

_____.

Here are some of the words I wrote down: I am blessed, chosen, holy, blameless, predestined, adopted, redeemed, forgiven, included, sealed, His possession.

Now do the same exercise for Ephesians 2:1-13.

Ephesians 2:5 I am

_____.

Ephesians 2:10 I am

_____.

Ephesians 2:8 I am

_____.

Ephesians 2:13 I am

_____.

These are the truths I took note of: I am alive in Him, saved by grace, God's handiwork (masterpiece), brought near to Him.

WEEK 1 .... WEEK 2 .... WEEK 3 .... WEEK 4 .... WEEK 5 .... WEEK 6 .... WEEK 7 .... WEEK 8

DAY 1

Look back earlier in today's study when you wrote down some of the labels you carry. In the section below, write down the negative labels you believe or have been given once more. Next to it, write out the words from Ephesians that speak truth against that lie.

So, with my example, it looks like this:

LIE: I am boring and excluded. TRUTH: I am chosen, included, God's masterpiece

LABEL/LIE	GOD'S TRUTH

Just like Moses, we all have lies about our true identity that are birthed out of our circumstances and our sin. As women married to men with sexual addiction, old insecurities frequently get amplified while new ones emerge. The insecurity and doubt can be crippling, just like they were for Moses, bringing fear and hesitancy to fulfill God's calling on our lives. But God doesn't want us to walk in the lies. He wants us to know the truth that leads to freedom (John 8:32). We are God's masterpiece, created in His image.

HEARTWORK

As we close out today's study, take some time to pray the words of truth from Ephesians out loud in thanksgiving ("Thank you, God, that I am accepted, thank you for making me your masterpiece," etc.).

As you pray, ask God to help you believe those truths.

On a few notecards, write down the verses that really spoke to you today about your identity in Christ. My favorites are Ephesians 1:11-13 and Ephesians 2:8-10. Write them down and put them in places in your home where you will see them frequently. Pray them over yourself when you are feeling insecure, inadequate and unloved. His truth will bring healing and hope to your heart.

CHARGE

The price Jesus paid for me determined my value. Any other assessment is a lie.

WORTH IT

John 10:11 "I am the good shepherd. The good shepherd lays down His life for the sheep."

WEEK 3 DAY 2

KEY THOUGHT: You are worth it because you are worth dying for.

On the heels of the women's rights movement, the French cosmetics company L'Oréal trademarked a new slogan, "Because I'm worth it." Their commercials in the 1970s featured beautiful women bragging that they were willing to spend more for L'Oréal hair color (a grand $2.75 at the time!) because they were worth it.

The irony is that this is a cosmetics company… a company that uses beautiful, skinny women with perfect hair and skin to advertise products that will make you feel more confident about yourself. It contradicts the very message that, on your own, you are worth it. Just use our overpriced product, and you will find your self-worth.

As women, we are bombarded on all sides with ways we can improve our self-worth. It's discussed extensively on talk shows, in countless books, and in our children's schools. The positive quotes captured on inspirational wall hangings in our homes and classrooms sound great. Quotes like:

"To thine own self be true." —William Shakespeare

"No one can make you feel inferior without your consent." —Eleanor Roosevelt

"Accept everything about yourself—I mean everything. You are you and that is the beginning and the end—no apologies, no regrets." —Henry A. Kissinger

"Be yourself; everyone else is already taken." —Oscar Wilde

"Parents need to fill a child's bucket of self-esteem so high that the rest of the world can't poke enough holes to drain it dry." —Alvin Price

On the surface these quotes are motivational and empowering, but what is the foundation for the ideas being expressed? What about when I don't feel good about myself, can I just glance over at a motivational poster or apply some almond-spice hair color to my grays and I'll finally feel worthy?

WEEK 1 .... WEEK 2 .... WEEK 3 .... WEEK 4 .... WEEK 5 .... WEEK 6 .... WEEK 7 .... WEEK 8

DAY 2

As I shared in my story in chapter two, after my husband had a relapse into his sexual addiction, my self-esteem spiraled out of control quickly. I was depressed and angry, desperate to find help and hope. I had no confidence in who I was as a wife or a woman, and I was craving the truth. One of the greatest resources that helped me find that truth was the book *The Search for Significance*, by Robert S. McGee.

I cannot recommend this book enough. It would be a great follow-up after you complete this study. McGee includes so many great truths that are impossible to cover in just one lesson, but I've included some highlights below. As you read the excerpts, underline the portions that strike a chord in your heart and then answer the thought-provoking questions that correspond to the reading.

> The man or woman who lives only for the love and attention of others is never satisfied—at least, not for long. Despite our efforts, we will never find lasting, fulfilling peace if we must continually prove ourselves to others. Our desire to be loved and accepted is a symptom of a deeper need—the need that frequently governs our behavior and is the primary source of our emotional pain. Often unrecognized, this is our need for self-worth.[11]

Why do you think the author says that our desire to be accepted governs our behavior? Have you found this to be true in your own life?

_____

_____

_____

_____

_____

_____

McGee shares more truth about how we look to the wrong source for self-worth:

> Since the fall, man has often failed to turn to God for the truth about himself. Instead, he has looked to others to meet his inescapable need for self-worth. *I am what others say I am,* he has reasoned. *I will find my value in their opinions of me.*
>
> Isn't it amazing that we turn to others who have a perspective as limited and darkened as our own to discover our worth! Rather than relying on God's steady, uplifting reassurance of who we are, we depend on others who base our worth on our ability to meet their standards. Our true value is not based on our behavior or the approval of others but on what God's Word says is true of us.

WEEK 1 .... WEEK 2 .... WEEK 3 .... WEEK 4 .... WEEK 5 .... WEEK 6 .... WEEK 7 .... WEEK 8

DAY 2

If we base our worth solidly on the truths of God's Word, then our behavior will often reflect His love, grace, and power. But if we base our worth on our abilities or the fickle approval of others, then our behavior will reflect the insecurity, fear, and anger that come from such instability.[12]

Why do you think we look to others instead of God for our approval?

_____

_____

_____

_____

_____

Take some time and think about the people in your life that you look to most for your approval. Write their names down on the lines below. What are some of the messages you have received from these people about your worth? Feel free to include both positive and negative examples. Make sure to include your husband. How has his sexual addiction impacted your view of self?

_____

_____

_____

_____

_____

If you remember John 10:10, a verse we have referenced multiple times in this study, you will recall that God desires to bring us life. But our enemy, Satan, comes only to steal, kill and destroy. This is why Satan "continues to deceive people, including many Christians, into believing that the basis of their worth is their performance and their ability to please others."[13]

WEEK 1 .... WEEK 2 .... WEEK 3 .... WEEK 4 .... WEEK 5 .... WEEK 6 .... WEEK 7 .... WEEK 8

DAY 2

McGee says that Satan uses this equation to deceive us:

Self-Worth = Performance + Others' Opinions

How many times a day does our enemy use this lie to make us feel insignificant and unloved? It's a formula that sets us up for disaster and depression. According to Satan, your value is dependent on your actions and other people's perception of you. What impossible standards to live up to! Our performance, even when we are at our best, will eventually fail to meet someone's standards or opinions. Our enemy knows the goal is unachievable and unmeasurable. It stands in stark opposition to the truth that God loves us without any effort on our part (1 John 4:19).

Satan gets into our thoughts and causes us to doubt the truth because he knows the truth will set us free (John 8:32). The truth is that we serve a Savior who is unwavering in His love and care for us.

> We do not have to be successful or pleasing to others to have a healthy sense of self-esteem and worth. That worth has freely and conclusively been given to us by God. Failure and/or disapproval of others can't take it away! Therefore, we can conclude, *It would be nice to be approved by my parents (or whomever), but if they don't approve of me, I'm still loved and accepted by God.* Do you see the difference? The *have-to* mentality is sheer slavery to performance and the opinions of others, but we are secure and free in Christ. Christ is the source of our security; Christ is the basis of our worth; Christ is the only one who promises and never fails.[14]

Let's dive into the Scriptures and uncover some truths about how worthy we are in God's eyes. Open your Bible and read John 10:1-15.

What does the hired hand do for the sheep in this parable (verse 12)? What does the Good Shepherd do for His sheep (verse 15)?

_____

_____

_____

_____

_____

_____

_____

Although the hired hands in this parable seemingly care for the sheep, they do not love the sheep enough to sacrifice themselves for it. It's such a powerful picture of why we should place our trust in God rather than man. When trouble comes, man will eventually run the other way. But God rushes in and saves us from disaster. He alone truly knows us and will do whatever it takes to protect us from the enemy who wants to steal, kill and destroy (verse 10).

How does this parable impact you? Write down your thoughts.

_____

_____

_____

_____

_____

_____

_____

_____

_____

_____

_____

_____

Now let's look at the concept of self-worth from a different passage. Turn to 1 John 4:7-10 and answer the questions below.

Where does love come from (verse 7)? _____.

Complete the blank from verse 8: God is _____.

How did God show His love to us (verse 9-10)? _____.

DAY 2

HEARTWORK

The challenge for us is to choose to listen to God instead of man. After reading this passage, the choice seems obvious. God's love towards us is unlimited and unchanging. He will never fail us.

Take some time to pray and ask God to help you look to Him alone for your self-worth. Thank Him for loving you freely.

CHARGE

The price Jesus paid for me determined my value. Any other assessment is a lie.

SEARCH FOR SIGNIFICANCE

Romans 5:1 "Therefore, since we have been justified through faith, we have peace with God through our Lord Jesus Christ."

WEEK 3 DAY 3

KEY THOUGHT: Your true value lies in what Christ has done for you, not in what you do or what others think.

Yesterday we started to look at the basic lie that Satan speaks over us to make us feel unworthy. Glance back at yesterday's lesson and write down the equation below:

$$Self\text{-}worth = \underline{\hspace{3cm}} + \underline{\hspace{4cm}}$$

Today we are going to take a deeper look at this idea and break it down into the false beliefs that Satan whispers in our ears. McGee covers four different false beliefs in his book, but I am going to focus on the first two for this study. If you want to dive deeper into all four, I really do recommend reading this book! Also, in Appendix G you will find a chart that summarizes all four false beliefs and the Scriptural answer to each one.

FALSE BELIEF #1:

The Performance Trap: *"I must meet certain standards in order to feel good about myself."*

A primary deception all of us tend to believe is that success will bring fulfillment and happiness. Again and again, we've tried to measure up, thinking that if we could meet certain standards we would feel good about ourselves. But again and again, we've failed and have felt miserable. Even if we succeed on a fairly regular basis, occasional failure may be so devastating that it dominates our perception of ourselves.[15]

The consequences of basing our self-worth on our performance are far-reaching and include the fear of failure, perfectionism, manipulating others, and withdrawal from healthy risks.[16]

This false belief has been a huge struggle in my life. Growing up Catholic with a list of do's and don'ts definitely exacerbated my natural tendency towards perfectionism. I had to get all A's, I had to be the best at sports, I had to be the best behaved and most responsible.

In high school, we had an all-girls gym class. The private school I went to was small, so we combined grades for this class. My sister is only eleven months younger than I am, so we were in gym together. She was naturally more athletic than I was, and so I worked really hard to be just as good as she was or better.

One year, while running the dreaded one mile for the presidential fitness test, I was at the head of the pack. The course was new, and I didn't know where to go after the half-mile mark. I turned the wrong way and was way off track by the time I realized I had taken a faulty turn. Desperate to win, I pushed with everything I had to catch up to the rest of the girls. My sister and I ended up tying for first, running across the finish line at the exact same moment.

As soon as the race ended, I crumbled into a heap on the asphalt and began sobbing through my shortened breath, "I tied her! NO! I can't believe we tied!" All the other students in the class looked at me with disbelief, and I remember at least one girl saying, "you are so mean!"

I wanted to win, to be the best. I didn't care how that made my sister feel or how it made me appear in front of others. I was angry and disappointed with my effort, even though it could be argued that I technically crossed the line first after running at least an extra quarter mile. My perceived failure caused me to think less of myself and bring pain to one of the most important people in my life.

What about you? Have you, like me, literally gone to great lengths to outperform someone else? Do you feel the constant need to meet a certain standard to feel good about yourself? This false belief may come into play for you because of your husband's sexual addiction. Perhaps you feel that if you just tried harder to be a better wife then your husband would stop struggling with lust. Journal your thoughts below.

_____

_____

_____

_____

_____

_____

_____

_____

DAY 3

The amazing thing is that God doesn't require us to perform at a certain standard in order to be loved. We have been justified through faith, or "placed in right standing before God."[17] The book of Romans sheds light on this concept of **justification**:

Romans 4:4-8

4 When people work, their wages are not a gift, but something they have earned. **5** But people are counted as righteous, not because of their work, but because of their faith in God who forgives sinners. **6** David also spoke of this when he described the happiness of those who are declared righteous without working for it: **7** "Oh, what joy for those whose disobedience is forgiven, whose sins are put out of sight. **8** Yes, what joy for those whose record the Lord has cleared of sin." (NLT)

Romans 5:1

Therefore, since we have been made right in God's sight by faith, we have peace with God because of what Jesus Christ our Lord has done for us.

What does Paul say makes us righteous in God's sight?

_____

What is the result of justification? Look at Romans 4:7-8 and Romans 5:1 for the answer.

_____

_____

_____

Because of Jesus' sacrifice on the cross, we have been justified by faith. "Because of justification, I bear Christ's righteousness, and I am therefore fully pleasing to the Father."[18]

How does this truth impact you? How would your view of self change if you were able to fully realize the fact that God loves you regardless of performance?

_____

_____

_____

WEEK 1 .... WEEK 2 .... WEEK 3 .... WEEK 4 .... WEEK 5 .... WEEK 6 .... WEEK 7 .... WEEK 8

DAY 3

_____

_____

_____

_____

FALSE BELIEF #2:

The Approval Addiction: *"I must be approved (accepted) by others to feel good about myself."*

We can ultimately seek either the approval of men or of God as the basis of our self-worth. We cannot seek both. God wants to be the Lord of our lives, and He is unwilling to share that rightful lordship with anyone else. Therefore, the only way we can overcome the fear of rejection is to value the constant approval of God over the conditional approval of people.[19]

The consequences of constantly seeking others' approval are the "fear of rejection, attempts to please others at any cost, overly sensitive to criticism, and withdrawal from others to avoid disapproval.[20]

Again, this false belief has been a huge struggle for me as well. I long for approval from people, even people I don't like. If I know that someone doesn't like me or is upset with me, I try everything in my power to earn their approval. I have changed how I act, what I wear, and what I say all in an attempt to gain others' praise. The compliments are never enough, and the criticism always weighs heavier in the balance. One insult or disapproving comment negates any positive words I have received up until that moment.

What about you? How important is the approval of others in your life? Does it affect how you act or speak?

_____

_____

_____

_____

_____

The need for approval has also played a role in my relationship with my husband and our sex life. I said yes to certain activities in the bedroom because I wanted to please him, even though I was uncomfortable.

WEEK 1 .... WEEK 2 .... WEEK 3 .... WEEK 4 .... WEEK 5 .... WEEK 6 .... WEEK 7 .... WEEK 8

DAY 3

How has your need for approval impacted your relationship with your husband? How has it impacted your sexual relationship with him?

_____

_____

_____

_____

_____

God's Word again gives us the truth to combat the lie that we need approval from others. The answer to this addiction comes through **reconciliation.**

Write out Colossians 1:21-22 below.

_____

_____

_____

_____

_____

McGee gives us more insight into how God presents us holy in His sight through reconciliation. Underline the phrases that speak to you as you read these excerpts:

> Reconciliation means that although I was at one time hostile toward God and alienated from Him, I am now forgiven and have been brought into an intimate relationship with Him. Consequently, I am totally accepted by God.[21]

> We can do nothing to contribute to Christ's free gift of salvation; furthermore, if we base our self-worth on the approval of others, then we are actually saying that our ability to please others is of greater value than Christ's payment. We will begin to discover true freedom and maturity in Christ only when we understand that our lives mean much more than what success or the approval of others can bring.[22]

WEEK 1 .... WEEK 2 .... WEEK 3 .... WEEK 4 .... WEEK 5 .... WEEK 6 .... WEEK 7 .... WEEK 8

DAY 3

Do you recognize that Christ's death on the cross speaks such great volumes about your worth? You are so valuable to Him that He died for you. The message of love communicated by His sacrifice far outweighs others' opinions and approval. It also outweighs the disapproval you feel when your husband turns to pornography.

If you truly believed that Christ fully approves of you, how would that change the way you view yourself? How would this truth impact your response the next time you discovered your husband was looking at pornography?

_____

_____

_____

_____

_____

_____

_____

_____

_____

_____

 ## HEARTWORK

We are going to close out today with a few different passages that talk about our value to God. After you read each one, write down which lie (Performance Trap or Approval Addict or both) that it combats and why.

Psalm 139:14-18

_____

_____

_____

WEEK 1 .... WEEK 2 .... WEEK 3 .... WEEK 4 .... WEEK 5 .... WEEK 6 .... WEEK 7 .... WEEK 8

DAY 3

1 Peter 2:9-10

_____

_____

_____

Romans 15:7

_____

_____

_____

Colossians 2:13-15

_____

_____

_____

Spend some time in prayer thanking God that you don't have to earn His approval or live for others. Thank Him for accepting you through Christ's death on the cross.

CHARGE

The price Jesus paid for me determined my value. Any other assessment is a lie.

GOOD ENOUGH

Psalm 73:25-26 "Whom have I in heaven but you? And earth has nothing I desire besides you. My flesh and my heart may fail, but God is the strength of my heart and my portion forever."

WEEK 3 DAY 4

KEY THOUGHT: You don't have to be good enough. God is good, and He is enough.

Every time I make a trip to our local buy-in-bulk store, I experience an overwhelming sense of contentment when all the bags and boxes get unpacked at home. Typically, I stand back with both refrigerator doors wide open and let out a huge sigh of relief. My heart is happy when I see that every bin, shelf and drawer is full to capacity… and I'm also glad I won't have to do that chore again for another few weeks! The relief I experience on these shopping trips comes from knowing that my family will be taken care of, that they will be satisfied.

Because both my husband and I grew up in large families where money was tight, there were many times when food was scarce in the house. We didn't starve by any means, but it was carefully portioned out for the week so that we could make it to the next paycheck. We made frequent trips to the food bank. I remember being so jealous of my friends at school that actually got to eat BOTH the snack cakes in the double pack. And there was one Thanksgiving when someone dropped off a turkey and all the fixings because we just didn't have the money that year. There just never seemed to be enough, and deep down it made me question if God was good. Was He able to fulfill my deepest desires? My fear and mistrust of His ability to provide led me to a life of **striving** for more, so I could fill in the missing gaps.

When you are married to someone with a sexual addiction, fear of "the missing gaps" is often present. Your husband's betrayal leads to mistrust and fear that he will never be able to care for you the way your heart desires. For me, those fears also lead to a **constant striving** in order to be good enough for him, hoping that would make him love me more. I have spent many late nights lying awake, wondering what I could do to make myself better for my husband. If I could just be more for him somehow, maybe he wouldn't want to look at porn. I spun my wheels, trying to be more pretty, more patient, more forgiving, even more sexual. The problem is that my extra effort could never be the solution to the real problem. Deep down my husband wanted more, he wanted to be filled and satisfied. And I wanted more, too, the same feeling of true satisfaction. We were looking to each other to meet that desire, when we should have been looking to our Savior.

God has created within each one of us a deep desire for Him, a longing that only He alone can fill. When we place our hope in anyone or anything but Him, our true desires will remain unfulfilled. It all goes back to the Garden of Eden. We covered the Creation in week one of our study, but let's take another look through a different lens.

In Genesis 1:31-2:1, the Bible says, "God saw all that He had made, and it was very good... Thus the heavens and the earth were completed in all their vast array." Note the words used to describe his creation: **very good, completed.** Then in Genesis 2:9 we read, "The Lord God made all kinds of trees grow out of the ground—trees that were pleasing to the eye and good for food. In the middle of the garden were the tree of life and the tree of the knowledge of good and evil." We discover in this verse that **ALL** the trees were pleasing and **GOOD** for food.

God's creation was **GOOD,** and it was **ENOUGH.** There was nothing left for God to do, His creation was a complete work. He created a world for Adam and Eve that was sustaining, pleasing and beautiful. Man was satisfied in God's presence, until the truth about God's good provision was tainted by a lie.

Open your Bible and read Genesis 2:16. Write it down on the lines below.

_____

_____

Now read Genesis 3:1-7. What question did Satan ask Eve in verse 1?

_____

_____

Notice how Satan twisted God's command from Genesis 2:16. God said they could eat from any tree except one, Satan asked if God told them not to eat from any tree at all. He drew her attention away from **all God had provided** to focus on the **one thing** she couldn't have. After Satan distracted her from the truth, he then planted a lie: "No, you will not die; you will be like God." The serpent called God a liar and promised Eve that if she took what she wanted, she could be like God.

Satan convinced her that she didn't **have enough** and that she **wasn't enough**. He made her believe that God was withholding something that would make her life better and make her a more complete person. Once Eve bought the lie, she took things into her own hands literally by taking the fruit and eating it. At the heart of this seemingly simple and innocent act was a deeper issue. Eve was seeking to be like God, discontent with whom He had made her to be. If she could be like God, she would no longer need to be dependent on Him, the very Creator who breathed life into her body.

Unfortunately, eating the fruit did not bring the satisfaction that she was hoping for. She did not get the upgrade she expected. Instead, she was left feeling naked and ashamed, having her eyes opened to sin and its consequences (Genesis 3:7).

We repeat Eve's sinful choice every time we search after things other than God to satisfy our deepest desires and longings. How often do we take our eyes off of all the good things that God has provided for us and look at the one thing we don't have? We long for the piece of forbidden fruit to bring us satisfaction when we have access to the One whose presence brings us "fullness of joy" (Psalm 16:11). For your husband, that thing is frequently pornography. But what about you?

What things in your life have you longed for that you believe will finally make you feel complete, like you have enough and are enough? What has the pursuit of these things brought into your life? Are they ever fully satisfying? Perhaps it is motherhood, or a best friend, or the dream job. For me, I spent the longest time looking to my spouse to make me feel like a complete person. Take some time to honestly answer these questions on the lines below.

_____

_____

_____

_____

_____

_____

_____

_____

_____

_____

When we choose to believe God is good and that He is enough, we can rest in who He has made us to be and the circumstances He allows in our life. Psalm 34 sheds some light on this idea.

DAY 4

Read Psalm 34:1-10 below.

1 I will *praise* the Lord at all times. I will constantly speak his praises.

2 I will boast only in the Lord; let all who are helpless take heart.

3 Come, let us tell of the Lord's greatness; let us exalt his name together.

4 I prayed to the Lord, and he answered me. He freed me from all my fears.

5 Those who *look to him* for help will be radiant with joy; no shadow of shame will darken their faces.

6 In my desperation I *prayed,* and the Lord listened; he saved me from all my troubles.

7 For the angel of the Lord is a guard; he surrounds and defends all who fear him.

8 Taste and see that the Lord is good. Oh, the joys of those who take refuge in him!

9 Fear the Lord, you his godly people, for those who fear him will have all they need.

10 Even strong young lions sometimes go hungry, but those who *trust* in the Lord will lack no good thing.

In verses 8–10, circle the words that indicate how God is both good and enough.

I love how verse 8 says, "taste and see that the Lord is good." Eve saw the fruit and tasted it, but it wasn't good. It brought sin, evil and shame into the world. *She took her eyes off of her Creator and looked to His creation.* But when we see and taste what the Lord has done, it will bring us joy instead of shame (verse 5 and 8).

Reread Psalm 34:1-10 once again and this time underline the action words the Psalmist uses to talk about his relationship with God. Each verse has at least one. I've done a few above in bold italic as examples.

In verses 4-7, what does the Psalmist say God will do for those who seek after Him and call on His name?

_____

_____

_____

WEEK 1 .... WEEK 2 .... WEEK 3 .... WEEK 4 .... WEEK 5 .... WEEK 6 .... WEEK 7 .... WEEK 8

DAY 4

When you choose to believe that God is good and that He is enough, your identity won't be shaken when your husband struggles with sexual sin. Instead of crumbling in despair and defeat, we can run to our Savior who will carry us through the struggle. God is our "refuge and strength, a very present help in trouble" (Psalm 46:1). He has our best in mind, working all things together for good, even though we may never fully understand it (Romans 8:28, Isaiah 55:8).

Christ alone can satisfy our heart's deepest longings and desires. The lyrics to a worship song have been running through my mind over and over as I write this lesson:

> All of you is more than enough for all of me
> For every thirst and every need
> You satisfy me with Your love
> And all I have in You is more than enough[23]

Not only is God enough, but He is more than enough!

Read Ephesians 3:20-21. What does the writer say God is able to do (second half of verse 20)?

_____

_____

_____

_____

God can do above and beyond all that we can ask or even imagine! He is more than enough. In Exodus 16, He provided more than enough daily manna for the Israelites for forty years. In 1 Kings 17, He provided more than enough oil and flour to feed Elijah and his friends until the drought ended. In Matthew 15, Jesus provided more than enough bread for four thousand men. Our God is a good God who gives us more than enough.

Do you believe that God is good and that He gives more than enough? How would believing this truth change the way you see yourself? How would believing this truth change the way you respond to your spouse's sexual addiction? Before you answer, read the verse listed at the top of today's lesson (Psalm 73:25-26).

_____

_____

_____

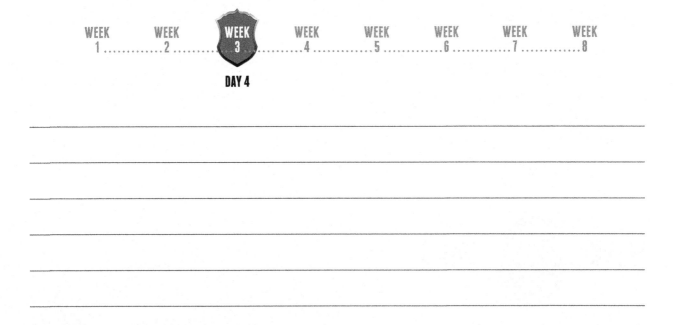

WEEK 1 .... WEEK 2 .... WEEK 3 .... WEEK 4 .... WEEK 5 .... WEEK 6 .... WEEK 7 .... WEEK 8

DAY 4

_____

_____

_____

_____

_____

_____

_____

HEARTWORK

Let's finish today with a famous Psalm. Psalm 23 beautifully speaks of God's goodness and provision. As we close, pray these verses out loud to your God.

The LORD is my shepherd, I lack nothing. He makes me lie down in green pastures,

he leads me beside quiet waters, he refreshes my soul.

He guides me along the right paths for his name's sake.

Even though I walk through the darkest valley, I will fear no evil, for you are with me; your rod and your staff, they comfort me.

You prepare a table before me in the presence of my enemies. You anoint my head with oil; my cup overflows.

Surely your goodness and love will follow me all the days of my life, and I will dwell in the house of the LORD forever.

CHARGE

The price Jesus paid for me determined my value. Any other assessment is a lie.

CALLED DAUGHTER

Luke 8:47-48 "Then the woman, seeing that she could not go unnoticed, came trembling and fell at his feet. In the presence of all the people, she told why she had touched him and how she had been instantly healed. Then he said to her, 'Daughter, your faith has healed you. Go in peace.'"

WEEK 3 DAY 5

KEY THOUGHT: You have value because you are a child of God.

If you are a mom and you have a little girl, you know what a great joy and responsibility it is to have a daughter. I have had the privilege to raise both a son and a daughter, and there's something special about my relationship with each of my children. The unique part of having a little girl is having a "mini-me," another person in the family who can identify with the ups and downs of being female. You will commiserate with her over the inconvenience of always waiting in line for the public restroom. You will cry with her over a bowl of popcorn and a chick-flick. You will celebrate with her when she goes on her first date, gets her diploma, marries her best friend, gives birth to her own child.

If you aren't a mom, maybe you are a daughter who understands this special mother-daughter relationship. It's a unique and powerful bond. Storytellers have long understood the compelling nature of this connection, tugging at the heartstrings of their audiences with stories like Snow White and Cinderella. The death of a loving mother replaced by the presence of an evil one has a lasting impact on the young girl in each of these fairy tales, and as we watch their stories unfold, a deep sense of compassion stirs within us.

There's a story that's told in three of the four Gospels that tells of two daughters. Open your Bible and read Luke 8:40-56.

I love this story! There is so much to learn about how God loves the women He has created in this passage. In his commentary on the Gospel of Luke, Charles R. Swindoll sets the stage for this story and shows us how much is going on behind the scenes.

> As Jesus came ashore back from a trip to the region of Decapolis, the needs of two very different women demanded His attention. One was the daughter of a prominent leader in the Jewish community; the other, an anonymous social outcast. How He would address their competing needs would define His ministry in many ways. Would He favor the one promising greater political advantage? Would He help the helpless at the risk of alienating powerful friends? Or would class

distinction carry any weight at all with Jesus? Would He address the most pressing need and leave the less urgent for later?[24]

The females in this passage come from completely opposite worlds. The little girl was the daughter of a prominent Jewish leader, Jairus. He was a man of position and power, known well enough that his name gets mentioned in the Bible. The twelve-year-old girl was his only child and the apple of his eye. Jairus loved his daughter so much that he was willing to push his way through the enormous, crushing crowd and beg at Jesus' feet for Him to come and heal her. He unashamedly made his need known, hopeful that Jesus would listen and respond to his plea for help.

The woman described in Luke 8:43-48 was a nobody in her culture. She wasn't even named in this story, we just know her as the "sick woman" or "the woman with the issue of blood." Unlike Jairus' daughter, she was alone and uncherished because her illness left her untouchable. She was considered "unclean," and anyone who came into contact with the places she sat on or slept in was also considered unclean (Leviticus 15:25-30).

The continual flow of blood, a condition that she dealt with for twelve years, left her hopeless and penniless. It also brought her deep shame and emotional pain, for certainly she must have been the brunt of name-calling, scowling glares, and ostracization. She quietly lurked in the chaos of the crowd, waiting for a chance just to get close to Jesus. She didn't declare her need or ask for help like Jairus; instead, she lingered in the background, desperately hoping to be healed without anyone noticing her presence.

Swindoll elaborates on the dichotomy of the two situations:

> Interestingly, she (the sick woman) had been struggling with this illness for as long as the elder's daughter had been alive. During the same twelve years that this little girl had been the sunshine of Jairus's home, a hopelessly ill woman suffered in humiliation and discouragement. The official's only daughter—and perhaps only child—enjoyed privileged status in Jewish society; her father's wealth made her the potential prize of every suitor in Galilee. The unnamed woman, by contrast, existed on the periphery of the community and was not permitted to be intimate with any man.[25]

I love the details that Luke records for us in his Gospel, especially the wording in Luke 8:47-48, which isn't found in the other two Gospels. It's also our verse for the day. Write down the first sentence of verse 47 below.

_____

_____

Jesus is relentless in His pursuit of this woman. He inquires twice about who touched Him, unhindered by the crowd or Peter's puzzled response. She recognizes that she CANNOT GO UNNOTICED. The Savior of the world noticed this woman, this outcast, this seemingly insignificant person whose need paled in comparison to a young woman's imminent death.

WEEK 1 .... WEEK 2 .... WEEK 3 .... WEEK 4 .... WEEK 5 .... WEEK 6 .... WEEK 7 .... WEEK 8

DAY 5

This woman's story deeply resounds with me, especially in light of how I have felt as the wife of a sexually addicted man. Like her, I too, have felt unclean and unvalued. I have felt ostracized from society, afraid that if others knew about our secret they would look down on me as a bad wife. I have felt unnoticed, wondering if my husband truly saw me instead of a naked image.

Do you connect with this woman's story at all? What emotions do you think she felt that you can identify with?

_____

_____

_____

_____

_____

_____

Jesus noticed this woman because she was valuable to Him. He takes the time to stop and speak to her even though He has a very important and pressing need waiting for Him. Her touch and her faith brought her physical healing, but His words brought her emotional and spiritual healing.

> Jesus called the woman 'daughter,' not 'woman' (i.e., ma'am), as was the custom. He called her by a term of familial endearment, despite the fact that He was probably younger than she was. He declared that her faith had made the difference, without, of course, taking anything away from divine ability.[26]

In an instant, years of pain and shame melted away as she lay trembling at Jesus' feet. Her old title of "unclean" was gone and was replaced with "daughter." She must have felt so loved at that moment! He didn't reject her like everyone else had. He saw her heart, her pain, and her faith. He commended her actions, confirmed her healing, and sent her away with the word "peace."

No situation is too small for Jesus to take notice. When you come to Him and fall at His feet, He has time for you. He notices you. You are valuable to Him because you are His daughter. Perhaps your own sin struggles and your husband's feel like an incurable disease. Bring your pain and hopelessness to Jesus. He sees you, He hears you, and He loves you.

WEEK 1 .... WEEK 2 .... WEEK 3 .... WEEK 4 .... WEEK 5 .... WEEK 6 .... WEEK 7 .... WEEK 8

DAY 5

The love that unfolds from Jesus to both the unclean woman and the dying girl is so beautiful. How great is the Father's love for his girls! 1 John 3:1 says, "See what great love the Father has lavished on us, that we should be called children of God! And that is what we are!" If you have put your faith in Jesus, you have become His beloved daughter.

This picture of a father's love for his daughter plays itself out every day in my household. Just last night, my husband went out tie-shopping and brought home a new watch for our teenage daughter. Even when he isn't with her, he is thinking about her. He knows both her needs and her wants. He desires to lavish good things on her and make her feel special. His love for her is deep and unchanging, and he would do anything to protect her from pain or harm.

When our daughter was just four years old, we noticed a strange rash on her knuckles. She had small red raised bumps that wouldn't disappear. Our pediatrician recommended we go see a specialist at the University of Virginia. As my husband and I waited with our bouncy, spunky preschooler for the diagnosis, we grew more concerned by the minute. We didn't know what his prognosis was yet, but the doctor sent in residents to see if they could figure out what was wrong with her. Whispered guesses were thrown around the room as a gaggle of college boys gathered around and examined my daughter's knuckles.

We eventually were told that our daughter had juvenile dermatomyositis, an autoimmune disease that affects three out of one million children every year. It's a skin and muscle disease ("dermato", meaning skin; "myositis" meaning muscle inflammation) that causes a skin rash as well as muscle weakness and calcification.

Our minds were racing, and we did the worst possible thing when we got home. We googled the disease and found disturbing information that potentially linked dermatomyositis to cancer among other things. Both my husband and I were scared, unsure of what the future held for our little girl.

I remember my husband kneeling by our daughter's bed that night after she fell asleep, sobbing as he prayed over her body. I've heard my husband pray many times, but this night his prayers were different. He was begging God to heal our daughter, to give him the disease instead of her.

The doctor monitored her condition and gave us updates every few weeks, and then we had lab tests done. We were told to wait seven days and call back for the results. We waited breathlessly on the phone, and then the doctor told us that the disease was gone. He had no explanation and said we didn't need to come back. I can't explain to you the overwhelming joy and relief we felt when we heard that our daughter was healed! We fully believed that God took the disease away, and we made sure to tell the doctor that it was a miracle. To this day, my husband has the prescription paper with the note from the doctor to call back on the inside of his toolbox. It's a constant reminder of the prayers He answered that day. If we, as humans, can love our little girls so much, how much more does our Heavenly Father love us!

WEEK 1 .... WEEK 2 .... WEEK 3 .... WEEK 4 .... WEEK 5 .... WEEK 6 .... WEEK 7 .... WEEK 8

DAY 5

Throughout the Old Testament, God refers to His chosen people as the "daughters of Zion" (Isaiah 1:8, Jeremiah 4:31, Micah 4:13, Zechariah 2:10). His deep love for His daughter was and still is unfailing, in spite of her sinful idolatry.

Read Isaiah 49:14-16 and Zephaniah 3:14-17.

What do these passages say about how God feels about His daughter? How is His love evidenced?

Isaiah 49:14-16

_____

_____

_____

_____

_____

_____

_____

Zephaniah 3:14-17

_____

_____

_____

_____

_____

_____

_____

WEEK 1 .... WEEK 2 .... WEEK 3 .... WEEK 4 .... WEEK 5 .... WEEK 6 .... WEEK 7 .... WEEK 8

DAY 5

As a Christ-follower, you are adopted into God's family (John 1:12, Romans 8:14-17), and He has written you on the palms of His hands. He has not forgotten you, even if you have been forgotten by your own family. He rejoices over you with singing. How great is His love for you!

HEARTWORK

Like the woman in Luke 8, end today by kneeling at the feet of Jesus, not as a worthless woman, but as His daughter. Pour out your heart to Him. Tell Him about your wounds, your weaknesses, and your fears. Come to Him with confidence, knowing that He wants to listen and that He cares about you deeply.

Journal your prayer here.

_____

_____

_____

_____

_____

_____

_____

_____

_____

_____

_____

_____

_____

_____

WEEK 1 .... WEEK 2 .... WEEK 3 .... WEEK 4 .... WEEK 5 .... WEEK 6 .... WEEK 7 .... WEEK 8

DAY 5

WEEKEND HOMEWORK

Review all the note cards you have written so far with verses to memorize. They should include the verses from Ephesians 1 and 2 that you chose on Day 1 of this week, as well as Philippians 4:6-7, Psalm 73:25-26, Hebrews 4:15-16, and Ephesians 5:33.

CHARGE

The price Jesus paid for me determined my value. Any other assessment is a lie.

WEEK FOUR

LOVE IS A BATTLEFIELD

Ephesians 6:12 "For our struggle is not against flesh and blood, but against the rulers, against the authorities, against the powers of this dark world and against the spiritual forces of evil in the heavenly realms."

WEEK 4 DAY 1

KEY THOUGHT: There is a daily war being waged against your marriage.

I grew up in the 1980s, the decade that produced glam metal and MTV. Artists like Michael Jackson and Madonna rocked the charts, and big hair was everywhere. One of the most successful songs during that time was "Love is a Battlefield" by Pat Benatar.[27] The lyrics describe the emotional ebb and flow of love, the deep yearning for someone that is accompanied by heartache.

The song title aptly captures the theme of this chapter of study. Marriage can feel like a battlefield at times, especially when a sexual addiction is present. In order to have a healthy marriage, you must be willing to fight for it.

We have an enemy, Satan, that wants to see every marriage fail. In fact, he has targeted this relationship since the Garden of Eden, tempting Eve to sin and then convincing her husband to do the same. But why does he have his sights set on marriage? When a husband and wife truly love the way Christ loves, the impact is eternal and exponential. A godly marriage is a reflection of Christ's love for the church (Ephesians 5:21-33). It also is foundational to the future of humanity, creating generations of young men and women who will carry the gospel to the rest of the world (Genesis 1:28, Proverbs 22:6).

Pastor Steven J. Cole expounds on this concept, explaining how God not only designed marriage for human companionship, but also for a greater purpose:

> Marriage is a picture of the believer's relationship with God. After discussing marriage and quoting Genesis 2:24, Paul writes, "This mystery is great; but I am speaking with reference to Christ and the church" (Eph. 5:32). Marriage is an earthly picture of the spiritual relationship that exists between Christ, the bridegroom, and the church, His bride. The consummation of a marriage is referred to in the Bible as a man *knowing* his wife; even so, we can know Christ our bridegroom. A husband and wife are *one flesh*; we are one spirit with the Lord (1 Cor. 6:17). Just as the church is to be subject to Christ, so the wife is to be *subject* to her husband. Just as Christ *loves* the church,

— 94 —

WEEK 1 .... WEEK 2 .... WEEK 3 .... WEEK 4 .... WEEK 5 .... WEEK 6 .... WEEK 7 .... WEEK 8

DAY 1

so a husband is to love his wife. Just as the marital union results in *children*, so the union of the Lord and His church is to result in many offspring, to God's glory.

Someone has described marriage as God's doing with one man and one woman that which He is always trying to do within the world as a whole. That's why it's so important for you to work at developing a Christ-honoring relationship with your mate. You're working on a portrait of Christ and the church, and the world is looking over your shoulder. God's glory is at stake![28]

Have you ever thought about your marriage having a greater impact in God's story? What kind of picture is your marriage painting to a world that is watching?

_____

_____

_____

_____

In the book of Ephesians, Paul talks about marriage and parenting in chapters 5 and 6. Interestingly, after he talks about the basics of family life, Paul dives into a sermon about spiritual warfare. Our key verse for today reveals that our fight isn't with the man lying next to us in bed, but with an even bigger foe.

Read Ephesians 6:10-12. Who are we truly fighting a war against? List all three phrases at the end of verse 12 that describe our enemy.

_____

_____

_____

I don't think it's mere coincidence that Paul's call to battle follows his teaching about marriage and parenting. He recognized that the home is on the forefront of the fight between good and evil. When you get into an argument with your husband, there's an unseen war going on in the heavenlies. Just because you can't see it doesn't mean it's not taking place.

On the day you and your husband exchanged vows, you both enlisted to fight in the war against marriage and family. As a wife, you have a decision to make: Do I stand up and fight or do I sit on the sidelines and watch the enemy steal, kill and destroy (John 10:10)? As "one flesh" (Mark 10:6-9), you and your spouse have the power to

WEEK 1 .... WEEK 2 .... WEEK 3 .... WEEK 4 .... WEEK 5 .... WEEK 6 .... WEEK 7 .... WEEK 8

DAY 1

be a united force against the schemes of the devil. But if you choose to stand on the sidelines, unwilling to pick up your weapons, you are welcoming civil war into your home.

Sexual temptation is one of Satan's greatest tools in his evil game plan to divide and conquer in the home. Sexual addiction destroys trust and intimacy, and with it comes shame and fear. It also breeds anger in both the husband and wife. All of these stand in direct opposition to true, godly love (1 Corinthians 13:4-8).

I met with a friend when I started writing this study, and she gave me a very poignant word picture of how she felt about the battle with her husband's sexual addiction, relating it to an experience she had with her dog. She explained how one of her puppies came home covered in dog mess. He was unaware of how dirty and stinky he was from the waste, and playfully trounced right into the house. My friend was frustrated and angry, knowing that the cleanup process was going to be smelly and lengthy and that she would most likely get dirty. Even though it was a disgusting task, her love for her puppy gave her the will and the desire to carefully bathe him, scrub his fur, and comb all the filth out.

Over the course of your marriage, there will be many times when it will feel like you are in the midst of a big, smelly mess that your husband dragged into the house. You will have no desire to "clean up after him"; after all, you weren't the one who made the mess. But you vowed to honor and cherish this man, for better or worse. As a wife, you have a unique role to play in your husband's story; you have the chance to reflect God's love for him and grace toward him when he comes home dirty and smelly from sin. As his God-given helper (Genesis 2:18), you are also his battle buddy.

Galatians 6:1-3 sheds more light on this topic. I love the Amplified Bible version:

> **1** Brothers, if anyone is caught in any sin, you who are spiritual [that is, you who are responsive to the guidance of the Spirit] are to restore such a person in a spirit of gentleness [not with a sense of superiority or self-righteousness], keeping a watchful eye on yourself, so that you are not tempted as well. **2** Carry one another's burdens and in this way, you will fulfill the requirements of the law of Christ [that is, the law of Christian love]. **3** For if anyone thinks he is something [special] when [in fact] he is nothing [special except in his own eyes], he deceives himself.

How does this passage say we are supposed to deal with someone caught in a sin struggle? Whose guidance must we be following in the restoration process (verse 1)?

_____

_____

_____

WEEK 1 .... WEEK 2 .... WEEK 3 .... WEEK 4 .... WEEK 5 .... WEEK 6 .... WEEK 7 .... WEEK 8

DAY 1

What are we to guard against while we engage in this battle to restore (verse 1 and 3)? Why?

_____

_____

_____

I think a mind-shift when looking at sexual addiction is helpful in this process of restoration. When I began to view my husband as a wounded warrior instead of an evil enemy, I was able to approach him with love and gentleness. Satan was on the prowl, seeking to devour my husband (1 Peter 5:8). The battle for his heart had left us both battered and bruised. I could choose to pour salt in the wound, or I could apply healing to his bones through words filled with grace (Proverbs 16:24). This mind-shift, combined with the realization that I, too, am a sinner who has fallen short of grace, was very instrumental in the restoration process.

But how does a wife stand by her man in the battle without becoming overwhelmed by the attack? A sexual addiction is a heavy "burden" that can weigh down both a husband and his wife. Personally, when I know all the details about my husband's struggle with lust, I can quickly spiral into depression and self-doubt. I strongly believe that the wife should not be the husband's sole source of accountability, support and restoration; *he also needs reinforcement troops.*

In our marriage, we came up with a battle plan so that my husband was able to be accountable and honest with me about his sexual sin while still protecting my heart. I have the freedom to ask if he is struggling with sexual sin, whenever I want, and he needs to respond truthfully with a yes or no. It's important not to dig for specific details that will only bring deeper pain and fear; just a simple, "are you struggling right now?" is sufficient.

If he admits that he is on the losing side of the battle with lust (more than just the occasional impure thought or quick second glance), then the next step is for him to meet with his accountability partner. My husband has someone in his life that is a godly husband and father, but also a man who understands the struggle for sexual integrity. This accountability partner is willing to ask the tough questions and give godly counsel.

Read Ecclesiastes 4:9-12, listed below in the NLT version:

> Two people are better off than one, for they can help each other succeed. If one person falls, the other can reach out and help. But someone who falls alone is in real trouble. Likewise, two people lying close together can keep each other warm. But how can one be warm alone? A person standing alone can be attacked and defeated, but two can stand back-to-back and conquer. Three are even better, for a triple-braided cord is not easily broken.

WEEK 1 .... WEEK 2 .... WEEK 3 .... WEEK 4 .... WEEK 5 .... WEEK 6 .... WEEK 7 .... WEEK 8

DAY 1

How does this passage apply to what you have been reading so far?

_____

_____

_____

_____

I consider my husband's accountability partner and myself to be the other two strands for my husband's triple-braided cord. The cord also widens to include many other friends and mentors that know him well enough to call out his sin when necessary. They have "got his back" and stand with him in the battle, ready to defend our marriage and conquer the enemy.

We have found that honesty is a key step to victory. Satan wants us to isolate ourselves when we sin and keep us in fear of what others will say or think. Ironically, the more honest my husband has been with other men, the more he has found that he is not alone in his battle. It creates an environment of trust and vulnerability, the kind of gentle and loving care that we read about in Galatians 6 that allows us to help others in their time of need. Each honest conversation invites other men into the battle with my husband, and these honest conversations are crucial to accountability.

I have mentors and friends as well that are part of my "triple-braided cord." They are women that truly love Jesus and who will point me back to Him instead of engaging in a husband-bashing session. When my marriage is in a dark place, I seek them out, looking for godly wisdom that will challenge my heart and help me see truth. Again, honesty and transparency are the cornerstone of these accountability partnerships.

Do you have people in your life that are willing to go into battle with you? Does your husband? If so, list their names below and spend some time thanking God for your "battle buddies."

_____

_____

_____

_____

If the answer is no, what steps can you take to find someone to stand by you and your husband as you fight for your marriage? I prayed for years that God would give me a good friend to "do life with." Prayer is one step, another would be to get involved with a local community of believers. If you aren't plugged in to a local church, you are

WEEK 1 . . . . WEEK 2 . . . . WEEK 3 . . . . **WEEK 4** . . . . WEEK 5 . . . . WEEK 6 . . . . WEEK 7 . . . . WEEK 8

DAY 1

failing to tap into a powerful resource. Our relationships with our church friends have been the difference-maker in our marriage. Hebrews 10:24-25 admonishes us to continue to meet together as Christ-followers so we can encourage each other and "motivate one another to acts of love and good works." God didn't intend for us to walk through life alone and without support, and the local church is His family, your family.

Indeed, love is a battlefield. We are engaged in a war that won't end until Jesus returns and Satan is thrown into the lake of fire (Revelation 20:10). But we have a Savior that promises He will never leave us or forsake us (Deuteronomy 31:6, Hebrews 13:5). We can be strong and have confidence in our God who has overcome the world (John 16:33). And He has given us fellow warriors to fight in the war.

HEARTWORK

Over the next few days we will explore the weapons and strategies God has given us to go into battle. As we end today, take some time to write a prayer to God below. If you are ready to stand and fight, proclaim it! If you are scared to go to war, tell Him about it. If you are weary from fighting, ask God to refresh your soul. "Come to me, all you who are weary and burdened, and I will give you rest" (Matthew 11:28). Ask Him to give you people to keep both you and your husband accountable as you go into battle.

_____

_____

_____

_____

_____

_____

_____

_____

CHARGE

I have one enemy and it is not my husband. I will suit up and I will fight.

KNOWING IS HALF THE BATTLE

Ephesians 6:10-11 "Finally, be strong in the Lord and in his mighty power. Put on the full armor of God, so that you can take your stand against the devil's schemes."

WEEK 4 DAY 2

KEY THOUGHT: God has given us armor to help us in the battle against Satan.

To continue on with the 1980s reference from yesterday, I'd like to introduce you to another famous icon from that decade. G.I. Joe, a toy action figure soldier created by Hasbro, was made into a cartoon in the mid 1980s. At the end of each episode, a different character from the show would dispense wisdom through the TV screen about topics like telling the truth, stranger danger, and even how to stop a nosebleed. The clip would end a bunch of kids saying, "Now we know!" and the cartoon hero replied, "And knowing is half the battle!"

As cheesy as it sounds, (and quite funny now that I re-watch the clips courtesy of the internet), there's a lot of truth in that statement. It's not enough to know you are in a battle, you've actually got to do something about it. When my husband signed up for the military after our nation was attacked on September 11, he was very aware that America was at war. He recognized that he was committing to a real fight, not a fictional version without bloodshed and bullets like the G.I. Joe cartoon he had grown up watching in the 80s. Like all other soldiers who join the military with the right intentions, my husband didn't feel like he had done his part until he went overseas on a mission. He didn't want to just know about the fight, he wanted to go.

That war was obvious. In the days and months following September 11, 2001, all you had to do was turn on the news and you could see the devastation from the terrorist attack. But the attacks on our homes aren't always easily recognizable. We get in a rut and assume that daily arguments are "just how it is" when you are married. We start to just carry on, barely surviving as prisoners of war in our own home. We start to slowly bleed out from the wounds created from our harsh words (Proverbs 12:18), leaving our relationship weak and vulnerable.

As I prepared to write this chapter, my marriage was "in a funk," as I like to call it. My husband and I just couldn't get along, and we were fighting almost every day. We had two of the worst arguments we've had in a long time, the kind of fights that you still remember years later and wish had never happened. After weeks of going back and forth with each other, walking on eggshells and just hoping for a good day together, the irony of it all hit me like a ton of bricks. In the midst of writing about spiritual warfare, I had neglected to see that there was a

WEEK 1 .... WEEK 2 .... WEEK 3 .... WEEK 4 .... WEEK 5 .... WEEK 6 .... WEEK 7 .... WEEK 8

DAY 2

huge battle taking place in my own home. Once I finally recognized what was going on, I was vigilant to grab hold of my spiritual weapons and start fighting the real enemy instead of my husband.

Victory comes when we recognize the fight and then move to action with effective and powerful weapons. We've been given both offensive and defensive equipment to go into battle, and it's referred to in Scripture as the armor of God.

Read Ephesians 6:10-18. Then, on the lines below, list the six pieces of armor in these verses.

_____

_____

_____

_____

_____

_____

THE BELT OF TRUTH

This article of clothing isn't something you would normally think of when you consider battle gear, but it was essential for the Roman soldier. It had loops on it to store the soldier's swords and darts, as well as a place to keep his ration sack. It also kept all of his clothing tied securely in place, so he could be ready to fight at a moment's notice. The belt was foundational and critical to his safety and preparation in battle.

Why do you think Paul said to put on the belt of truth first?

_____

_____

_____

Read the following passages and summarize what each says about truth.

John 8:31-32

_____

_____

WEEK 1 .... WEEK 2 .... WEEK 3 .... WEEK 4 .... WEEK 5 .... WEEK 6 .... WEEK 7 .... WEEK 8

DAY 2

John 14:6

_____

_____

1 John 5:20

_____

_____

We are secure in our identity and free from the bondage of sin because of the truth of the gospel. His truth, found in His Word, keeps the rest of our armor firmly in place. We stand in confidence knowing who He is and who we are in Him. The lies that the devil throws at us will not shake us because we stand upon the truth that we are secure in Christ and loved by Him.

BREASTPLATE OF RIGHTEOUSNESS

The breastplate was attached to the belt by leather straps. It protected the heart, as well as the other vital organs in the abdominal area.

Read Proverbs 4:23 and write it out below.

_____

_____

_____

As women it's so easy to let our hearts (emotions) rule our thoughts and behavior. The breastplate of righteousness is an important part of our battle gear as wives, especially when dealing with the carnage that results from a pornography addiction. Our hearts can be so easily "broken" when we allow our husband's addiction to determine our worth. That's why Paul tells us to put on righteousness. We are not worthless or unloved, as our enemy and our human hearts would have us believe. We are treasured and loved because of Christ's death on the cross (Romans 3:23-25), we stand righteous and forgiven before Him.

How difficult is it for you to "guard your heart"? How would your emotional response to your husband's addiction change if you walked in Christ's righteousness instead of fleshly condemnation?

_____

_____

WEEK 1 .... WEEK 2 .... WEEK 3 .... **WEEK 4** .... WEEK 5 .... WEEK 6 .... WEEK 7 .... WEEK 8

DAY 2

_____

_____

_____

_____

SHOES OF THE GOSPEL OF PEACE

Our shoes take us places. They protect our feet for the journey ahead. They give us stability on rocky ground. Our shoes indicate we are ready to go. The shoes mentioned here are extraordinary because they are trade-marked by peace.

Isaiah 52:7 says, "How beautiful on the mountains are the feet of those who bring good news, who proclaim peace, who bring good tidings, who proclaim salvation.'"

In Matthew 5:9, we read, "Blessed are the peacemakers, for they will be called children of God."

After reading these two verses, what words are used to describe those who pursue peace?

_____

_____

_____

_____

The right pair of shoes make all the difference. When our feet are laced up securely with the gospel, we bring peace wherever we go… including our homes. Sometimes war requires us to diffuse a situation rather than escalate it. When we acknowledge the fullness of grace that has been given to us because of Christ's death on the cross, we can bring that same grace and peace wherever we go. The security that comes when we stand in His forgiveness gives us steady footing on even the most difficult terrain.

SHIELD OF FAITH

Paul tells us directly in Ephesians 6:16 that the shield of faith is used to "extinguish all the flaming arrows of the evil one." Satan uses "flaming arrows" or "fiery darts" to destroy homes every day through the sin of lust. How many families and churches do you know that have been destroyed by infidelity? Satan is constantly launching fiery arrows at both you and your husband, waiting for you to have your guard down. But God has overcome the world and does not leave us defenseless against these attacks. When you hold up the shield of faith, it not only catches the fiery darts, it extinguishes them.

DAY 2

Open your Bible and read John 16:33. Write down the last sentence below.

_____

_____

Now read 1 John 5:1-5.

According to this passage, specifically verses 4-5, what happens when we have FAITH in the Son of God?

_____

_____

_____

Our God has overcome the world, and He gives us the power through Him to have victory over this world as well. Satan may hurl temptations and accusations toward you in this life, but he cannot touch your eternal destiny. The devil is guaranteed a loss, and he knows it, so he tries every trick in the book to make us feel defeated. But the truth that shields us is this: The One who has purchased your freedom from sin has also guaranteed your "victory over sin and death through our Lord Jesus Christ" (1 Corinthians 15:57).

HELMET OF SALVATION

A helmet protects your skull, which in turn protects your brain, where your thoughts are stored. The battle for the mind is the most crucial one, because our thoughts determine our attitudes and actions. Satan knows that the battle for the human soul is won or lost within the mind. He won't stop deceiving unbelievers and tempting believers until Christ comes back.

Satan's tried and true weapon is deceit, and his use of the lie dates all the way back to the beginning of time. He wants to keep you trapped in fear, doubt and insecurity. If he can get you to believe lies, then he can influence your emotions and actions.

2 Timothy 1:7 (NKJV) says, "God has not given us a spirit of fear, but of power and of love and of a sound mind." I love this verse so much that I have committed it to memory. If a thought is bringing fear, then it is from the enemy. To combat the lies that produce fear, we must know the truth that saves, which is God's word.

My mentor shared a story with me about how her husband, Joel, (founder of Proven Men) was given a letter filled with accusations. Some of them were true, the sinful results of sexual addiction, but many were false. For a long time, Joel and Theresa were unable to let go of the anger and hurt that they experienced from the condemning spirit of the letter. They decided to burn the letter as a sacrifice to God, taking responsibility for how Joel's addiction had wounded others but then moving on through the forgiveness that comes from

WEEK 1 .... WEEK 2 .... WEEK 3 .... WEEK 4 .... WEEK 5 .... WEEK 6 .... WEEK 7 .... WEEK 8

DAY 2

the shed blood of Christ. Their decision to put to rest the lies and shame from the past was a decision to take up the helmet of salvation and put down their anxieties so that God's peace would guard their hearts and minds (Philippians 4:6-7).

Putting on the helmet of salvation means we "take captive every thought to make it obedient to Christ" (2 Corinthians 10:5). We acknowledge the lies and then put them in their correct place... at the foot of the cross, where all condemnation and shame was destroyed through Christ's death (Romans 8:1).

SWORD OF THE SPIRIT

This final piece of armor is our one piece of offensive weaponry, the Word of God. If you grew up in the church, you are familiar with the Bible being called a sword. We are going to cover this weapon in greater detail in tomorrow's lesson as it applies to the battle against sexual addiction. I can't wait to cover the material with you!

One final thought as we close out today: In both Ephesians 6:11 and 13, Paul says we should put on the FULL armor of God. If you leave one part of your body unprotected, the enemy will aim for it. Putting on the full armor of God isn't just a cute idea, it's a command in Scripture. Are you ready for war?

When I was a teenager, my mom made us put on the armor of God every day. I hated it at the time, it made me feel so silly as I said each piece out loud. But I am so grateful for it now... she knew the seriousness of the battle for our hearts and wanted us to be protected from head to toe. I'm asking you to do the same thing. Put on the FULL armor of God, every day. Don't leave yourself vulnerable. You are more than a conqueror in Christ Jesus! (Romans 8:37-39)

HEARTWORK

End today by praying each piece of armor over yourself. Visualize every part as you "put it on." I added a beautiful printout in Appendix B of a female warrior wearing her spiritual armor. Put it in a place of prominence so you can remember every day to put on your battle gear.

CHARGE

I have one enemy and it is not my husband. I will suit up and I will fight.

POWER OF THE WRITTEN WORD

Hebrews 4:12 "For the word of God is alive and active. Sharper than any double-edged sword, it penetrates even to dividing soul and spirit, joints and marrow; it judges the thoughts and attitudes of the heart."

WEEK 4 DAY 3

KEY THOUGHT: God's Word is a love letter, a light, and it's alive. When we read it, study it, and know the Word, it brings life!

Yesterday we briefly mentioned the last piece of armor, the Sword of the Spirit, which is God's Word (the Bible). Our verse for today, Hebrews 4:12, also compares the Word of God to a sword. It cuts deep into our spiritual being and brings discernment to our innermost thoughts and feelings. It is alive and active through the power of the Holy Spirit. By the end of this lesson, my hope is that you will realize what a powerful tool the Word of God is as you wage war against the enemy. Nothing else compares to the wisdom and comfort we receive when we open up the Bible and let its truths transform us from the inside out.

Throughout the Old and New Testament, the authors use beautiful descriptive language for the Word of God. Today we will explore three of them: God's Word is a love letter, a light, and alive.

THE WORD OF GOD IS A **LOVE LETTER**
When my husband left for U.S. Army basic training, we had only been married for a little over two years. I already knew from the extended summer months of long-distance dating during college that lack of communication is hard on a relationship, so I was nervous about the toll that the time apart would have on our marriage during his time at Basic.

The only communication that privates (brand new military recruits) were allowed to have with the outside world was good old-fashioned snail mail. Occasionally a phone call home was permitted, but they were brief and weren't guaranteed. In fact, the drill sergeant would use the phone privileges as leverage against the privates. Using the phone wasn't a right, and my husband remembers the opportunity being yanked away from the group multiple times while he was training at Fort Jackson.

So, the handwritten note became our trusted way of communicating with one another. I cherished each letter my husband wrote to me during basic training. I could hear his voice with every written line. No detail was boring to me because I missed him desperately.

WEEK 1 .... WEEK 2 .... WEEK 3 .... WEEK 4 .... WEEK 5 .... WEEK 6 .... WEEK 7 .... WEEK 8

DAY 3

My husband's letters were love notes to me. He told me how important I was to him, and how much he missed both me and our son. He shared his victories and struggles as well as his dreams for our future. We were so young back then and had no clue what life was going to bring, but one thing was certain—we were in it together.

While my husband was gone, I read each letter over and over. I couldn't wait until I received a new one, anxiously waiting each day for the mail to come. And he did the same, standing each day in the mail-call line, hoping and praying that I had written him one in return. To this day, every letter that he wrote during basic training, as well as all the letters he sent when he got deployed to Iraq, are stored safely in a box. They will be cherished for the rest of my life.

One morning, as I was rereading one of my husband's letters, the Lord spoke to my heart. I could hear Him telling me that His written Words, the ones found in the Bible, were so much sweeter than my husband's. As much as my husband loved me, his love paled in comparison to the way God cared for me. If that was true, why would I not want to spend just as much time in His Word? Why wasn't I just as excited to find a quiet space and pour over His sweet messages to me?

God knows you better and loves you so much more than anyone on earth ever could. The Bible is His love letter to you! Why would you and I not want to sit and read his loving words over and over? Listen to these words from Scripture. Fill in each blank with the word LOVE.

Ephesians 2:4-5 "But because of his great _____ for us, God, who is rich in mercy, made us alive with Christ even when we were dead in transgressions—it is by grace you have been saved."

1 John 4:7-8 "Dear friends, let us _____ one another, for _____ comes from God. Everyone who loves has been born of God and knows God. Whoever does not love does not know God, because God is _____."

Psalm 86:15 "But you, Lord, are a compassionate and gracious God, slow to anger, abounding in _____ and faithfulness."

1 John 3:1 "See what great _____ the Father has lavished on us, that we should be called children of God! And that is what we are!"

Romans 8:35, 37-39 "Who shall separate us from the _____ of Christ? Shall trouble or hardship or persecution or famine or nakedness or danger or sword? No, in all these things we are more than conquerors through him who loved us. For I am convinced that neither death nor life, neither angels nor demons, neither the present nor the future, nor any powers, neither height nor depth, nor anything else in all creation, will be able to separate us from the _____ of God that is in Christ Jesus our Lord."

WEEK 1 .... WEEK 2 .... WEEK 3 .... WEEK 4 .... WEEK 5 .... WEEK 6 .... WEEK 7 .... WEEK 8

DAY 3

All of these verses speak about God's great love for us, and there are so many more throughout Scripture! When you spend time reading the Bible, you will discover your value in God's eyes. You will understand that your worth is not linked to your husband's sin but your Savior's sacrifice. He LOVES YOU SO MUCH that He gave His life for you! There is no greater love (John 15:13).

THE WORD OF GOD IS **A LIGHT.**
Read Psalm 119:105 and 130, then write them out below:

_____

_____

_____

_____

I love this comparison! God's Word brings light into the darkness. This verse is so helpful for us as wives dealing with a sexually addicted spouse. When your partner embraces a sexual addiction, he is walking in darkness (1 John 1:5-7). At times, the darkness was tangible in our home; I could feel it hovering around me while my husband and I were having sex (Ephesians 6:12). It wasn't a physical darkness just because we had the lights turned off; it was a spiritual, psychological and emotional darkness that was draining the life out of our marriage. Lust had blanketed true intimacy with a tarry mixture of fear, guilt and shame.

Paul reminds believers in Ephesians 5:3-4 that, as God's children, there shouldn't even be a "hint of sexual immorality" and the "fruitless deeds of darkness" among them. He then explains what our lives should look like instead. Read Ephesians 5:8-13 and fill in the blanks accordingly:

For you were once darkness, but now you are _____. Live as _____

_____

Find out _____.
Everything exposed _____.

According to verse 9, what are the three fruits of the light?
1. _____
2. _____
3. _____

If you know Christ as Savior, you are now LIGHT IN THE LORD! And when you spend time reading His Word, you are holding up a light for your path that can not be dimmed. God's truth "shines in the darkness, and the darkness has not overcome it" (John 1:5).

WEEK 1 .... WEEK 2 .... WEEK 3 .... WEEK 4 .... WEEK 5 .... WEEK 6 .... WEEK 7 .... WEEK 8

DAY 3

When you pick up the Sword of the Spirit, which is the Word of God (Ephesians 6:17), you cut through the darkness. It's what gives you discernment when you have that gut feeling that something "just isn't right" between you and your husband. You usher in goodness, righteousness and truth to expose the lies that have been living within the walls of your home.

Because we are engaged in a spiritual battle, the residing darkness will fight for its territory. Most men aren't quick to let go of the addiction that they have fed and nurtured for years. Lazy love is convenient and seems controlled in their sexual fantasy world, and the enemy knows that. Your husband may fight you tooth and nail when you speak biblical truth as you pursue maturity in Christ (Ephesians 4:14-15). But we have hope as we look to God's Word for direction.

Read Psalm 18:28-32.

How does God come to our aid in our fight against the darkness? Write down your observations below.

_____

_____

_____

I love how these verses remind us that God alone is our security, our rock, our shield. How often do we put our hope in our husbands to be the one we lean on? With the confusion and fear that can swirl around a sexual addiction, He keeps our lamps burning and turns our darkness into light. He arms us with strength and brings security in the midst of disaster.

THE WORD OF GOD IS **ALIVE.**

Not only is God's Word a love letter and a light, but it is also alive! Open your Bible to each one of the passages below and write down the portion that illustrates how God's Word is living.

2 Timothy 3:16-17

_____

_____

Matthew 4:4

_____

_____

WEEK 1 .... WEEK 2 .... WEEK 3 .... WEEK 4 .... WEEK 5 .... WEEK 6 .... WEEK 7 .... WEEK 8

DAY 3

John 6:61-69 (look specifically at verses 63 and 68)

_____

_____

_____

_____

_____

Through the power of the Holy Spirit, Scripture speaks to us. 2 Timothy explains that the Bible is "God-breathed" and is useful for every situation that we encounter in this life. It equips us for "every good work." I have opened its pages so many times and read words that specifically speak to my heart and bring wisdom for the circumstances I am encountering that very day. Even as I have been writing this study, His Word has come into my mind to direct the content.

Have you experienced the living power of reading God's Word? Write down a time when you felt God literally breathing life into your soul through the Scriptures. If you haven't experienced that, I want you to read Psalm 19:7-11 and write down a short prayer in the lines below asking God to give you an encounter with His Word in the way described by the Psalmist.

_____

_____

_____

_____

There is so much to be gained when we open God's Word! We can gain wisdom and encouragement from friends and from books, but truly the greatest instruction and hope comes from the Scriptures.

What would you say to the military wife who only glances at the envelope of her deployed husband's letter and throws it in a pile? Or the mom who walks into a pitch-black room with Legos covering the floor who refuses to flip on the light switch? Or the runner who has just completed a marathon and sits down at the kitchen table but never takes a bite out of the gourmet meal prepared just for her? Each one of these women would be considered foolish and ignorant. They may seem like silly comparisons; but in all reality, we have access to the most

beautiful love letter, the brightest light, and living nourishment for our souls, yet we refuse to utilize it. How are we supposed to understand what God wants us to do, how He feels about us, without listening to His Words?

You, my dear soldier, are engaged in a battle, and you must take up your Sword. It will comfort your heart, light your way, and nourish your soul.

HEARTWORK

As we end today, think about your daily routine. Before you started this study, was reading the Bible a priority? If your answer was no, what can you change in your schedule to make time for it? Write down a time and place that you will commit to read God's Word every day after you finish this study. Ask God to reveal to you where He would like you to dive into His Word after you finish this study. Write it down below for accountability.

TIME OF DAY:

PLACE:

WHAT TO STUDY:

CHARGE

I have one enemy and it is not my husband. I will suit up and I will fight.

POWER OF THE SPOKEN WORD

Ephesians 6:18 "And pray in the Spirit on all occasions with all kinds of prayers and requests. With this in mind, be alert and always keep on praying for all the Lord's people."

WEEK 4 DAY 4

KEY THOUGHT: Fight your enemy on your knees.

Yesterday we zeroed in on a specific piece of the armor of God, the Sword of the Spirit. Today we focus on a piece of battle gear that is sometimes looked over. When you read Ephesians 6:10-18, you'll notice that nothing covers the knees or shins. Many commentators have noted that this omission is intentional because, as believers, we should be fighting from our knees through prayer. I agree, and here's why: Right after Paul lists the all the components of the spiritual battle gear in chapter 6, he gives one final instruction to end his letter to the church in Ephesus: **PRAY.**

In just a few short verses, Ephesians 6:18-20, at the end of his letter, Paul unpacks an enormous amount of information about prayer:

> And pray in the Spirit on all occasions with all kinds of prayers and requests. With this in mind, be alert and always keep on praying for all the Lord's people. Pray also for me, that whenever I speak, words may be given me so that I will fearlessly make known the mystery of the gospel, for which I am an ambassador in chains. Pray that I may declare it fearlessly, as I should.

Let's look a little closer. Paul tells us:
HOW TO PRAY—in the Spirit
WHEN TO PRAY—on all occasions, always
WHAT TO PRAY—all kinds of prayers and requests
WHO TO PRAY FOR—all the Lord's people

Did you notice the grand and encompassing words Paul uses repeatedly? With a closer look you'll see he uses ALL and ALWAYS. There's no limit on prayer! Do it all the time, for everyone, with all kinds of prayers! You don't need a special person, building, or words to talk to God. You just need to do it!

WEEK 1 .... WEEK 2 .... WEEK 3 .... WEEK 4 .... WEEK 5 .... WEEK 6 .... WEEK 7 .... WEEK 8

DAY 4

I am in no way an expert on prayer. To be honest, writing today's lesson intimidated me, and I delayed writing it for weeks. Even though I've been praying since I could speak and can still quote all the lines from the Our Father and Hail Mary from my Catholic days, I struggle with prayer. I'm guessing that if you are anything like me, you have felt at loss for words sometimes when you talk to God. Or think you are praying the wrong way. Or that your prayers are hitting the ceiling.

When my marriage was in the midst of the "dark days," prayer was not my first inclination. I wanted to talk to someone, but not God. I wanted a listening ear and an understanding heart, and I sought that out in the people surrounding me. Instead of talking to God about my husband's pornography addiction, I talked to everyone else: my friends, my sister, my mom, my counselor. I cried with them as I shared my fear, my anxiety, my hurt, my disappointment. During those heart-to-hearts I was treated with care and compassion from others who loved both me and my husband. But, even though it felt great to be heard and understood, when I walked away from our time together the issue still remained: My husband and I were in a dark place in our marriage, and a ninety-minute venting session wasn't going to change my husband's heart, or my own, for that matter. It served as a nice Band-Aid for the wounds, but it couldn't do the deep healing work that our souls actually needed.

Why is it so easy to talk to other people about our hurts instead of to the One who can actually do something about them? God gave us earthly companions to encourage us on the journey (1 Thessalonians 5:11, Hebrews 3:13), but their support is supplementary. Only God can HEAR and ANSWER prayer. He knows about your husband's sexual addiction, and He cares. He knows about your wounded heart, and He cares. One of my favorite verses in Scripture is 1 Peter 5:7, "Cast all your anxiety on Him because He cares for you." He is available any time of the day or night to listen (Psalm 121). Not only does He listen and care, but He has the power to change hearts and lives.

Today's study will be a bit different than the other days we've done together so far. Rather than try to explain why we should pray, how we should pray, and what happens when we pray, I'm going to ask the true Guide to reveal those truths to your heart—the Holy Spirit.

John 16:13 says the Spirit will "guide you into all truth." 1 Corinthians 2:12 says that as believers we have received the Spirit "from God, so that we may understand what God has freely given us." God can and will reveal His truth to you through His Spirit, and He will even pray for you when you don't know how!

Read Romans 8:26-27. What two things does this passage say the Holy Spirit does for us?

_____

_____

WEEK 1 .... WEEK 2 .... WEEK 3 .... WEEK 4 .... WEEK 5 .... WEEK 6 .... WEEK 7 .... WEEK 8

DAY 4

The rest of today's study will be passages of Scripture that talk about prayer. There's a journaling portion under each passage for you to note what the Holy Spirit is revealing to you. No commentary, just you and God in a read-and-respond time. Approach each section of verses with the same questions we used when looking at Ephesians 6 in the beginning of our lesson. Each passage will answer one or more of these questions:

HOW SHOULD I PRAY?
WHEN SHOULD I PRAY?
WHAT SHOULD I PRAY FOR?
WHO SHOULD I PRAY FOR?
WHAT HAPPENS WHEN I PRAY?

Read the passages below. Pay attention to which question(s) the verses answer. What is the Holy Spirit revealing to you about prayer in each passage?

James 5:13-16

_____

_____

_____

Matthew 6:3-13

_____

_____

_____

Psalm 5:1-3

_____

_____

_____

Philippians 4:6-7

_____

_____

_____

Hebrews 4:14-16

_____

_____

_____

Psalm 27:7-10

_____

_____

_____

Psalm 34:1-6

_____

_____

_____

Ephesians 3:14-21

_____

_____

_____

WEEK 1 .... WEEK 2 .... WEEK 3 .... WEEK 4 .... WEEK 5 .... WEEK 6 .... WEEK 7 .... WEEK 8

DAY 4

The last one you read is the portion of Scripture that I pray all the time for myself and others, including you, the reader. I love it so much and have used it so frequently that I made it into a print design that I have in my home. I want you to have it in your home as well. You'll find it under APPENDIX E.

HEARTWORK

As you end today, put what you've learned into practice. Find a quiet space and kneel down. Pray Ephesians 3:14-21 (APPENDIX E) over yourself, and then again over your husband. Remember that as you kneel in prayer you are actually marching into battle. And God gives us the victory through our Lord Jesus Christ! (1 Corinthians 15:57)

CHARGE

I have one enemy and it is not my husband. I will suit up and I will fight.

POWER OF THE KNOWN WORD

Philippians 4:8 "Finally, brothers and sisters, whatever is true, whatever is noble, whatever is right, whatever is pure, whatever is lovely, whatever is admirable— if anything is excellent or praiseworthy—think about such things."

WEEK 4 DAY 5

KEY THOUGHT: Wallpaper your mind with God's truth.

The other day my teenage son was helping his dad change the oil in our vehicles. Running back and forth from the basement to the driveway with all the tools, my son breathlessly said to me with a smile, "Man, if a robber ever showed up at our house, he wouldn't stand a chance!"

He was confident in his father's ability and training as a soldier to use the tools to keep our family safe. His comment made me think about how our enemy doesn't stand a chance against us when we are in Christ. "You, dear children, are from God and have overcome them, because the one who is in you is greater than the one who is in the world" (1 John 4:4). We have effective and powerful tools to defeat the enemy, we just need to pick them up and confidently use them, knowing that the victory is ours through Christ!

This entire chapter has been all about spiritual warfare. So far we've talked about how we must recognize the battle (day one) and then gear up for it with our armor (day two). Our greatest weapons are listening to God speak through His Word (day three) and talking to God through prayer (day four). As we finish up, we are going to look at one more vital weapon that will help us stand our ground when going to battle against sin and addiction—memorizing God's Word.

With the technology we have available to us and the widespread accessibility of the Bible, why should we bother to memorize God's Word? You can open its pages or search on the internet for a specific verse any time you want. The truth of the matter is that when you are tempted or being told lies by Satan, you have a crucial window of time to take hold of his fiery darts and extinguish them. In order to do that, you must have knowledge of what Scripture says so that you can access it whenever and wherever you are.

2 Corinthians 10:3-5 shows us this principle:

> For though we live in the world, we do not wage war as the world does. The weapons we fight with are not the weapons of the world. On the contrary, they have divine power to demolish strongholds.

We demolish arguments and every pretension that sets itself up against the knowledge of God, and we take captive every thought to make it obedient to Christ.

I love the way Paul gives us a battle strategy in this passage, just like he does in Ephesians 6. He again reminds us that our fight is a spiritual one. We go into war with God-given weapons that give us the power to destroy the strongholds of the devil. The Word of God is your Sword, and it cuts through Satan's attacks and lies.

A sword must be ready at a moment's notice. Imagine a soldier going into battle without his sword, but instead a handwritten note in his sheath that contains detailed directions on where to find it. By the time he reads the note and locates his weapon, the enemy will have attacked and inflicted a severe or fatal wound. No soldier would be allowed to go into battle without having his weapon readily accessible and functional for the fight. In the same way, when your enemy attacks, you need to know where your Sword is.

If you have to stop to rifle through the Scriptures or Google to find a verse, you have wasted precious moments in battle. You give your mind the chance to go down an unhealthy path, or strong-place of the devil (2 Corinthians 10:4), and quickly spiral out of control until you find yourself acting out your insecurities and fears.

Let me give you a practical, everyday example of how God's Word helps me break down every thought and take hold of it to make it obey Christ (2 Corinthians 10:5). I struggle with worry and fear on a daily basis, as do many people. I am constantly in my own head, suffering from an overactive mind. Because of my husband's job in the military, I have been alone many nights while he was away on training or a mobilization, leaving me mentally vulnerable. Late at night is prime hunting ground for Satan! In the dark, alone with my thoughts, I would worry myself into sleepless nights. A google search for Bible verses about worry at 3:00 a.m. is not very effective, to say the least. In those moments, my mind can go to terrible places, imagining my worst fears coming true with every creaky sound coming from the hallway.

As soon as the fearful and anxious thoughts start to flood my mind, I recognize the attacks from Satan and begin to fight back with a whole arsenal of verses that I have memorized on fear and anxiety. Verses like these:

> 2 Timothy 1:7 (NKJV)
> For God has not given us a spirit of fear, but of power and of love and of a sound mind.
>
> 1 Peter 5:7 (NIV)
> Cast all your anxiety on him because he cares for you.
>
> Isaiah 26:3 (NKJV)
> You keep him in perfect peace whose mind is stayed on you, because he trusts in you.
>
> Psalm 56:3 (HCSB)
> When I am afraid, I will trust in you.

WEEK 1 .... WEEK 2 .... WEEK 3 .... WEEK 4 .... WEEK 5 .... WEEK 6 .... WEEK 7 .... WEEK 8

DAY 5

Psalm 4:8 (NKJV)

I will both lie down in peace, and sleep; For You alone, O Lord, make me dwell in safety.

***Side note: The different versions listed actually reflect the version I was exposed to or chose to read during the time period when they were memorized. I love that the verses I know reflect a different stage in my spiritual development. The version doesn't matter, but the content does.

While lying there in the pitch black, all of these verses pop into my head because I have memorized them over the years. I can't always remember the reference or the exact wording, but I know the truth found within: When I am filled with anxiety, I must turn to God and trust in Him. I repeat them over and over to myself as I lie in bed, sometimes out loud. The truth of God's Word defeats Satan's lies.

Jesus also models this behavior for us in Matthew 4:1-11. Open your Bible and read the passage, then answer these questions:

How long did Jesus spend in the wilderness? Why was He vulnerable after this time?

_____

_____

_____

How many different times did Satan tempt Jesus? What did he tempt Christ with?
What does this teach us about Satan?

_____

_____

_____

How did Jesus combat the temptation? What eventually happened (verse 11)?

_____

_____

_____

I love that Jesus, who is the very Word Himself (John 1:1), knew Scripture (Matthew 5:21, 13:14-15) and spoke it out loud to defeat the enemy (Matthew 4:1-11). As His followers, we should also make it a high priority and believe in its power to make the enemy leave!

Satan prowls around like a roaring lion waiting for someone to devour (1 Peter 5:8). He studies us carefully, determining the most strategic time to attack. Have you ever watched a lion hunting his prey on one of those animal channels on TV? The lion singles out an animal that is slow, weak or tired, and his prey is usually alone or isolated from the group. Just like a lion, Satan waits for the best time to pounce on his target. Satan tempted Christ after He spent forty days without food or human companionship. Just like with Jesus, he knows when we are weak and seeks to take advantage of us whenever he gets the chance.

Satan also knows the battle is won and lost within the mind. If he can plant a lie in our brains and get us to believe it, all he has to do is sit back and watch us self-destruct. It's like a stick of dynamite. Satan sets the spark to the end of the fuse and watches the lie work its way into our minds, burning until it explodes and damaging everything in its path. For your husband, lust is a weak spot that Satan will try to expose again and again. If he can get your husband to believe that he can take "just a peek" or that his impure thoughts are not harming anyone, then the explosive, self-destructive process has been put into motion.

Not only does your husband's lust create devastation in his own heart and mind, but also in yours. Satan knows that sexual addiction can be a two-for-one deal because as husband and wife you are one flesh. Your husband's sexual addiction creates an environment of vulnerability for the both of you. When you discover that your husband is struggling with lust, Satan sees it as an opportunity to trigger the insecurities and lies that have plagued you since childhood (I'm ugly, I deserve this, I don't measure up, It's always my fault, I'm worthless, etc.). Knowing Scripture and repeating it to yourself is the best way to diffuse his lies.

So, how can you identify when a thought is an attack from Satan? Our verse for today, Philippians 4:8, gives some insight. Let's backtrack a few verses to get the overall picture. Keep in mind the importance of context when reading and memorizing Scripture! We can't just pick and choose verses from the Bible, a la carte style. Knowing the historical context, the author, and the audience is critical to give us an accurate interpretation. In this passage from Philippians, Paul is writing to a local church of believers, so we can take his encouragement and apply it to our lives as well:

Philippians 4:6-8
6 Do not be anxious about anything, but in every situation, by prayer and petition, with thanksgiving, present your requests to God. **7** And the peace of God, which transcends all understanding, will guard your hearts and your minds in Christ Jesus. **8** Finally, brothers and sisters, whatever is true, whatever is noble, whatever is right, whatever is pure, whatever is lovely, whatever is admirable—if anything is excellent or praiseworthy—think about such things.

One of the first things I notice here is that Paul commands us not to be anxious. Anxiety does not come from God! Read 1 Timothy 1:7 from earlier in today's lesson. If your thoughts are bringing fear or worry, then they are from the devil.

How does Paul say we are supposed to handle anxiety according to Philippians 4 (verse 6)? What will be the result (verse 7)?

_____

_____

_____

Continuing on, Paul tells us how to protect our mind through spiritual weapons like prayer. He then tells us what kind of thoughts we should have in verse 8. What does Paul say we should think on?

_____

_____

_____

Here lies the key to identify the attack of the enemy! Ask yourself, "Is this thought true? Is it noble? Is it right, pure, lovely, admirable, excellent and praiseworthy?" If the answer is no to any one of those, then those are not God-given thoughts, and you need to immediately extinguish the fiery darts by heaping Scripture on top of it!

Let's put into practice what we have been talking about. What are your weaknesses, the strongholds of your mind? I have listed some of the ones that I struggle with in APPENDIX C, along with accompanying Bible verses to combat the lies. To finish today's study, pick two verses from the lists and then write them out on a notecard. Then read the tips in APPENDIX D on how to memorize Scripture more effectively. When you have time and have memorized those two verses (days when you don't have any of this study to do, weekends would be great!), go back through and pick a few more. Once you've done that, take some time and find some verses on your own and do the same.

One final note: When you take time to memorize Scripture, not only is it beneficial for you, but also for those that God has entrusted to you. In order to fight for your husband, your family, and your friends, you must know how to wield your Sword to block the daggers that Satan is throwing at them as well.

When I sit across the table from a woman who has just discovered her husband has a pornography addiction, my common-sense answers lack the power and authority that come from God's Word. In those moments, God

reminds me of all the Scriptures I have learned over the years so that I can speak His Words to bring comfort and direction. When my kids are fearful or lonely, the Holy Spirit prompts me in a similar way as I advise and encourage them on their journey. Your battle readiness and effectiveness increase every time you memorize another Bible verse because you are equipped to protect and fend off another one of Satan's lies, whether they are directed at you or those you love. Don't just memorize God's Word for yourself, memorize it for your loved ones!

My prayer for you today is that you will find this to be true in your own life:

"I know of no other single practice in the Christian life more rewarding... than memorizing Scripture... No other single exercise pays greater spiritual dividends..." *~Charles Swindoll*

HEARTWORK

Now turn to Appendix C to start writing and praying your new verses.

HOMEWORK

At the end of Appendix C there is a space for you to do your own research for verses you want to memorize. Take some time and add your struggles and corresponding verses. Pick two and write them out on note cards. Add them to the verses you are memorizing.

CHARGE

I have one enemy and it is not my husband. I will suit up and I will fight.

PW

WEEK FIVE

A "WE THING"

Romans 8:18 "I consider that our present sufferings are not worth comparing with the glory that will be revealed in us."

WEEK 5 DAY 1

KEY THOUGHT: Marriage isn't a "me thing"; it's a "we thing."

Now that we have laid a foundation of truth in identity and learned about the war our enemy is waging against us every day, let's look at some combat strategies (mind-sets). There are practical steps that can be taken to jump start the redemption of our marriages. Jesus promises that the cross He has asked us to pick up is easy (Matthew 16:24) and provides soul rest (Matthew 11:29). It might not feel comfortable or convenient at first, but it is the better way! Trust Him.

I'd like to introduce you to someone who was highly instrumental in my healing journey, my good friend, Theresa. She is a professional counselor and also the wife of Joel, the founder of "Proven Men." Proven Men is the study that serves as the blueprint for this one. It has been instrumental in the transformation of thousands of men struggling with sexual integrity, including my own husband.

I came to Theresa at a turning point, much like where we are now in this study. Like you, I understood that pornography and sexual addiction are harmful because I had experienced the devastation firsthand. My husband and I had already been to marriage counseling, but I needed someone to show me how to be what she calls a "safe wife." Theresa was willing to walk with me through the rough months ahead and give me godly wisdom on how to love my husband and honor my marriage.

Here's a bit of insight from her:

> Like most of you doing this study, I was devastated by my husband's infidelity and disgusted by his addiction. To say I was angry was putting it mildly. After my initial shock wore off, I became very angry. Angry over his betrayal and enraged that I had to deal with this addiction he brought into our marriage. I originally viewed it as a "he" problem, and he needed to get some help.

He did get help. One day as I was pouring out my heart to the Lord over how much Joel had broken my heart, God clearly said to me, "this marriage isn't about you, it's a *we*." I always knew that marriage took two people and that we all have issues we bring into our marriages from our past relationships to our familial relationships. Yet this seemed so much bigger. I mean, I was sinned against by my husband, so *he* should fix it. It involves *me* as much as *he* has to earn my trust back. Most of that is true. But in order for my marriage to get healthy, I needed to be part of the solution, not focused on being a victim. You see, I was raised in an alcoholic home whose hallmark was denial and silence. The family was invested in surviving, not thriving. Their concept of *we* was to remain silent and move on. So the challenge for me was to be an active participant who does not remain silent but is part of the solution, not the problem.

God made it clear that I was responsible for my own actions before Him, regardless of what my husband did. So, if this was the case, I needed to be the helpmate that God originally intended. The *we* and/or team approach is something we see in Scripture very clearly through the Trinity. They each have their own roles and responsibilities yet act as a unified one. *We* for me as a wife meant doing what it took to make Joel's healing path to God possible. Now hear me clearly, I am not saying I am responsible for his sobriety or keeping himself pure. That was something between God and Joel. I am NOT his accountability partner; I am NOT his watchdog. He does not have to check in with me, and I don't demand to see his phone or computer every night. What I do is help him and trust that God will reveal what I need to know.

Joel thought it was best if we did not watch TV for a year. As much as that was something I was going to miss, I sacrificed, and we found other ways to connect by playing games. Going to the mall was another trigger, so we avoided malls. Magazines coming in the mail were a problem, so I got the mail ahead of him.

This does not mean that Joel was not working on a game plan. He would communicate what he was learning about himself and how he was struggling. Honest communication is a key component to healing. Learning to hear hard truth from my husband without condemning or shaming was a challenge for me; but, as we communicated more, I was able to find ways to be his helpmate.

It was clear that my biggest struggle was not learning to trust Joel but trusting in God. Having a consistent quiet time to reflect on my relationship with God and Joel was key. I also found a godly woman who would tell me the hard things I needed to hear, not just a listening ear.

REFLECTION:

What stuck out to you as you read through Theresa's experiences? Write down some advice she gave that you can incorporate into your marriage moving forward.

_____

_____

_____

_____

_____

_____

Theresa shared with me a few Bible passages that were a great encouragement to her during her struggle with Joel's infidelity. One of them, Romans 8:18, is at the top of our lesson today.

Read it now and answer this question:

What does God promise He is doing in us through the sufferings we experience on earth?

_____

_____

Another portion of Scripture that was especially helpful to Theresa was Hebrews 11 and 12. At the same time that Joel was struggling with his sexual addiction, Theresa was grieving their inability to have children. During those long months she often turned to the "heroes of faith" listed in Hebrews 11. It affirmed the truth that, just like Noah and Abraham and Joseph, God was working out something in her heart through the testing of her faith. Hebrews 12 gives us great encouragement following all the stories in Hebrews 11.

Read Hebrews 12:1-2 below:

> Therefore, since we are surrounded by such a great cloud of witnesses, let us throw off everything that hinders and the sin that so easily entangles. And let us run with perseverance the race marked out for us, fixing our eyes on Jesus, the pioneer and perfecter of faith. For the joy set before him he endured the cross, scorning its shame, and sat down at the right hand of the throne of God.

DAY 1

Jesus Himself had to endure great trials as a human before reaching the finish line. We too have our own crosses to bear before we complete our earthly journey (Matthew 16:24). When we feel hindered or entangled, we can look to Jesus, who has already completed His race. He is both the "pioneer and perfecter of faith" and is interceding for us as He sits at God's right hand (Romans 8:34, Colossians 3:1-4). Jesus has seen it through from beginning to end and promises to never leave or forsake us (Deuteronomy 31:6,8).

This chapter of our study is all about *we*. You and your husband are in this thing together. But there will be many times when you feel alone. That's when it's important to remember that you have Jesus by your side.

Not only do you have Him, but you also have a "great cloud of witnesses." Theresa is part of my "cloud." In order to continue on in the race, we need to have people in front of us, cheering us on. People who know how it feels to fall, to be exhausted, to want the race to be over. Individuals who know the struggle but continue on in spite of the hindrances and point us to the One who is waiting at the finish line.

I encourage you to ask a few people you trust to be your "Theresa" as you continue on. Ask them to pray for you. Seek godly wisdom from them. Don't share just to gossip about your spouse but truly get biblical counsel on how to love and respect your husband through the darkness.

HEARTWORK

Who is part of your great cloud of witnesses? Write their names below and pray about how to connect with them, asking God for wisdom. If you don't have anyone that comes to mind, write a prayer below asking God to give you someone to encourage you in your faith.

_____

_____

_____

_____

CHARGE

We are on the same team. I will be an ally, not an adversary. This is the only way we can win.

IN THE BEGINNING–GOD'S ORIGINAL PLAN

Genesis 2:24 "That is why a man leaves his father and mother and is united to his wife, and they become one flesh."

WEEK **5** DAY 2

KEY THOUGHT: Man needed a complement and community. Woman was the answer to his needs.

The Bible starts out with these very well known words: "In the beginning, God created the heavens and the earth." The creation narrative follows, and as we read it we can visualize a blank canvas being beautifully painted by a masterful Artist. In just the first two chapters of the first book of the Bible (Genesis), we uncover many truths about God's nature through the creation process. Upon careful examination, this famous passage also reveals a great deal about God's intent for man and woman and the marriage relationship. In order for us to understand how to find our way back from the devastation caused by sexual sin, we need to understand first what God's original plan was for humanity and the marriage relationship.

THE CONCEPT OF COMMUNITY AND COMPLEMENTS

God is *like* a community

Read Genesis 1:1-2, Genesis 1:26, and Colossians 1:15-16.

Write down the phrases that indicate that God is like a community. Who are the three distinct persons that constitute God?

_____

_____

_____

_____

_____

WEEK 1 .... WEEK 2 .... WEEK 3 .... WEEK 4 .... WEEK 5 .... WEEK 6 .... WEEK 7 .... WEEK 8

DAY 2

God created complements in nature

Genesis 1:2-19 tells about all the complementary elements God placed within our universe. Read through these verses and fill in the corresponding complement:

Light and _____   Land and _____

Day and _____   Plants and _____

Water and _____   Sun and _____

God created community among living creatures

Read Genesis 1:20-22, 2:18-20.
God also formed community within nature. List the beings he created (note the plurals!).

_____

_____

_____

Everything God designed up until this point had a counterpart, except one—the man. When God created the first human being, he gave Adam nutrition (garden and trees, Genesis 2:8), a mission (to work the Garden and watch over it, Genesis 2:15), and a position (authority over living creatures, Genesis 2:19-20). But even though Adam had all he needed to thrive physically, he had no one he could share life with, no community, no complement.

Adam initially had two relationships, illustrated by these arrows:

GOD

↓

ADAM

↓

CREATION

He was **UNDER the authority of God** and had **authority OVER** the **land** and **animals**. Two relationships vertical in nature, but not one that was horizontal. No one to partner with, to share experiences with on the same level. God, in His wisdom, knew that man also needed a counterpart, and so he created the first woman.

WEEK 1 .... WEEK 2 .... WEEK 3 .... WEEK 4 .... WEEK 5 .... WEEK 6 .... WEEK 7 .... WEEK 8

DAY 2

Read Genesis 2:18 again, followed by verses 21-25.

> Eve was the answer to Adam's "community gap," the only thing he created with the capacity to change the "not good" (Genesis 2:18) into "very good" (Genesis 1:31).

I love Genesis 2:23 in the New Living Translation of the Bible:

> "At last!" the man exclaimed. "This one is bone from my bone, and flesh from my flesh! She will be called 'woman,' because she was taken from 'man.'"

Adam was relieved and excited when God designed woman. WOW! Finally! "This one" was just like him! Someone who could understand him, partner with him, and be the "helper who is just right for him" (Genesis 2:18). God changes the *me* into a *we* by creating a friendship and partnership between the first man and woman. Note that Adam was born into a relationship with God, but Eve was born into a relationship with both man and God. We have never been alone.

Notice that God created the woman from the inner chamber of man. He didn't create her from an external feature, like his arm or a strand of hair. He designed her from man's ribs, the internal shield that protects most of the vital organs, including the heart and lungs.

Also notice he didn't create another man. He created an entirely new gender. Man didn't need someone exactly like him, but someone to complement and fulfill him. Both man and woman are created in God's image, reflecting unique aspects of His nature. Each gender is different, but both are necessary.

Genesis 2:24-25 reveals the great beauty and mystery of marriage.

> That is why a man leaves his father and mother and is united to his wife, and they become one flesh. Adam and his wife were both naked, and they felt no shame.

Before sin entered the world, man and woman were together in every sense of the word. They enjoyed God's presence together. They were naked together without fear or shame. Every human longs to be seen, to be known, and to be loved. The most beautiful expression of this desire is sexual intimacy.

Before sin entered the world, man and woman experienced love in its purest form—one flesh, naked, and unashamed (Genesis 2:24-25). But after the fall of man, Adam and Eve experienced blame and shame (Genesis 3). Every human relationship is now tainted by sin, and mankind is vainly trying to replicate the euphoria that existed in Eden. Perhaps this is why your husband's betrayal seems so devastating and personal; it stands in stark opposition to what once existed at the beginning of time.

Right now, I realize you are hurting, wondering why we are reading about creation instead of tackling your husband's pornography problem. God's best and original plan will point us in the direction we need to be going. In this sin-ravaged world, marriage will never get back to Garden of Eden status, but through Jesus Christ, we can

experience glimpses of it through His redemption and forgiveness. When both a husband and wife allow God's grace to flow through them, they can experience marriage in its purest state, without sin, shame and mistrust.

How do the passages we read today make you feel about your role as a woman within God's original and perfect design to fill man's needs? Reflect on some of the key phrases in Genesis:

It is not good for man to be alone (needs community).

I will make a helper suitable for him (complement).

HEARTWORK

Take some time to pray as you end today's lesson and *ask God* to reveal how He has designed you as the perfect complement for your husband. Then write down some of the ways He has specifically created you for him.

_____

_____

_____

_____

_____

_____

CHARGE

We are on the same team. I will be an ally, not an adversary. This is the only way we can win.

STAND BY YOUR MAN

Genesis 2:18 "It is not good for man to be alone. I will make a helper suitable for him."

WEEK 5 DAY 3

KEY THOUGHT: Woman was given the divine opportunity and responsibility to help man.

"You can be my helper." Moms and preschool teachers everywhere take advantage of this phrase daily, allowing little hands to "help." Help translates into cracking the eggs or being the line leader. Frequently, it's no help at all... the eggs drip all over the counter or the bickering in the line trumps any useful efforts.

Perhaps that's why we cringe when we read about Eve's original design to be "Helper." In my mind, I presume that means the female was incapable, unqualified, or too weak to take on the lead role. This simple word has a much deeper meaning than you may realize. Let's take a closer look.

In her book, *What's It Like to Be Married to Me?*, Linda Dillow discusses this idea of the word "helper." She explains that "helper" is actually the same word God uses to describe Himself. The wording in Genesis 2:18 where Eve is called a "suitable helper" comes from the Hebrew word *Ezer*. The use of the word *Ezer* in reference to God occurs twenty-one times in the Old Testament.[29]

READ these Psalms and **write down** the phrases that describe God as our helper.

Psalm 33:20

_____

Psalm 70:5

_____

WEEK 1 .... WEEK 2 .... WEEK 3 .... WEEK 4 .... WEEK 5 .... WEEK 6 .... WEEK 7 .... WEEK 8

DAY 3

Psalm 115:9

_____

Psalm 118:7

_____

Psalm 121:1-2

_____

A few noteworthy things stick out in these passages. The word "help" is frequently paired with words like "deliverer" and "shield," indicating protection in the face of danger or oppression. So often as women when we hear the word "helper," we immediately think it means "lesser than," someone who isn't capable to do the task but is permitted to assist, like in the case of the toddler asking to help mix the brownies. But these passages indicate the exact opposite. *A helper is someone fully capable, someone who comes in at a time of great need to bring relief and safety.*

Here's an illustration from my daily life that I think gives a good picture of "helper." Our kids are masters of the "divide and conquer" technique. It usually goes something like this:

KID: "Hey Dad, can I have some soda?"
DAD: "Nope, it's too late, and you've already had enough sugary stuff today."
KID: "But Dad..."
DAD: "The answer is no."
15 minutes later...
KID: "Hey Mom, can I have some soda?"
ME: "Sure, no problem!"
KID: "Thanks Mom!"
Dad enters the room.
DAD: "Didn't I tell you no soda?"
KID: "But Mom said yes!"
MOM: "I did... why not?"
DAD: "I said no, it's way too late."
MOM: "Oh, come on, babe."
DAD: "NATIONWIDE!"

That's his code word, his indicator that he needs me to stand by him. If you've ever seen the Nationwide insurance commercials, you know their tagline and jingle: "Nationwide is on your side." When my husband says

WEEK 1 .... WEEK 2 .... WEEK 3 .... WEEK 4 ....  WEEK 5 .... WEEK 6 .... WEEK 7 .... WEEK 8

DAY 3

"nationwide," that is my indicator that he needs me to stand by him. He wants my support and encouragement so that we can stand as a united front to defeat the enemy (in this case, our children!).

Our true enemy, Satan, desires to divide and conquer in our marriage. He knows our God-given role as helper and often targets wives. In fact, that's what he did in the Garden of Eden. He tempted Eve first. Rather than being Adam's helper and defender, she invited sin into their marriage and became the tool Satan used to bring them both down. She took the fruit, ate it, and then gave it to her husband who was standing right by her (Genesis 3:1-7). This biblical example illustrates the great influence in your husband's life, your marriage, and your future.

Linda Dillow expands on the idea of helper:

> God takes this strong name, *Ezer,* and says, "Now you, the one called wife, have the same privilege and the responsibility that I have. I give you one of my names, Helper. Being a helper is godlike. As I come alongside you as your Helper, I ask you to come alongside your husband, and fill his respect gap as his personal, private, intimate helper. *Only you* will become his intimate ally, his closest companion."[30]

This can seem like a daunting task, to be our husband's sole helper. But we aren't alone. God is helping us help our man. And He is also helping our husbands at the same time. If we are believers, He is at work changing us both and strengthening us to be more like Him (2 Corinthians 3:18).

Please note that being his helper doesn't mean that we must take responsibility for his actions. It means that we come alongside as a support. Our significant other needs to own their own healing. We cannot do that for them as much as we might like to take control over their behavior. Trying to micromanage his actions comes down to self-preservation… we never want to be hurt, caught off-guard, or disappointed by his behavior. We can't make our men leaders, only God can do that. How much different things would be if Adam would have taken leadership and told Eve to remember what God said and told Satan "NO." This is what we want our husbands to do—say no to sexual addiction and temptation and take spiritual leadership back!

Dillow provides a great question we can ask our husbands: "What practically can I do in this season of life to be a help to you?" It's a worthwhile question to ask. For the purpose of this study, I want to refine the question. How can we be a helper without being a stumbling block or a controller?

In my marriage, being a helper to my husband meant going into battle with him to fight the sexual addiction. I cancelled my *Victoria's Secret* magazine subscription and stopped watching certain TV shows. Together we created guidelines for how frequently we should have sex to help avoid temptation. For a season, we got rid of the internet completely in our home, which was a significant sacrifice on my part since I needed the internet for my part-time job. Every day I went to someone else's home to work so that the temptation to look at online pornography was erased.

Take some time as we end today's study to write down a few ways you think you can be a "helper" to your husband. Be thorough as you answer—how can I help him physically, emotionally, mentally, spiritually? Before you go to bed, ask him the same question and listen thoughtfully. Pray first before you ask, that God would soften His heart to give you an honest response. The ways that you thought might be helpful could be way off target, so getting his feedback is paramount. Add his answers to yours and find creative ways this week to put his suggestions into practice. And don't be hurt if he doesn't ask you the same questions back—remember you are only responsible for yourself and your role in the marriage.

Here are some questions for you to ponder and write down. Spend time talking with God before and after writing answers to each of these questions as well.

 ## HEARTWORK

TO ASK YOURSELF:
How can I physically help my husband during this season?
How can I emotionally help my husband during this season?
How can I mentally help my husband during this season?
How can I spiritually help my husband during this season?

_____

_____

_____

_____

_____

_____

_____

_____

_____

_____

TO ASK YOUR HUSBAND:
How can I physically help you during this season?
How can I emotionally help you during this season?
How can I mentally help you during this season?
How can I spiritually help you during this season?

_____
_____
_____
_____
_____
_____
_____
_____
_____
_____

CHARGE

We are on the same team. I will be an ally, not an adversary. This is the only way we can win.

EMPATHY

Hebrews 4:15-16 "We do not have a high priest who is unable to empathize with our weaknesses, but we have one who has been tempted in every way, just as we are—yet he did not sin. Let us then approach God's throne of grace with confidence, so that we may receive mercy and find grace to help us in our time of need."

WEEK 5 DAY 4

KEY THOUGHT: Empathy transforms judgment into partnership.

It's slightly embarrassing, but I am just going to own it: I love reality TV. I have watched countless people get voted off the island, crowned as the best singer, or proclaimed winner for being a successful loser. After analyzing my affinity for these shows, I now realize I am drawn to them because I interject my own life into the participants' lives. My ability to relate to each character in the show, or empathize, gives me the opportunity to identify with or judge them based on their circumstances.

For example, if the brunette, middle-aged, hardworking housewife survives elimination, I experience a sense of elation. Somehow it makes me feel validated if she sticks around for another episode because she represents me. Or, if I can't empathize with their story, then I can judge them. Such as the obnoxious frat boy with the inflated ego. I'm ecstatic when he gets eliminated. I have deemed him unworthy of the million dollars and the prestigious title based on my perception of his character, which stands in stark contrast to mine. My life, my behavior, my standards are superior, so he deserves to go. The sweet mama of two, the contestant most like me, needs another week to make it to the top.

My newest reality obsession is a show called *Fit to Fat to Fit*. Each episode of this show plays out the same way (which, don't all reality shows do that? You'd think I would be over it by now with the predictable outcome). There is an overweight client and an exceptionally fit personal trainer. The client is intimidated by their trainer and thinks that they can't possibly understand what it is like to be fat. The trainer believes the client is lazy and has chosen to be overweight. They think the solution is to convince them to put down the candy bar and pick up some weights and self-discipline instead. Typically, most trainers in these weight-loss type reality shows will shame, guilt and scare their clients into losing weight.

But there's something special about this particular show. The personal trainer chooses to gain an excessive amount of weight over a four-month period, so they can relate to, or empathize with, their overweight client. This revelation from trainer to client is usually met with great disbelief and frequently tears. "Why would you do that to yourself?" is often the immediate response. Then comes the moment when the personal trainer, now about forty

WEEK 1 .... WEEK 2 .... WEEK 3 .... WEEK 4 .... WEEK 5 .... WEEK 6 .... WEEK 7 .... WEEK 8

DAY 4

to sixty pounds heavier from gorging out on cheese fries and doughnuts, sees the client for the first time. There's a nervous vulnerability from the trainer that awkwardly collides with surprise and relief from the client. In that moment, they are experiencing the impact of empathy, and it propels them into their journey to get fit together.

Webster's dictionary defines empathy as the ability to share someone else's feelings. We all long to be seen, validated, and understood. Empathy makes this possible. **When empathy is realized and appreciated, it has the power to transform judgment into partnership.** Like in the example of the TV show, the trainer feels empathy toward their client because they now understand how it feels to be addicted to sugar, to lack the energy to get up in the morning, to be insecure because their clothes won't fit. Suddenly there's a little more compassion extended during the workout because both the trainer and client are struggling to bang out twenty-five burpees. The client is motivated to change because they know their trainer sacrificed their body and health to get fat. Together they struggle to move from obesity to physical fitness with understanding and compassion.

Empathy is one of the most powerful tools you will have on this journey. Author, college professor, and speaker Brené Brown puts it this way: "Empathy is the antidote to shame. If you put shame in a petri dish, it needs three things to grow exponentially: secrecy, silence, and judgment. If you put the same amount of shame in a petri dish and douse it with empathy, it can't survive. The two most powerful words when we're in a struggle are, 'me too.'"[31]

When I finally realized that I was just as much a sinner as my husband, my heart softened toward him. We tend to categorize sin, to treat certain behaviors with a greater level of disgust. I viewed his sin as worse than mine. God doesn't have a sin-meter or a consequence chart. Yes, certain sins are hated by God (Proverbs 6:16-19), but all sin has the same result: death. Romans 6:23 states, "For the wages of sin is death, but the gift of God is eternal life in Christ Jesus our Lord." (NIV)

While I may not have had a sexual addiction, I certainly had a problem with jealousy. And pride. And selfishness… the list goes on. And we all have the same sin struggle, don't we?

OUR SIN

Look up these verses and write down a brief summary of each in your own words.

Romans 3:23

_____

_____

Romans 3:9-10

_____

_____

DAY 4

James 2:10

_____

_____

What do all of these passages say about humanity and your sin?

_____

_____

According to **Romans 6:23**, what was the price for our sin?

_____

GOD'S RESPONSE

Look up **Hebrews 4:14-16**

How does Jesus empathize with us? (verses 14-15)

_____

_____

What is our natural response when we realize Jesus understands our struggles? (verses 1-6)

_____

_____

How does it make you feel to know that the one who created you also understands you in every way?

_____

_____

2 Corinthians 5:21—God made him who had no sin to be sin for us, so that in him we might become the righteousness of God.

I Peter 2:21-24—To this you were called, because Christ suffered for you, leaving you an example, that you should follow in his steps. "He committed no sin, and no deceit was found in his mouth." When they hurled their insults at him, he did not retaliate; when he suffered, he made no threats. Instead, he entrusted himself

WEEK 1 .... WEEK 2 .... WEEK 3 .... WEEK 4 .... WEEK 5 .... WEEK 6 .... WEEK 7 .... WEEK 8

DAY 4

to him who judges justly. "He himself bore our sins" in his body on the cross, so that we might die to sins and live for righteousness; "by his wounds you have been healed."

These passages highlight the fact that although Jesus was without sin, He took ownership of ours. He bore our sin and became sin, so we could become righteousness.

HEARTWORK

How do these truths impact your soul? How does it impact the way you should respond to your spouse's struggle with sexual addiction?

These truths may be difficult to embrace. Your pain, your disappointment, your hopes and dreams are being devastated by a man who promised to love, protect and be faithful. Hang in there, God will meet you in this place of pain.

Write out a letter to God and tell Him about your pain, keeping in mind that He understands.

_____

_____

_____

_____

_____

_____

_____

Now write Hebrews 4:15-16 out on a card and put it in a place you will see every day as a reminder of God's love, grace and mercy. Ask Him to help you embrace and believe His truth, and to give you the strength to extend the same compassion He has for you to your husband.

CHARGE

We are on the same team. I will be an ally, not an adversary. This is the only way we can win.

WHAT TO WEAR–ACTIVE EMPATHY

Colossians 3:12-14 "Therefore, as God's chosen people, holy and dearly loved, clothe yourselves with compassion, kindness, humility, gentleness and patience. Bear with each other and forgive one another if any of you has a grievance against someone. Forgive as the Lord forgave you. And over all these virtues put on love, which binds them all together in perfect unity."

WEEK 5 DAY 5

KEY THOUGHT: How we respond to our spouse's sexual addiction is a daily choice.

One of the main discussions I have with women when talking about their husband's sexual addiction is how his sin makes them feel. They want to know if their feelings are normal and how they should respond to them. This is an important question to tackle and one that needs to be addressed in this study. How can I love my husband, help my husband, and be intimate with my husband when I feel so angry and hurt?

In his book, *False Intimacy,* Dr. Schaumburg talks at great length about the normal responses a wife has when learning about her husband's sexual addiction. I felt validated when I read through his list, knowing that I wasn't alone in my struggle. Below is a synopsis. As you read through it, underline the phrases that best describe how you've been feeling. Feel free to jot additional thoughts or feelings in the margins.

>**FEELINGS of FEAR:** "How will my spouse respond to me if I get involved in this problem? My whole life will disintegrate, and I won't survive. I don't want to do anything, and yet I do." Because you are afraid, you can choose to numb yourself. The most important issue, however, is not what will happen if the sexual addiction is addressed, but what is happening right now—to you, your spouse, and possibly your children. A little more of your feminine soul dies each day as you choose to live with sexual addiction.

>**FEELINGS of ANGER:** You will feel deep anger because it is so hard to believe that someone who has exchanged marriage vows with you and declared his love for you would have so little regard for you—your emotions, your health, your family. Anger reflects your deeper hurt. It is justified, given your spouse's betrayal. You may even be angry at God: "He allowed me to marry someone who has this problem. I prayed and really wanted His will. Why did He allow this to happen?"

>**FEELINGS of BETRAYAL:** Betrayal is part of the deep hurt you feel. "How could he do this to me?" It's essential that you acknowledge this hurt and disappointment. The ideal image

WEEK 1 .... WEEK 2 .... WEEK 3 .... WEEK 4 .... **WEEK 5** .... WEEK 6 .... WEEK 7 .... WEEK 8

DAY 5

of your life has been shattered. You must deal with the fact that you don't even know the person you married. You wonder if you'll ever be able to trust your spouse—or anyone close to you—again.

FEELINGS of LOSS of PERMANENCE: Sexual addiction changes a couple's life forever. They can't go back to what life was like before. Their world is unraveling. Sexually addictive behavior may drastically alter or even destroy reputations, careers, and families. Although life may never be the same, it won't necessarily be worse. When a husband and wife work together to deal with sexual addiction, positive changes can take place in their overall relationship and their relationship with God.

FEELINGS of WITHDRAWAL and DEPRESSION: You simply can't face the mountain of pain and the day-to-day challenges of dealing with a sexually addicted spouse. Hope seems too distant. You withdraw, trying to insulate yourself from the struggle and the pain. However, long-term withdrawal will damage both you and your spouse. Your addicted spouse needs your support and love, even if he is hostile and doesn't want to address the real problems. It's vital that you realize how important a role you can play in helping both of you recover from the effects of sexual addiction.

FEELINGS REGARDING SEXUAL INTIMACY: The quality of the sexual relationship in a marriage is usually severely effected when one spouse is sexually addicted. In fact, real intimacy may not have existed for years. You may try to control your spouse's sexual behavior through your own sexual responses, trying to defend yourself from the helplessness you feel and protect yourself from more pain and disappointment. For example, the wife of a sex addict may participate in sexual activities that are distasteful or immoral in order to have control of the situation. Others may avoid sex entirely, feeling like sex objects.

FEELINGS of GUILT: You may feel like you are the primary cause of your spouse's sexual addiction. "If only I had been more sexually available this wouldn't have happened." You may have done or said things that impacted sexual expression in your marriage, but don't allow guilt to minimize the extent and consequences of your spouse's addiction. Lack of sexual interest isn't a primary cause of sexual addiction. The root usually goes back to adolescence and deep spiritual issues. Instead of focusing on guilt, concentrate on whatever you can do to support your spouse emotionally and guide him toward restoration.[32]

I hope that reading through that list in some way validated your feelings. There's great comfort in knowing that you aren't alone and that your responses are normal. As wives, we have to be able to learn how to deal with our feelings and respond with God's heart in the midst of pain and disappointment.

We discover how to respond this way in the book of Colossians. Read through our key verse found at the beginning of today's lesson.

I love how Paul uses the metaphor of getting dressed to illustrate how we are to respond to our fleshly desires. It's particularly powerful to us as women, knowing how much care and attention we put into getting dressed each day. There's a great feeling of satisfaction when you step out into the world wearing an outfit that makes you feel confident. But putting together that outfit takes careful time and consideration. That same principle applies to the way we respond daily to sin and disappointment.

Paul tells us to clothe ourselves because our flesh is our style, not God's. Our flesh needs to be taken off; it's what comes naturally, but it's old and smelly and ill-fitting. We have to be intentional to put on the "outfits" He has designed for us. The clothing God has for us is new and beautiful and is the perfect outfit. The more we put it on by practicing it, the more it will become "our style."

In Colossians 3, Paul outlines what we are to "put off" and instead "put on."
READ Colossians 3:1-15
In the chart below, write down all the phrases that tell us what to put off and what to put on.

TAKE OFF (verses 8–9)	PUT ON (verses 12–14)

I was talking to a friend about her journey after her husband was unfaithful, and this passage transformed her perspective. The verses in Colossians revealed to her how we can respond with Jesus' love in spite of experiencing deep emotional pain. She explained how verses 12-13 declare our position in Christ: We are CHOSEN, HOLY, DEARLY LOVED and FORGIVEN. If we believe these things, then we are secure in our position. We are valuable because He has chosen us. Through Him we experience the joy and peace that results from being forgiven and loved. He enables us to respond like Him out of a grateful heart.

Jesus clothed Himself with humanity. He experienced hunger, pain, loss, and loneliness. Then He died in our place on the cross. He did all this so that we could experience His grace and love. And He calls us to extend that

same love to others, even when they hurt us. He asks us to forgive, without limitation. We can overflow with His love because we are secure, knowing that our identity is in Christ and that He alone can fill our deepest needs.

Picture in your mind your outfit of choice each month when you are on your cycle. If you are like me, it's probably some kind of stretchy pants and oversized sweatshirt. It's definitely not my most flattering look. Imagine wearing that for a week straight and then throwing it into the bottom of the laundry hamper. Would you pull that outfit out of the heap and wear it to a job interview or a concert to see your favorite band? No way! Why? It's smelly and gross! Just because something is comfortable doesn't mean we need to put it on. Our sinful flesh is the easy go-to, but we are now "hidden with Christ in God" and should reflect His glory!

It's a choice. Daily. Just like the choice about what to wear. Are you going to choose the dirty, oversized, smelly outfit? Or are you going to carefully choose each article of clothing and bind it all together with love?

Galatians 3:26-27 "So in Christ Jesus you are all children of God through faith, for all of you who were baptized into Christ have clothed yourselves with Christ."

Romans 13:14 "Rather, clothe yourselves with the Lord Jesus Christ, and do not think about how to gratify the desires of the flesh."

Reread Colossians 3:12-14 out loud.
How does it feel knowing that, in Christ, you are chosen, holy, dearly loved, and forgiven?

_____

_____

_____

_____

How does Christ's forgiveness and love impact how you respond to your husband and his sin struggle? Is God pressing a current behavior or attitude that needs to be confessed? What is it?

_____

_____

_____

_____

WEEK 1 .... WEEK 2 .... WEEK 3 .... WEEK 4 .... WEEK 5 .... WEEK 6 .... WEEK 7 .... WEEK 8

DAY 5

HEARTWORK

Ask God to soften your heart toward your husband. Pray that God would help you see your husband the way He does. If he is a believer, then your husband is chosen, holy and dearly loved in Christ. If he isn't a follower of Christ, then your husband is still someone that God has made in His image and desires to see come to forgiveness and repentance (2 Peter 3:9, Luke 19:10).

What will you have to relinquish if you make the choice to clothe yourself daily with God's compassion and love? Give this careful consideration. For example, it could mean embracing and dealing with your hurt rather than responding in anger. Perhaps it means going to God first instead of others when you are feeling betrayed. Maybe it means that you stop waiting for the other shoe to drop, expecting your husband to constantly fail you. Or it could mean that you stop choosing to have a victim mentality. For me, it means that I choose to close my mouth when I want to give a sarcastic jab or an unfair "you never" or "you always" blanket statement.

Below write out what it will cost you to love this way. Then take time to process it in prayer with Jesus.

_____

_____

_____

_____

_____

_____

_____

_____

_____

_____

WEEK 1 .... WEEK 2 .... WEEK 3 .... WEEK 4 .... WEEK 5 .... WEEK 6 .... WEEK 7 .... WEEK 8

DAY 5

Putting off the old and putting on the new is not an easy task. It's only possible through the power of the Holy Spirit. God wants to make His strength perfect through your weakness, and that comes from moment to moment complete dependence on Him (2 Corinthians 12:9). Ask God to give you HIS strength to daily choose to clothe yourself with compassion, kindness, humility, gentleness, patience and love.

HOMEWORK

READ HEBREWS 11 and 12. Read it through three or four times, then write out the verses that seem most profound to you. Think of the implications of the verses you chose, careful not to disregard the context in which they were written. What do they say about God? What do they say about God's people?

CHARGE

We are on the same team. I will be an ally, not an adversary. This is the only way we can win.

PW

WEEK SIX

RUBIES

Proverbs 31:10 "A wife of noble character who can find? She is worth far more than rubies."

WEEK 6 DAY 1

KEY THOUGHT: A safe wife brings good, not harm, to her husband.

This week we are going to look at the concept of being a "safe wife." Based on our study in chapter 1, we have identified that sex addicts use pornography/fantasy as a way to escape from reality. The consumer engages in sexual fantasy so he/she can ignore or withdraw from real relationships in an attempt to meet relational needs in a safe and controlled environment.

Your spouse's decision to look at pornography is not your fault. He has made the choice to withdraw into a fake fantasy world rather than pursue true intimacy in marriage. Please hear that loud and clear. BUT, as godly wives, we can provide a safe and loving environment for our husbands that calls him out of withdrawal and into true intimacy. So, what does this kind of wife look like?

There's pressure as a woman to have it all and be it all. The lyrics to a 1980s perfume commercial, *Enjoli,* describe the expectations we often feel as women:

> I can put the wash on the line, feed the kids.
> Get dressed, pass out the kisses, and get to work by five of nine.
> I can bring home the bacon, fry it up in a pan,
> and never let you forget you're a man. Cause I'm a woman![33]

As women we have this idea that we have to do everything perfectly, with ease and without breaking a sweat. Do you relate to this idea? What expectations and standards do you feel you have to live up to? Where do those messages come from? Journal your thoughts below.

_____

_____

_____

WEEK 1 .... WEEK 2 .... WEEK 3 .... WEEK 4 .... WEEK 5 .... WEEK 6 .... WEEK 7 .... WEEK 8

DAY 1

_____

_____

_____

The expectations that society places on us or that we place on ourselves are unattainable and constantly changing. Rather than measuring our worth by the world's standards, we should be looking instead at God's standards. So, what does God say about wives? The answer comes through the words of Proverbs 31.

Recently I have been poring over these verses, one by one, to learn more. Who is this godly woman and how can I become more like her? What does she look like? Are the expectations I have for myself in line with the Proverbs 31 woman? A specific portion of this passage challenged me deeply.

Read Proverbs 31:10-12 and write it out below.

_____

_____

_____

_____

_____

_____

_____

The NIV calls this woman a wife of noble character. She is a competent woman according to the New Living Translation, both "virtuous" and "capable." In the New American Standard Bible, she is called "excellent." The words used to describe her have the same contextual meaning as those used for the men chosen by Moses in Exodus 18:20 to lead and judge the Israelites.

Verse 10 says that this woman is a **treasure**. She is uncommon; sought after but rarely found. She is worth the seeking, more valuable than rubies. Why is this woman compared to a ruby? Rubies are rare and precious gems and were considered more valuable than all others in ancient history. According to Nina Switzer-Spano, instructor of gemology at Gemological Institute of America, "Rubies have remained popular for millennia because they are beautiful stones that evoke love, romance, and power. Here's vivid proof of our fondness for them: rubies can still command the highest per-carat price of all colored stones."

WEEK 1 .... WEEK 2 .... WEEK 3 .... WEEK 4 .... WEEK 5 .... WEEK 6 .... WEEK 7 .... WEEK 8

DAY 1

The fact that this woman is considered more valuable than rubies in the Bible is something special to note. Read **Proverbs 3:13-15** and **Proverbs 20:15**. What other things does Scripture say are more precious than rubies?

_____

_____

_____

This noble woman is considered to be just as valuable as wisdom and knowledge, both of which the Bible says we should try to get no matter what the cost (Proverbs 4:7).

Verse 11 reveals that she is **trustworthy**. Again, I love the New Living Translation, "Her husband can trust her, and she will greatly enrich his life." Other versions state "the heart of her husband trusts in her." This small phrase points to the concept of the safe wife. Her husband finds a sense of security and rest when she is by his side. She is his soft place to land. She improves the quality of his life. He trusts her implicitly.

Verse 12 is where the idea of being a safe wife really comes home: "She brings him good, not harm (or evil, depending on the version), all the days of her life." I realized as I read it over and over that this portion of Scripture holds a critical truth for us as wives. EVERYTHING I do or say involving my husband should be GOOD, from now until the day I die. It boils down to this one question: Is what I am saying right now and doing right now bringing good to my husband?

When you are married to someone with a sinful addiction, it's hard to want to seek their good. Our natural response is retribution for the evil that they are inviting into our home. Perhaps you want to seek revenge because your husband is failing to meet your needs. But this passage calls us to a higher standard.

Do you struggle with the idea of wanting to do good for your husband? What feelings, thoughts and justifications come to mind? Take a moment to list them.

_____

_____

_____

_____

_____

_____

It's difficult to feel loving toward your husband when he is walking in sin, especially if he is unrepentant and continues to fail. You may have the same question that the disciples did when they asked Jesus how many times they must forgive someone. His answer was seventy times seven. That's a lot of forgiving and may seem impossible, but the Bible does not give us an escape clause. Our attitude and actions toward our spouses must be for their good in spite of their sinful behavior. "She brings him **GOOD,** not harm, **ALL** the days of her life." I am accountable for my own responses, every day for the rest of my life, regardless of how I feel. I must choose to extend grace to my husband just as Jesus did to me (Ephesians 4:32). A safe wife provides an environment where grace flourishes.

So, what does this look like? Does that mean you just allow your husband to continue on in his addiction, never saying a word or standing up for the truth? No! It means not gossiping about your husband's addiction to every woman you know. It means praying for him every day. It means asking God to empower you with the Holy Spirit so that you can make the difficult choice to act in a good, loving manner, regardless of your feelings. It means honoring his authority as the God-appointed leader of your household. It means using your words to build him up according to what he needs (Ephesians 4:29). 1 Peter 3:1-2 reminds us that we can quietly "win over" our husbands by the purity and reverence of our lives.

There's another portion of Proverbs 31 that I find so encouraging as I struggle with how to be a godly wife. Verse 25 says, "She is clothed with strength and dignity; she can laugh at the days to come." It's a reminder to me that I don't have to hang my head in shame because of my husband's sin struggle. We can be submissive and honoring to our husbands while maintaining our strength and dignity. We don't have to be browbeaten doormats. Your identity is not tied to your husband's sin cycle. My identity is not tied to my husband's sin cycle.

This kind of mind-set will require a great strength and dignity that can only come through Jesus Christ. A strength that enables you to bite your tongue instead of reciprocating in anger. A dignity that will remind you of your worth in Christ Jesus regardless of your husband's sinful actions. We must daily clothe ourselves with strength and dignity and pair them with "the unfading beauty of a gentle and quiet spirit, which is of great worth in God's sight" (1 Peter 3:4). This will transform us into the godly wife that is a true treasure, more valuable than rubies.

Take some time to honestly answer this question:

What attitudes do I have that bring harm to my husband? What actions? Write them out below.

_____

_____

_____

_____

WEEK 1 .... WEEK 2 .... WEEK 3 .... WEEK 4 .... WEEK 5 .... **WEEK 6** .... WEEK 7 .... WEEK 8

DAY 1

_____

_____

_____

_____

Take a few moments to pray over these thoughts and attitudes, asking God to forgive you for the moments that you have sinned out of anger against your husband.

What actions and attitudes can you begin to implement that will bring good to your husband instead?

_____

_____

_____

_____

_____

_____

_____

HEARTWORK

I want to challenge you to start practicing a new rhythm in your life. Start asking yourself throughout the day, "Are my words/actions bringing good to my husband right now?" This question is critical when you feel yourself starting to get impatient or angry. If the answer is no, stop immediately and ask God to give you a deep love for your husband that would seek to bring him good, in that very moment… not because he necessarily deserves it, but because it honors the Lord.

CHARGE

What seems impossible is only an opportunity for miracles. I am brave and will act courageously in faith.

RESPOND

James 5:16 "Therefore confess your sins to each other and pray for each other so that you may be healed. The prayer of a righteous person is powerful and effective."

WEEK 6 DAY 2

KEY THOUGHT: How we respond to our husband's sexual addiction has great impact on his road to recovery.

When your husband's addiction is revealed, whether by his own choice or by your discovery, it will be one of the most vulnerable moments of his life. He will feel naked, exposed, afraid and defensive because of his sin, just like Adam did in the Garden of Eden (Genesis 3:1-13). How you respond in that moment has great significance. Today we will explore how a "safe wife" will listen to her husband's confession and then turn her focus to prayer.

If your husband has made the decision to confess on his own, he will most likely be very aware of his vulnerability. The fear of shame and vulnerability was the very thing that kept my husband silent for years, trapped and alone in his struggle. He repeatedly buried the gentle stirrings inside that called him to confess and be free of the guilt and shame, petrified that he would be thrown out of the church with pitchforks and torches. His story is not unique. How many of us, myself included, think, "If people knew what I was really like, what I really thought, what I have done, I would be rejected. I'm a freak. No one will like me if I let them see the real me, my weaknesses."

Have you ever had to tell someone about a significant sin in your life? How did you feel when you confessed? What were your fears?

_____

_____

_____

_____

_____

_____

WEEK 1 .... WEEK 2 .... WEEK 3 .... WEEK 4 .... WEEK 5 .... **WEEK 6** .... WEEK 7 .... WEEK 8

DAY 2

If your husband's addiction was discovered rather than confessed, which happened in our marriage the second time I found out he was struggling, he may become angry or defensive. He has built a world around himself where he feels accepted, in control, and physically desired. He is powerful in his world of false intimacy where no one has expectations or criticism, only admiration and a desire to please. The idea of losing that comfort and control may result in an all-out war.

Have you ever been discovered or called out for your sin? What was your response? What were your feelings towards that person who "called you out"?

_____

_____

_____

_____

_____

_____

_____

No matter what the circumstances, our response as a wife is critical. It's important to note that vulnerability requires bravery. To quote speaker Brené Brown, "Vulnerability is not weakness; it's pure courage. Vulnerability requires emotional risk and exposure. It's our most accurate measurement of courage—to let ourselves be seen, to be honest."[34] It doesn't matter whether your husband chose to be vulnerable through confessing his sin or was forced into it by being caught in his sin; your response will have a profound and lasting impact in both scenarios. I've done it the right way and the wrong way.

When my husband first confessed, the Lord had been softening my heart for months. The pages of my journal from that season of life went something like this:

> God, I know you are preparing my heart. I don't know for what, by whatever it is, give me the strength to respond with your love.

On a cold Sunday morning in a high school hallway, my husband admitted to me that had a pornography addiction. At that moment, I truly believe the Holy Spirit spoke through me. I whispered words of love as I cried and hugged him. My heart felt compassion because I knew how difficult it was for my husband to admit he was struggling.

WEEK 1 .... WEEK 2 .... WEEK 3 .... WEEK 4 .... WEEK 5 .... **WEEK 6** .... WEEK 7 .... WEEK 8

DAY 2

When my husband was discovered during a relapse years later, my heart was not so compassionate. We had already been through the battle, sought godly counsel, talked through the pain and insecurity that pornography brought into our life. This time around I was angry and felt like a complete idiot. How could I have missed the signs after going through this all before? My response was far from loving and forgiving.

So how are we to respond when we discover our husband's sexual addiction, whether it's confessed or stumbled upon? There's a beautiful story in the Gospels that shows us how Jesus responded. In John 8, we find the beautiful story of a woman caught in sexual sin. Take a few minutes and read **John 8:1-11**. Write out verses 10 and 11 below.

_____

_____

_____

_____

_____

Note the ways that Jesus DIDN'T respond to this woman. He didn't get angry, threatening her with a list of painful consequences. He didn't embarrass her as she stood there, vulnerable in front of the group of religious leaders. He didn't tell her, "Oh, it's OK," and give her permission to remain in her life of sin. He called her to repentance, to leave behind her life of sin. He offered her grace and forgiveness. His extension of love pointed her to repentance.

Just like those people crowded around the woman with stones in hand, it's easy for us as wives to have a righteous attitude when we find out our husband has a sexual addiction. It's natural to start categorizing their sin as more severe than ours, more deserving of shame and punishment. But Jesus reminds us in His calm and quiet way that none of us are without sin. **We have no right to condemn our husbands because we too are guilty of walking in sin.** How I wish I had read that portion of Scripture and allowed it to impact me when I heard about my husband's relapse!

Romans 2:1-4 boldly calls us out when we pass judgment on others for their sin:

> You, therefore, have no excuse, you who pass judgment on someone else, for at whatever point you judge another, you are condemning yourself, because you who pass judgment do the same things. Now we know that God's judgment against those who do such things is based on truth. So when you, a mere human being, pass judgment on them and yet do the same things, do you think you will escape God's judgment? Or do you show contempt for the riches of his kindness, forbearance and patience, not realizing that God's kindness is intended to lead you to repentance?

WEEK 1 .... WEEK 2 .... WEEK 3 .... WEEK 4 .... WEEK 5 .... **WEEK 6** .... WEEK 7 .... WEEK 8

DAY 2

Yes, our husbands' behavior is sinful. Yes, it impacts us greatly. Yes, like all sin, it is costly (Romans 6:23). But God alone is the Righteous Judge, and if He is willing to extend forgiveness and love then as His followers we must do the same:

> Forgiveness is a gift that God means for you to receive and then pass along to others. It may be the most costly gift you will ever give; yet, precisely because it is so costly, it is also one of the clearest ways you can show God's love as his image bearers.[35]

This mandate to love and forgive is repeated throughout the New Testament. Read the following passages and write them out on the lines below.

1 Peter 4:8

_____

_____

_____

_____

Colossians 3:13

_____

_____

_____

_____

What do these verses say to you?

_____

_____

_____

_____

WEEK 1 .... WEEK 2 .... WEEK 3 .... WEEK 4 .... WEEK 5 .... **WEEK 6** .... WEEK 7 .... WEEK 8

DAY 2

Practically speaking, how do we put forgiveness into motion? The Bible verse we started out with today gives us some direction.

Write out James 5:16 below.

_____

_____

_____

_____

What does James tell us to do when someone confesses their sin?

_____

What will be the end result if we follow this instruction (last part of the verse)?

_____

Your initial response to your husband is just a first step in the direction of healing and forgiveness. In your flesh, you will experience a flood of emotions. You will want to know details. Don't push for them. Getting all the journalist details (who, what, when, why, and how) will only be more painful for you. As wives it's tempting to believe that if we know all the specifics, then perhaps we can control our husband's behavior so he won't be a repeat offender. That's a faulty assumption. James 5:16 tells us that our response shouldn't be to dig deeper into the sin, *but instead dig deep into prayer.*

I love how the New Living Translation states James 5:16, "Confess your sins to each other and **pray** for each other so that you may be **healed**. The **earnest** prayer of a **righteous** person has great **power** and produces **wonderful results**."

There is great power and comfort found through prayer! Listen to this encouragement from Psalm 34 about how God responds to the prayers of a righteous person:

> The eyes of the Lord are on the righteous, and his ears are attentive to their cry; but the face of the Lord is against those who do evil, to blot out their name from the earth.

> The righteous cry out, and the Lord hears them; he delivers them from all their troubles.

> The Lord is close to the brokenhearted and saves those who are crushed in spirit.

> The righteous person may have many troubles, but the Lord delivers him from them all; he protects all his bones, not one of them will be broken.

WEEK 1 .... WEEK 2 .... WEEK 3 .... WEEK 4 .... WEEK 5 .... WEEK 6 .... WEEK 7 .... WEEK 8

DAY 2

You may be troubled, brokenhearted, and crushed in spirit, but God hears your prayers. His ears are listening to your cries when you come to Him, believing in faith that He alone can sustain you through this difficult season. The righteous will walk by faith (Habakkuk 2:4), looking to God for strength to endure and press on.

HEARTWORK

As you end today's lesson, put James 5:16 into action. Pray earnestly for your husband's healing. Pray that God will lead him to confession and genuine repentance.

Pray that you will respond to your husband with grace, love and forgiveness, in spite of his sinful actions. Pray that God would produce a righteousness in you as you pursue His heart instead of your fleshly feelings.

CHARGE

What seems impossible is only an opportunity for miracles. I am brave and will act courageously in faith.

REVENGE

Romans 12:19-21 "Do not take revenge, my dear friends, but leave room for God's wrath, for it is written: 'It is mine to avenge; I will repay,'" says the Lord. On the contrary: "If your enemy is hungry, feed him; if he is thirsty, give him something to drink. In doing this, you will heap burning coals on his head." Do not be overcome by evil, but overcome evil with good.

WEEK 6 DAY 3

KEY THOUGHT: The safe wife pursues forgiveness and restoration, not revenge.

The verses quoted above hung on the upstairs wall of my childhood home. My mom gave us 50 cents apiece for every verse we wrote out and colored to make homemade art. Not very much money, for sure, but this verse is so much more valuable to me now than the pocket change I earned illustrating it. Verse 21 has come in handy many times as I deal with difficult people. It is also a verse I quote frequently to my children as they interact with bullies at school.

This passage has also been instrumental when responding to my husband's "evil," his pornography addiction. There was a time in my marriage when I definitely viewed my husband as an enemy. As we have discussed in previous chapters, a sexual addiction is a deep betrayal by the one who promised to love and protect "as long as we both shall live."

Yesterday we talked about our initial response to the confession (voluntary or involuntary) of a sexual addiction. Over the next two days, as we continue with the theme of being a safe wife, we will talk about the difficult subject of how to put love and forgiveness into action. How do we respond with a Christlike heart and mind when our husbands' actions seem more like those of an enemy rather than a lover?

Let's turn to Dr. Schaumburg and pages from his book, *False Intimacy,* again for insight on this issue.

> Within each of us lies the tendency to want people to pay for their sins—especially if they commit sins against us. But God calls us to overcome evil with good. He calls us to be involved in *RESTORATION,* not in vengeful acts (Romans 12:19-21). Each of us involved in the *ministry of healing* must be willing to *love sex addicts through the power of God, surprising them* with what they *don't deserve* and offering them *mercy, forgiveness and joy that only God can provide.*

WEEK 1 .... WEEK 2 .... WEEK 3 .... WEEK 4 .... WEEK 5 .... WEEK 6 .... WEEK 7 .... WEEK 8

DAY 3

Loving those who are sexually addicted in the power of God's love entails a process of offering them what is *not* deserved so they might be *restored* to our Lord, to others, and to us. Properly understood, *love is the greatest gift each of us can offer*. When love is given to those held captive by the sins of sexual addiction and spiritual adultery, it reaches out with God's power to *astound* sinners. It *destroys* the power of sin over their lives. It *contradicts all the false intimacy within sexual addiction* and calls forth sinners to express true love because they have been loved so deeply.[36]

I have italicized the sections that impacted me personally. Now REREAD it, and as you do, UNDERLINE or CIRCLE the phrases that speak to your heart and challenge you.

On the lines below, journal about your typical response to your husband's pornography addiction. What do you think drives those responses?

_____

_____

_____

_____

_____

_____

Because it's been so long since my husband's admission of addiction, sometimes I can forget how deeply angry and sad I was during that difficult season. But then something happened to our family just this weekend that brought all of those feelings immediately back to the surface.

We had our first big snow this past weekend, the kind of snow that makes me giddy inside like a little girl. Something about waking up to the white falling flakes brings back wonderful childhood memories of sledding and playing in the snow. So, when my daughter asked if she could take our family dog up the street to go sledding with her cousins, I only slightly hesitated to say yes. She's a young teenager and I'm not quite comfortable with the idea of her walking around the neighborhood alone, but I figured our dog, Charlie, would be able to keep her safe.

Little did I know that Charlie was the one I should have been worried about instead. While traipsing out in the snow, Charlie was involved in a terrible accident that left him bloody and severely injured. Unfortunately, we had to put him down because the recovery would be painful and expensive, and he was already an old dog with significant health issues. His injuries were the result of an unfortunate accident, but the individuals who were part of the incident never apologized and actually blamed our dog for the situation.

WEEK 1 .... WEEK 2 .... WEEK 3 .... WEEK 4 .... WEEK 5 .... WEEK 6 .... WEEK 7 .... WEEK 8

DAY 3

Even as I type these words, the desire to seek revenge in my life is very real. I'm angry at the injustice of the situation. I'm frustrated by my inability to change the circumstances. I felt guilty that I allowed our dog to leave the safety of my home to go play in the snow. I'm heartbroken that Charlie's last experience in life left him in deep pain and shock.

I want things to go back to the way they were moments before I heard about what happened, a home filled with joy over the beauty of the snow and a few days off from work and school. Instead of sledding and sleeping in, we spent our time burying our dog in the frozen dirt and crying ourselves to sleep.

This incident has reminded me of the deep anger and vengeance that we feel as wives when we discover our husband has a sexual addiction. The inner dialogue that is going on in my head about our dog is very similar to how I felt when my husband had his relapse. I felt wronged, angry, guilty, betrayed, and sad. I desperately wanted revenge, for him to hurt as deeply as I did, to pay for what he put me through.

The emotions and feelings that result from your significant other's deep betrayal are normal. But as Christ-followers, we are called to respond out of His love and forgiveness instead of our fleshly feelings. Learning how to forgive in the midst of deep pain requires an intentional shift in our thinking. Rather than focus on what was done **TO US by our husband**, we need to put our focus on what was done **FOR US by Jesus** on the cross. When we think about Jesus' great sacrifice and love for us, we embrace an "attitude of gratitude." True appreciation for Christ's death on the cross produces a thankful heart that recognizes you'd be lost without Him. It changes our fleshly response from "look what my husband did to me!" to "what can I do for my husband?" to show him Christlike love.

On the surface this idea sounds beautiful. But, like me, I am sure you have deep concerns about your husband's response to your selfless love. What if my husband doesn't respond with gratitude, love, or a changed heart? What if I pray for him and extend grace and he doesn't get healed? Will he misinterpret my kindness as weakness and continue in his addiction? Won't he just walk all over me? How can I just "forgive and forget"?

I love how Dr. Schaumburg responds to these concerns:

> Such a love is not weak. It requires courage, power, strength, and humility of heart. It is willing to engage in ministry regardless of the cost or the calculated chance of victory. It calls us to forsake emotional safety, motivates us to selflessness, and empowers us to respond in humble dependence on God. Such a love is a natural response to gaining from God what we don't deserve, which frees us to give the same to others. This love can then confront the sins of sexual addiction and spiritual adultery, regardless of the sex addict's response.[37]

Read over the quote once more and **circle** the qualities it will require in you to love this way.

The Bible passage at the beginning of this lesson says that we are to overcome evil with good. Is this even possible? To love and forgive, without a desire for revenge, even if your spouse decides not to repent?

WEEK 1 .... WEEK 2 .... WEEK 3 .... WEEK 4 .... WEEK 5 .... WEEK 6 .... WEEK 7 .... WEEK 8

DAY 3

Read Romans 5:6-8. Write out verse 8 below.

_____

_____

_____

This passage illustrates God's love and forgiveness for us, extended without any requirements on our end. He gives lavishly, whether we choose to accept it or not.

Now read Ephesians 4:32 and write it out.

_____

_____

_____

When we grasp the depths of God's love made manifest through forgiveness, our response is a willingness to give it away to others. Unfortunately, this response is in conflict with our human nature. Our flesh seeks after revenge and wants the offender to pay for their wrongdoing. The godly response is difficult to put into action when we have been wounded so deeply by our significant other.

Extending forgiveness instead of revenge calls for a shift in our mind-set. This mind-set change happens when I "recognize that God in Christ has forgiven me in the midst of my own sin, so I can by the strength of the Holy Spirit forgive my husband in the midst of his."[38]

What has been your definition of forgiveness? Do you believe that it is a one-time event, or an ongoing process? Does it mean that you just "forgive and forget" the sinful behavior, or just ignore it? Journal your thoughts below.

_____

_____

_____

In his article, "Forgive and Forget and Other Myths of Forgiveness," professional counselor Dan Allender reveals the faulty assumption that forgiveness is a one-time event where you decide to forget what has been done in order to move on from the pain. As you read the excerpt below, underline any statements that make you pause and reconsider your concept of forgiveness.

DAY 3

Forgiveness is too often seen as merely an exercise in releasing bad feelings and **ignoring** past harm, **pretending** all is well. Yet nothing could be further from the truth. True forgiveness often deepens internal passion and sorrow. Yet it is a powerful agent in a process that can transform both the forgiver and the forgiven. It is a gift that pierces a hardened, defensive heart with rays of redemptive kindness.

Many attempt to put their injuries behind them through a dramatic, climactic, once-and-for-all deliverance from anger. They **assume** that forgiving involves a sudden, marked change from being filled with bitterness and hatred to a state of untroubled peace. Those who hold this view refer to forgiveness as a finished event ("It took years before I forgave my father") rather than an ongoing work of the Spirit of God.

It is **naïve** to believe that forgiving another for any one failure or for a lifetime of harm is ever entirely finished. In truth, the more fully we face the harm we have suffered, the more deeply we must forgive. Forgiving another is an ongoing process, rather than a once-and-for-all event.

I was struck by the phrase, "true forgiveness often deepens internal passion and sorrow." What do you think that means?

_____

_____

_____

For me, that means that when I choose to forgive, I also choose to face the reality of what was done to me and the resulting pain, which may be difficult to internalize and process. Just like a wound cannot be treated if it's not correctly diagnosed, likewise you must take careful inventory of sinful behavior in order to get emotional and spiritual healing.

For the next few minutes I want you to carefully consider the areas where you have been wounded by your husband. In what ways has he sinned against you? What have been the results of that sin? What areas do you need to extend forgiveness to him? Take some time to journal it out on the lines below.

_____

_____

_____

_____

Allender continues with some other statements that tie together the idea of acknowledging sinful behavior with our main verse for today, Romans 12:21.

> Forgiving does involve costly sacrifice, but it is not a weak, look-the-other-way pretense that all is well. Forgiveness involves a courageous commitment to "overcome evil with good" (Romans 12:21). And the good that is done is an assault against the inner cancer of arrogance and independence that, left unchecked, will eat away at the offender's soul.

> **Overlooking harm** in order to achieve a **sentimental** but not substantive **peace actually encourages sin.** When we put the best construction around a sinful behavior ("Dad has never been very emotional" or "What do you expect of someone who grew up in a dysfunctional family?") we deny the full extent of the harm, and **we neglect our part in dealing with their sin.**

> Overlooking harm also destroys one of the purposes of our relationships. Am I just to love you? Or do I offer a taste of the Spirit's kindness and strength by disrupting your sin and enticing your soul with a taste of a better life? I believe forgiveness is a weapon of wisdom that is designed to disrupt and entice.

By choosing to fully acknowledge sin and then forgive, we overcome evil with good. It's an ongoing process that forces us to look deeply at sin (both our own and our husband's) and then turn our gaze onto the one who has fully forgiven us, Jesus Christ. He alone can heal and restore, calling us into a full life where we are not ruled by sin.

HEARTWORK

As we end today, **read Psalm 32.** It's a psalm that expresses great joy upon the realization of forgiveness. His grace will guide you as you obey the commission to extend this forgiveness to your spouse and to others, especially as you continue to process through the pain that was a result of their sin against you.

Spend some time in prayer thanking God for His forgiveness and love. Pray that you will extend it graciously to your husband. Pray that your husband will be able to respond with gratitude and repentance as he receives both God's forgiveness and yours.

CHARGE

What seems impossible is only an opportunity for miracles. I am brave and will act courageously in faith.

RESTORATION

Galatians 6:1a "Brothers and sisters, if someone is caught in a sin, you who live by the Spirit should restore that person gently."

WEEK 6 DAY 4

KEY THOUGHT: Forgiveness + Repentance = Restoration

Today we will explore the call to restore those caught in sin. As a safe wife, we must not only learn how to forgive, but also how to do the ongoing work of repairing the marriage relationship.

Jesus tells a parable in Luke 15 that beautifully illustrates this idea of restoration.

Open your Bible and **read Luke 15:11-24.**

This well-known parable is one of my favorites. There's so much to learn about God's heart of forgiveness that we can apply to our marriages, especially when our husband has a sexual addiction.

Here's a few key observations that stand out when reading this passage.

1. Sin is costly, for both the offender and the offended. The son's decision to walk away with his father's inheritance had negative financial, physical and emotional repercussions for both of them. Not only did he lose all that his father had earned through years of hard work, he also lost time spent together, growing in their relationship. As a mom, I can imagine the emotional turmoil that the father must have experienced, worrying day and night until his son returned back home. How must the son have felt, so far from home, with no one who truly cared for him the way his father did? The son's selfishness cost them both dearly.

    Wilkerson talks about the great cost of forgiveness of sin:
    "The fact that God has given forgiveness freely doesn't mean it was cheap. It cost Him His Son, worth more than the whole world. And before it cost Jesus the pain and agony of crucifixion, it cost him a life of humility."

WEEK   WEEK   WEEK   WEEK   WEEK   WEEK   WEEK   WEEK
1 .... 2 .... 3 .... 4 .... 5 .... 6 .... 7 8

DAY 4

2. Sin has natural consequences. When the younger son decided to walk in sin, the father did not run after him. He allowed the son to suffer the repercussions of his choices.
Again, Wilkerson explains: "Sin causes damage that cannot always be undone and sets things in motion that cannot always be stopped. We reap what we sow (Galatians 6:7-8). When we forgive someone, it is not always wise—if it is even possible—to spare them the consequences of their sin."

    For some wives, there is a felt need to protect the husband from the ramifications of their sexual addiction. If we step in the way (covering his tracks at work, not letting others step in to help confront) then we may be removing the catalyst for repentance. The negative effects of sinful behavior are typically the very thing that cause sinners to evaluate their choices and "come to their senses" (verse 17).

3. True restoration cannot be experienced without true repentance. The father was ready and waiting for his son's return. He was keeping vigilant watch and saw him from "a long way off" (verse 20). We can forgive our husbands, but we must be watching for signs of true repentance so that we can be fully restored. True repentance requires humility, a physical turning from sin, and a recognition of the cost to both God and the injured party.

    Forgiveness is your decision, repentance is your husband's. Like God, we can forgive someone without them choosing to accept it and repent. So while we wait for their hearts to change, we watch and pray for it, just like the father in the parable.

    Wilkerson says it this way:

    "We should forgive even before the wrongdoer repents, and even if the wrongdoer never repents. 'While we were still sinners, Christ died for us' (Romans 5:8). God did not wait for us to repent before expressing his love toward us. Likewise, we can and should grant forgiveness to others, regardless of their repentance. This will lead some to ask, 'But if they never repent, isn't that like letting them get away with it?' Remember: when someone sins against you, he also sins against God. In *your* forgiveness, you turn him over to God, not primarily hoping that he will be punished by God but first with the hope that he will eventually repent and receive God's forgiveness. Every wrong will be made right in the end, one way or another (Romans 12:19). Ultimately, nobody gets away with anything."[39]

Take a few moments and record your thoughts on the three points listed above. What is God speaking to your heart through the parable of the lost son?

_____

_____

_____

WEEK 1 .... WEEK 2 .... WEEK 3 .... WEEK 4 .... WEEK 5 .... WEEK 6 .... WEEK 7 .... WEEK 8

DAY 4

_____

_____

_____

_____

_____

This parable is deeply personal to me because I have a prodigal in my life. Not a son, but another family member. This dear person in my life has been estranged from our family for over fifteen years. I'm not sure what made this person decide to cut off contact completely. Our continued attempts to make contact have unfortunately been met with hostility and aggression.

As the years have passed by, my family has mourned the loss of this relationship. There are nieces and nephews that have never been met, marriages that were unattended, holidays celebrated with no presents in this individual's name. The emotional weight of the distance between us is both heartbreaking and painful.

A few years ago, my maternal grandmother passed away from cancer, followed only weeks later by my paternal grandmother dying from a different form of the same disease. I felt compelled to give my estranged family member a phone call in the short time frame between their passing to inform them about what was going on in the family.

I'll never forget that moment. This family member didn't respond, I just got the answering machine. Instantly I burst into tears as I heard the familiar voice. It sounded the same after all these years. Memories flooded my mind and I so desperately wanted to reach through the phone and make him/her answer.

I could only choke out this short response through the tears: "Grandmom just passed away from cancer and Grammie is about to pass away too. I wanted to call to let you know. I love you, and I always will. Nothing will ever stop making me love you."

I'd love to say that this family member called me back. But they didn't. In fact, I don't know if they even listened to my voicemail. We experienced an additional layer of grief at my grandmothers' funerals, knowing that this person had made the choice to be "dead" to our immediate and extended family.

I pray for this family member often, begging and pleading to God for restoration both to Him and to our family. The more time passes, the more I wonder if it will ever happen. But I choose to believe that God loves this person more dearly than I do, that He is in control, and that He can heal the brokenness in our family.

WEEK 1 .... WEEK 2 .... WEEK 3 .... WEEK 4 .... WEEK 5 .... WEEK 6 .... WEEK 7 .... WEEK 8

DAY 4

Until then, we wait like the father in the parable. I've imagined the moment of return so many times. How would we all respond? It's a general consensus among my family that we would welcome this individual with open arms and tears of joy. Like the father in the story, I believe that we would be "filled with compassion," with arms wide open, ready to celebrate with everyone that has been part of our journey.

When your husband comes to you with a heart of repentance, are you filled with compassion like the father? Or does the pain and betrayal get in the way, whispering in your ear all the ways he hurt you? Do you cave in to your flesh, wanting to make him pay and punishing him further with your anger?

It may go against our human nature, but we must begin to approach relationships as other-centered rather than self-centered. The self-centered approach eventually leads to disappointment because our husband will never be able to fully meet our expectations or needs. We must have a ***passion to*** love that is stronger than the ***desire to be*** loved.[40]

Take a moment to think about that last quote from Wilkerson. What are your thoughts?

_____

_____

_____

_____

_____

_____

Philippians 2:3-4 puts this concept into words beautifully and practically. Write it out below:

_____

_____

_____

_____

What character trait is necessary for us to value others more than ourselves?

_____

WEEK 1 .... WEEK 2 .... WEEK 3 .... WEEK 4 .... WEEK 5 .... WEEK 6 .... WEEK 7 .... WEEK 8

DAY 4

We are called to humility, a "willingness to surrender our rights to our rights."[41] Humility must be accompanied by gentleness to move towards restoration instead of revenge (Galatians 6:1, today's theme verse).

Our example is Christ Himself:

> You must have the same attitude that Christ Jesus had. Though he was God, he did not think of equality with God as something to cling to. Instead, he gave up his divine privileges; he took the humble position of a slave and was born as a human being. When he appeared in human form, he humbled himself in obedience to God and died a criminal's death on a cross (Philippians 2:6-8, NLT).

In humility, Christ came and died for us, even though he was innocent. Instead of turning us away in guilt, His love calls us into the most endearing and trusting relationship—Father to child. This same humility and love are what Jesus says we must display to others, even when they have sinned against us, especially when they have sinned against us.

It's essential for you to communicate, with humility and gentleness, your desire for a restored relationship with your husband. Schaumburg gives us verbiage to express this sentiment:

> I'm committed to you, to seeing your life restored, to strengthening our relationship together, to getting closer to you and God in a stronger spiritual relationship.[42]

HEARTWORK

When the timing is right, in your own words, communicate your desire for restoration to your husband. Like the father in the story of the prodigal son, let him know that you are patiently waiting for him to come back into a healthy and loving relationship. If you don't have the desire, ask God to change your heart. Pray that He will give you a spirit that is others-centered rather than self-centered. Ask Him to give you the same humility that He had when He died on the cross for our sins. Finally, pray that God will bring your husband to repentance. Spend time now praying about all these things.

CHARGE

What seems impossible is only an opportunity for miracles. I am brave and will act courageously in faith.

RESPECT

Ephesians 5:33 "Each one of you also must love his wife as he loves himself, and the wife must respect her husband."

WEEK 6 DAY 5

KEY THOUGHT: A safe wife is a respectful wife.

I have a critical spirit. Anyone else? I can find something wrong in even the most positive situations. For example, recently I received a note of encouragement and the only thing I noticed was a misspelled word. I could blame it on the fact that I was an English Education major in college, but that's just an excuse.

I carry my criticism with me into my friendships, parenting, ministry and marriage. It is so easy for me to identify what everyone (including me) is doing wrong or how they could be doing it better. My eye for detail and perfectionistic tendencies are beneficial for my occupation and education, but can be deadly to relationships, especially my marriage.

The funny thing is that most of what I criticize my husband for doesn't really matter in the grand scheme of life. When I hear my kids bickering, I often ask, "Will this matter next week? Will you even remember what you are arguing about? If not, then it's not worth it." Those same questions can be applied to nitpicking at my husband. The dirty socks on the floor or the fact that he took five extra minutes to belly up to the table for dinner will not matter next week, and they definitely don't have any impact on eternity.

This does not mean that our husbands get a free pass to behave however they like and we have to keep our mouths shut. That is an archaic representation of biblical submission and respect for our husbands. What it does mean is that we have a voice, but as a safe wife we need to choose carefully how, when and why we choose to speak.

The way we speak to our husbands is one of the most important and difficult things to get right in order to have a healthy marriage. Our words have a great impact on our husband and his confidence, which is actually a lot more fragile than most men are willing to admit. The Bible actually addresses this very topic.

WEEK 1 .... WEEK 2 .... WEEK 3 .... WEEK 4 .... WEEK 5 .... WEEK 6 .... WEEK 7 .... WEEK 8

DAY 5

Write out Proverbs 21:9 and 19 below.

_____

_____

_____

_____

What kind of living conditions would be better than living with a quarrelsome wife? Living in a desert!!! I can't imagine how awful it would be to live in a desert, under the scorching hot sun with no water. But the Bible says that would be better than living with a nagging wife! Why do you think God compared a quarrelsome wife to the desert?

_____

_____

_____

_____

Now read Proverbs 27:15-16 and write it out below.

_____

_____

_____

_____

The Bible compares a nagging wife to three different natural occurrences—a constant drip during a rainstorm, the wind, and containing oil in your hand. No matter how hard you try, you can't get it to stop.

What kind of feelings and responses are accompanied by the inability to stop a constant annoyance? For me it's anger, impatience, frustration, aggravation, and sometimes even rage.

WEEK 1 .... WEEK 2 .... WEEK 3 .... WEEK 4 .... WEEK 5 .... WEEK 6 .... WEEK 7 .... WEEK 8

DAY 5

Take some time to evaluate and reflect on how often you nag your husband. What do you think it communicates to him? What is his response?

Write your thoughts below.

_____

_____

_____

_____

_____

_____

In contrast, the Bible actually calls us to speak words of encouragement rather than nagging.

Read Ephesians 4:29 and write it out below.

_____

_____

_____

_____

In her book, *What's It Like to Be Married to Me?*, author Linda Dillow expounds on the meaning of this passage.

> *Do not* speak dirty, rotten garbage words, literally. *Do* speak words that build up, meet the need of the moment, and give grace to the hearer.

> I love the way the Message renders Ephesians 4:29: 'Say only what helps, each word a gift.' Can you imagine how your husband would feel if each word you spoke to him was a gift? You would certainly be inviting him into emotional intimacy!

Dillow also explores the psychological effects that encouragement has on humans:

> Dr. Henry H. Goddary discovered that encouragement is actually an energy source, which can be measured in the laboratory. He pioneered studies using an instrument devised to measure fatigue. When an assistant would say to the tired child at the laboratory instrument, "You're doing

fine, John," the boy's energy curve would soar. Discouragement and faultfinding were found to have an opposite effect, which could also be measured. So when you encourage your husband, it pours courage and renewed strength in him, and when you criticize and complain, it drains him of courage and energy.[43]

While our words aren't the only indicator of respect, they certainly are a significant one. According to Luke 6:45, "the mouth speaks what the heart is full of." As wives, I think it's important for us to realize the impact of our words. Encouragement communicates respect. On day 1 of this week, we talked about how the godly, safe wife seeks good and not harm toward her husband. This principle can be applied here regarding our words. Ask yourself when you speak, "Are my words bringing good, not harm? Are they a gift or garbage?"

Our husbands need to feel our respect, to know we think they are a "big deal." If a husband senses disrespect or contempt from his wife, his responses may be severe. In his book *Love and Respect*, Emerson Eggerichs sheds light on this through two characters in the Old Testament: King Xerxes and Queen Vashti. In Esther 1, the king calls for the queen to appear before all the people and nobles, so she could display her beauty. For some reason, Vashti refuses, and the king calls for an immediate conference with all of his trusted advisors. They immediately removed her royal title and banished her from the king's presence forever.

> The male fear of contempt is dramatized in the first chapter of Esther. What was the fear? That wives would start to despise their husbands and defy them. The result: there would be no end to the contempt and anger poured out by wives on their husbands throughout the king's realm.

> Many husbands interpret criticism as contempt, and contempt is something men do not handle well. Wives must grasp that their husbands aren't half as big and strong and impervious to being hurt as they might seem. No matter how big they may be physically, emotionally they are vulnerable to what sounds like contempt.[44]

Scripture validates this concept, the male need for respect. In Ephesians 5, Paul gives us instructions for marriage. Men are called to "love their wives, just as Christ loved the church and gave Himself up for her. He who loves his wife loves himself" (verses 25, 28). Women are called to respect their husbands (verse 33).

As women, it's easy for us to recognize that we need love. We all crave it and seek after it. The greeting card industry wouldn't exist without women—we are constantly looking for ways to tangibly express the love we feel. While it's true that our husbands also need love, they thrive on respect.

Notice that Paul doesn't give any conditions that preclude us from respect. It's unconditional respect. We are familiar with the idea of unconditional love, and as women we embrace it. But we have been taught that "respect is earned, not given." Not according to Paul. We are called to respect our husbands, even at that moment it doesn't seem warranted.

As wives, our words to our husbands carry great power. I don't think it's coincidental that the writer of Proverbs 18 flowed from verses about using our tongue wisely into a verse about finding a wife.

Wise words satisfy like a good meal; the right words bring satisfaction. The tongue can bring death or life; those who love to talk will reap the consequences. The man who finds a wife finds a treasure, and he receives favor from the Lord (Proverbs 18:20-22).

HEARTWORK

As we close out our chapter on being a safe wife, I want you to complete what Linda Dillow calls a "respect exercise."[45]

Get out a piece of paper and pen and find a quiet place. Spend ten or fifteen minutes making a list of things you respect about your husband. When he isn't busy or distracted, say, "I was thinking about you today and several things about you that I respect, and I just want you to know I respect you." After saying you respect him, do not wait for any response. Just quietly start to leave the room. Be ready for him to inquire shortly after about what was on the list!

Write this version (Amplified Bible) of Ephesians 5:33 on a note card and place it somewhere you can see it every day.

"Let the wife see that she respects and reverences her husband [that she defers to him, praises him, and loves and admires him exceedingly]."

Pray that God will give you a deep and genuine respect for your husband and that it will be evident through your words and actions.

WEEKEND HOMEWORK

Read Appendix L and make sure to do the heartwork.

CHARGE

What seems impossible is only an opportunity for miracles. I am brave and will act courageously in faith.

PW

WEEK SEVEN

REAL INTIMACY

Genesis 2:25 "Adam and his wife were both naked, and they felt no shame."

WEEK 7 DAY 1

KEY THOUGHT: Real intimacy is characterized by vulnerability and trust.

We've spent six weeks talking about pornography and the painful struggles that result from the sinful patterns it creates. Perhaps one of the most difficult consequences to navigate is the impact it has on a couple's sex life. How do you resume having sex with someone who has misused it so profoundly? In this chapter, we will discuss how to get on a healthy path toward real intimacy within marriage.

Many wives have an extreme response to their husband's sexual addiction. They choose to be completely unavailable sexually, too angry and hurt to even consider being intimate with him again. Or they choose to be overly available, willing to do whatever their husband desires in order to keep the marriage intact. They hope that if they try to meet his every sexual whim, his addiction will end. Which end of the spectrum do you tend to find yourself on? Take a moment to consider how you have responded to your husband sexually since you discovered his addiction. Why do you think you respond that way? Record your thoughts below.

_____

_____

_____

_____

_____

Allow me to make a comparison that has been helpful for me regarding this issue:

Imagine one of your close friends comes to you and confesses that she is bulimic. She's been struggling with her relationship with food and body image for years and is tired of failing after countless attempts to get ahold of it on her own.

Would you tell your friend to stop eating altogether? Of course you wouldn't. Would you tell her that it's a hopeless cause and encourage her to continue to indulge without limits? Definitely not. Just like a person with an eating disorder needs to relearn how to have a healthy relationship with food, so a person with a sexual addiction needs to relearn how to have a healthy relationship with sex. Neither eliminating nor overindulging in sex is the right solution. A person with bulimia needs to have a complete mental overhaul on her approach to eating, and a sex addict needs to totally relearn how to approach sexual intimacy.

As a wife, you have a huge role in your spouse's rehabilitation. **Because God has designed sex to take place exclusively within marriage, you are your husband's greatest ally in the struggle to get back to real intimacy.** It's going to require lots of hard work and patience. It's going to mean that you will have to stand by as he experiences "withdrawals," patiently waiting out fits of anger or sulking. At times, it's going to mean that you will have to clean up the "vomit" that has resulted from his abuse of his drug of choice. But, it also means that you get to have a front-seat view of God's redemptive work in your husband's life.

You will be stretched in your faith as you learn to love selflessly and be the human reflection of God's grace and love toward all of His children. Even though you didn't choose this addiction, you chose to say "I do" for "better or for worse," and now is your chance to live it out. That includes resuming a sexual relationship even though it may be the very last thing you want to do. A skewed perception of food doesn't mean that a person should never eat again; a distorted view of intimacy doesn't mean that a person should never have sex again. There's a healthy balance that needs to be found, and it's called real intimacy.

Early on in our study, we identified three levels of intimacy: perfect, real and false. Perfect intimacy (Adam and Eve, naked and unashamed in the Garden of Eden) is unattainable in this life because it has been marred by sin. We are now left to pursue one of the other two options in our marriage: real or false intimacy. Let's review:

Real intimacy—the sexual and relational intimacy two spouses share within their committed, loving marriage. Self-doubts exist, but the couple communicates together and enjoys each other relationally and sexually. Given the reality of a world of imperfect relationships, both partners face disappointments. Within the enjoyment of real intimacy, both partners experience fear of being exposed, fear of abandonment, fear of loss of control, and fear of their respective sexual desires. In their sexual expression, both are dependent on and open to what the other spouse will do.

False intimacy—a self-created illusion to help a person avoid the pain inherent in real intimacy. This pursuit of happiness can lead to extreme behavior, many risks, and destructive consequences. The goal is essentially to control life by avoiding relational pain. A commitment to avoid being hurt or disappointed leads to destructive, out-of-control behaviors. As the sexual addict embraces what is false, the less he/she cares about what is good and loving—and the more he/she is captive to the desire to create a sense of control over life's circumstances. The addict is preoccupied with mood-altering sexual experiences and pursues them without regard for the consequences to health, family, and/or career.[46]

WEEK 1 .... WEEK 2 .... WEEK 3 .... WEEK 4 .... WEEK 5 .... WEEK 6 .... WEEK 7 .... WEEK 8

DAY 1

Notice the stark differences between real and false intimacy. Using the definitions above, answer the following questions that point out the disparities:

Real intimacy is a commitment to your spouse. What does a person walking in false intimacy pursue?

_____

_____

Real intimacy brings an understanding that disappointment and pain are unavoidable and must be faced. How does a person living in a world of false intimacy treat disappointment and pain?

_____

_____

What is the end result of real intimacy? What is the end result of false intimacy?

_____

_____

_____

Before you rush to judgment and self-righteousness of your husband and his desperate attempts to create a pain-free reality, take a few moments to examine your own heart. Your spouse may be pursuing false intimacy through sexual addiction, but is it possible that you are also pursuing a fake version of intimacy as well? Think about some of the things you turn to when you are feeling disappointed or want to escape. Food, romantic movies or books, a casual flirty relationship with someone at the office... all of these can be used as escape from reality into a fake world where you are in control and protected from the pain of true intimacy.

I found myself emotionally vulnerable after years of dealing with my husband's sexual addiction. I tried a few different methods of escape to avoid the pain. One of those was turning to other men for attention. I would try to make myself look pretty when I went out to get noticed. I longed to spend time with and talk to other men that made me feel valuable, and I began to give my heart away over time. Just like the woman at the well in John 4:1-26, I had been looking to other men in my life to quench my desire to be truly known and loved. My quest was false and selfish, and it never fulfilled my deepest longings. Thankfully, my pursuit of admiration and affection never resulted in an affair, but I knew in my heart that I was being emotionally unfaithful and walking in sin. My emotional infidelity had long-term consequences in our marriage, and it took years to heal the pain that my false intimacy had caused.

WEEK 1 .... WEEK 2 .... WEEK 3 .... WEEK 4 .... WEEK 5 .... WEEK 6 .... WEEK 7 .... WEEK 8

DAY 1

In her book *Hope After Betrayal*, Meg Wilson warns her readers about this vulnerability:

> Wounded women are vulnerable to an affair. One bit of attention from the wrong man can be like water to a dry sponge. Our need for assurance is at an all-time high: 'If another man is attracted to me, I must be okay.' It doesn't take much effort to put a tattered self-esteem that was naively placed in a husband's hand and place it in the hands of another man. It needs rather to be placed in the hands of God—the only place we'll find our true worth. Add to the vulnerability the false justification—'I'm only doing what my husband did'—and suddenly we're detoured down another wrong road. Be careful not to trade in one wound for a whole bundle of them.[47]

How I wish I had read these words years ago! Like my husband, I was pursuing false intimacy and justifying it! It's so easy to stand in judgment of our husbands, but we are also guilty of trying to avoid or numb pain through a false reality.

How about you? Take some time to journal your thoughts below about how you may be pursuing false intimacy.

_____

_____

_____

_____

_____

Deep wounds and genuine fear lie at the roots of our selfish attempts to avoid pain. We protect ourselves because we have been hurt in the past, or we don't want to be hurt in the future. Were you a victim of sexual abuse as a child? Or perhaps someone was sexually aggressive with you and disrespected your boundaries? Were you cheated on? Did you have a physically abusive mother or an absentee father? Or maybe you have been laughed at or ignored whenever you shared your own inadequacies or mistakes. All of these life circumstances create an environment of fear and apprehension regarding true intimacy.

What are some of your fears regarding real intimacy with your husband? Is it fear that he will take advantage of you, leave you, neglect your heart, not listen to your expressed wants and needs? Take some time and write them down, both your emotional fears and your sexual fears. Where do those fears come from?

_____

_____

WEEK 1 .... WEEK 2 .... WEEK 3 .... WEEK 4 .... WEEK 5 .... WEEK 6 .... WEEK 7 .... WEEK 8

DAY 1

_____

_____

_____

_____

_____

_____

_____

_____

_____

What do you think some of your husband's fears are regarding real intimacy? Think about some of the messages that he may have received throughout his life (you're not good enough, you will never succeed, you're stupid, ugly, fat, awkward, etc.). How have the lies that he has believed impacted him and caused him to live in fear of real intimacy?

_____

_____

_____

_____

SPECIAL NOTE: Let me pause here for a moment and address something that is significant to many women reading this study. If either you or your spouse have been sexually abused, you need to seek out godly counseling. This resource is meant to be a guide to help restore your relationship, but the wounds that result from sexual abuse need special care and attention. Navigating the waters of resuming sexual intimacy with your sexually addicted spouse may be especially difficult and painful, and counseling will help you work through your old wounds and triggers while addressing the new ones caused by your spouse.

WEEK 1 .... WEEK 2 .... WEEK 3 .... WEEK 4 .... WEEK 5 .... WEEK 6 .... WEEK 7 .... WEEK 8

DAY 1

If you are currently being sexually abused by your spouse (which includes exposure to pornography or forced sexual acts), that behavior is not honoring to you as a daughter of the King. Please know that you are not meant to live in a situation that brings you pain and shame. You need to reach out for help right away. Contact your local church or ask a friend if they know of any good Christian counselors. If the abuse is physical and has put you and/or your children in harm's way, seek out help from a Domestic Abuse hotline, Crisis Intervention center, or social services. **There is no shame in asking for help.**

If you are unsure of what sexual abuse entails, turn to Appendix F and read through the definition of sexual abuse taken from expert Dan Allender. Dan is a well-known and respected Christian therapist who has devoted his life to ministering to victims of sexual abuse and trauma. He has also written multiple books that deal with sexual abuse, and I highly recommend reading his work, *The Wounded Heart*. I read it with my counselor and gained so much wisdom and healing after reading his book. I realized that I had experienced some level of sexual abuse in both my childhood and my adult life, and I was finally able to understand why I responded to life in certain ways. Truly, it is a wonderful resource and I can't recommend it enough. If you feel like you don't have time to read the entire book, the link for Allender's booklet on sexual abuse, "When Trust is Lost: Healing for Victims of Sexual Abuse," is included in Appendix F.

Also included in this study is a friend's story of childhood sexual abuse and the hope she found in Christ after years of fear and shame. Her story is included in Appendix K.

———————————————

Although your heart may be wounded, you must be willing to pursue your husband intimately—both relationally and sexually. It requires real sacrifice, selflessness, humility, respect, and a heart of forgiveness. It's not easy, but it's what we are called to live out.

I love how Meg Wilson writes about the impact of real intimacy in marriage. As wives, we have a God-given calling to love our husbands in a special and exclusive way. Here's another snippet from her book *Hope After Betrayal*:

> Your husband's false sexual reality could never compare to the soul-satisfying blanket connection of real love, any more than a photo of a blanket can provide the same warmth as the real thing. As a wife, you can offer the lasting beauty of love and commitment that goes far deeper than anything that is solely physical. Companionship and support are the real cords that tie two people for life. Intimacy comes from this heart connection, and married sex is the physical expression of this emotional and spiritual closeness. Focusing on the external alone is incomplete; we can't use sex to work backwards toward real intimacy. This lack of intimacy is what the world offers, and is hollow and distorted compared to the real love God intended for husbands and wives.[48]

I love the word picture she gives with the blanket. Just like a photograph of a blanket can't provide warmth, a picture of a naked woman can't provide real intimacy. It's a false imitation, two dimensional and lacking any substance. Your calling as a wife is to embrace your spouse with the comforting blanket of sexual and relational intimacy. Your warmth and willingness to love your husband is true and lasting. And likewise, he is called to offer you the same warmth and comfort.

Consider the biblical story of Isaac and Rebekah. Open your Bible and read Genesis 24.

On the lines below, write down a few of the qualities that we discover about Rebekah (see verses 15-25, 57-58, and 64-65).

_____

_____

_____

_____

In Genesis 24:67, we read that Isaac brought Rebekah into the tent of his mother Sarah, and he married her. So Rebekah "became his wife, and he loved her; and Isaac was comforted after his mother's death."

The fact that Rebekah brought comfort to her husband's grieving soul shows the warmth that she brought to their relationship. I imagine that she was tired after her seventeen-day journey back to meet Isaac. I also imagine she was nervous and homesick after leaving her family to marry a complete stranger.

In spite of all the strange circumstances surrounding her betrothal, Rebekah looks beyond her own needs. She makes the choice to love her husband with vulnerability and trust. Her openness and servant's heart set the tone for their relationship. Isaac welcomes her into his mother's tent, a place that must have been filled with memories and strong emotions after her passing. Her kind-heartedness and openness become a soothing balm for his aching heart.

The story of Isaac and Rebekah provides a great example of real intimacy. Isaac came into the marriage sad and lonely, Rebekah entered it a stranger and a virgin. Both of them had insecurities and fears but chose to leave them outside the tent when they consummated their marriage. Their vulnerability from the very beginning set the tone for the relationship.

Reread verse 67 above. What did Isaac offer to Rebekah?

_____

What did Rebekah offer to Isaac?

_____

WEEK 1 · · · · · · · · WEEK 2 · · · · · · · · WEEK 3 · · · · · · · · WEEK 4 · · · · · · · · WEEK 5 · · · · · · · · WEEK 6 · · · · · · · · WEEK 7 · · · · · · · · WEEK 8

DAY 1

HEARTWORK

What about you? Do you set aside your insecurities and fears in order to have an open and real sexual relationship with your husband? What hinders you? As we continue on in the study, we will address the legitimate concerns you may have about being taken advantage of or enabling his addiction. But for now, think through what it would take for you to come to the marriage bed the same as Rebekah: respectful, selfless, and willing to give up comfort in order to be a source of comfort for your husband. Take some time to journal your thoughts below, then ask God to give you the desire and strength to love your husband in this way.

_____

_____

_____

_____

_____

_____

_____

_____

_____

_____

CHARGE

Real intimacy is critical for success. I will value my marriage enough to be vulnerable.

HEALTHY SEX

1 Corinthians 7:3 "The husband should fulfill his marital duty
to his wife, and likewise the wife to her husband."

WEEK 7 DAY 2

KEY THOUGHT: Within a healthy sexual relationship, both husband and
wife must be able to freely express their needs without fear or shame.

How are we as believers supposed to know what healthy sex looks like? When a sexual addiction is present in
a marriage, real intimacy may seem hard to find amidst all of the lies and shame. Fortunately, God gives us
guidelines throughout Scripture to show us the way.

It might be best to start with what real intimacy DOESN'T look like. God provides clear guidelines about sinful
sexual behavior: bestiality, homosexuality, adultery, prostitution, lustful thinking, and premarital sex are all
condemned by Him (Leviticus 20:9-21, 1 Corinthians 6:9, Hebrews 13:4). While God offers forgiveness for these
sins, He does not want "even a hint of sexual immorality, or of any kind of impurity, or of greed, because these
are improper for God's holy people" (Ephesians 5:3). If your husband is asking you to participate in or allow
any kind of this sexual behavior, then your answer can be a clear "no."

But what about the gray areas in between God's specific commands? What if both of you are longing for real
intimacy, but you aren't sure how to find it? When you are married to a sex addict, it can be very difficult to open
yourself up and be sexually vulnerable after you have been wounded so deeply. You may feel hopeless, angry
or confused when you think about having sex with your husband. It's OK to have mixed emotions about it. But
our emotions must not dictate our actions. God has called you, through His strength, to forgive your husband
and learn to love him wholly, even when he has wounded your heart. God calls us to love like He does. "But God
demonstrates his own love for us in this: While we were still sinners, Christ died for us" (Romans 5:8).

While God has called us to love greatly, He has not called us to be abused or ashamed in our marriages. 1
Corinthians 7:1-6 sheds some light on what healthy married sex should look like. Take a few moments and read
it for yourself.

In verses 3-5, Paul states that the husband and wife each have a duty to fulfill one another's sexual needs. We
are called to yield our bodies to each other sexually. When you are married, your body belongs to your spouse.

WEEK 1 .... WEEK 2 .... WEEK 3 .... WEEK 4 .... WEEK 5 .... WEEK 6 .... WEEK 7 .... WEEK 8

DAY 2

Likewise, your husband's body belongs to you. Sex is only God-honoring when it takes place between a husband and wife who are both submitting their own wants and desires in order to please their partner.

While God calls both the husband and wife to mutually yield to one another's needs, He doesn't call us to submit to every sexual request your spouse makes without concern for your own physical, emotional and spiritual well-being.

Genesis 2:24-25 gives us the appropriate filter for the kind of intimacy and sexual relationship that is both healthy and holy. It helps complete the picture of beautiful married sex, the kind of sex that God intended before sin entered into the world. Fill in the blanks below after reading those verses:

> That is why a man leaves his father and mother and is _____ to his wife, and they
> become _____. Adam and his wife were both _____, and they felt
> no _____.

There's a balance we find when we read Genesis 2 and 1 Corinthians 7 together. Here are some keywords that stick out to me when reading these passages:

UNITED, ONE FLESH, NAKED, NO SHAME (Genesis 2)

FULFILL, YIELD, DO NOT DEPRIVE, MUTUAL CONSENT (1 Corinthians 7)

I believe these verses hold the key to what real intimacy DOES look like: a unifying experience in which both partners experience freedom to express their needs without fear or shame. They willingly submit their own desires and bodies to one another. They don't deprive their partner sexually, unless it's for an agreed upon amount of time to grow deeper spiritually and individually through prayer.

At first glance when you read these verses, it might sound like God is calling you to be compliant to your husband's every sexual desire. But if you look closer, you'll actually see how God provides guidelines that promote a loving and gentle care of the wife sexually.

1 Corinthians 7:3 in the NKJV reads this way: "Let the husband render to his wife the affection due her, and likewise also the wife to her husband." David Guzik expounds on the importance of the word **affection** found in this verse:

> The affection due her is an important phrase; since Paul meant this to apply to every Christian marriage, it shows that *every* wife has affection due her. Paul doesn't think only the young or pretty or submissive wives are due affection; every wife is due affection! It is wrong for him to withhold affection from his wife.

> Paul also emphasizes what the woman needs: not merely sexual relations, but the affection due her. If a husband is having sexual relations with his wife, but without true affection, he is not giving his wife what she is due.

Affection also reminds us that when a couple is unable—for physical or other reasons—to have a complete sexual relationship, they can still have an *affectionate* relationship, and thus fulfill God's purpose for these commands.[49]

"The affection due her" means that he must learn to pursue you, which includes more than just the sex act. In order for a woman to feel sexually free, she must feel emotionally safe. Kind words, genuine compliments, non-sexual touch, time spent together in non-distracted conversation, and acts of service all communicate love and affection.

What does affection look like for you? Have you ever communicated that to your husband? Why or why not? Journal your thoughts below.

_____

_____

_____

_____

_____

_____

Not only does God provide for an affectionate relationship in marriage, He also makes provision for a safe and respectful relationship. Think back to Genesis 2 where the Bible says that Adam and Eve became "one flesh," "naked and unashamed." Healthy and real intimacy results in a unity that can't be achieved in any other human relationship. It is characterized by openness, security, and freedom. It does NOT bring fear, shame, or division.

If what your husband is asking you to do makes you feel ashamed, then his request is not God-honoring and you should NOT say yes. The shame that results from a sexual addiction causes us to want to hide behind lies and guilt. Like Adam and Eve in the Garden of Eden, we all have the propensity to shift blame to someone else (Adam) or pull them into our sinful behavior (Eve) so that we don't have to stand alone in the shame. But it doesn't have to be that way. Your husband's sin and shame do not need to become yours, and you have the right to guard your own heart by saying "no" to his sinful requests. Proverbs 4:23 says, "Above all else, guard your heart, for everything you do flows from it." Rather than join your husband in his sin and shame, God can use you to help pull him out of it.

So how do you recognize shame? Simply put, shame focuses on self and my sin instead of the Savior and His sacrifice.

WEEK 1 . . . . WEEK 2 . . . . WEEK 3 . . . . WEEK 4 . . . . WEEK 5 . . . . WEEK 6 . . . . WEEK 7 . . . . WEEK 8

DAY 2

College professor and self-proclaimed "researcher-storyteller" Brené Brown has an amazing TED talk called "Listening to Shame" that is definitely worth viewing! I've quoted her multiple times already in the past few chapters. In her talk she reveals the voice of shame, the words it whispers into our ears:

"You're not good enough."

"I am bad."

"I am a mistake."

"Who do you think you are?"[50]

She explains that we all feel shame, but we experience it differently based upon gender.

> Women feel shame when they can't measure up to all the competing, conflicting expectations of who we are supposed to be. For men, shame is one thing: do not be perceived as weak. You show me a woman who can sit with a man in real vulnerability and fear, I'll show you a woman who has done incredible work. Show me a man who can sit with a woman who has just had it, she can't do it all anymore... he really listens, I'll show you a guy who has done a lot of work. Shame is an epidemic in our culture. To get out from underneath it, to find our way back to each other, we have to understand how it affects us and how it affects the way we are looking at each other.

What kind of shameful thoughts have you had as a result of your failure to meet perceived expectations? What kind of shameful thoughts do you think your husband carries? Journal your responses below.

_____

_____

_____

_____

_____

_____

While shame may be experienced differently, it has the same results for both men and women. Shame keeps us in the dark. Shame paralyzes us with fear. Shame holds us back from real hope and healing. Shame is the enemy of real intimacy. God does not want us to walk in shame! He bore the weight of shame for us on the cross so that we wouldn't have to carry it.

WEEK 1 .... WEEK 2 .... WEEK 3 .... WEEK 4 .... WEEK 5 .... WEEK 6 .... WEEK 7 .... WEEK 8

DAY 2

I love these verses that talk about the freedom we have from the bondage of sin and shame through Christ's sacrifice on the cross:

Hebrews 12:1-3, NLT

Therefore, since we are surrounded by such a huge crowd of witnesses to the life of faith, let us strip off every weight that slows us down, especially the sin that so easily trips us up. And let us run with endurance the race God has set before us. We do this by keeping our eyes on Jesus, the champion who initiates and perfects our faith. Because of the joy awaiting him, he endured the cross, disregarding its shame. Now he is seated in the place of honor beside God's throne. Think of all the hostility he endured from sinful people; then you won't become weary and give up.

1 Peter 2:24-25

He personally carried our sins in His body on the cross so that we can be dead to sin and live for what is right. By His wounds, you are healed. Once you were like sheep who wandered away. But now you have turned to your Shepherd, the Guardian of your souls.

Jesus absorbed the pain and the price of sin on the cross. As His sheep, we must not carry it anymore! He is the Guardian of our souls, and He wants us to experience wholeness and healing.

Now take a few moments and write out each one of these verses:

Psalm 3:3

_____

_____

Romans 8:1

_____

_____

2 Timothy 1:7

_____

_____

After reading all five of these passages, what is God's perspective on shame?

WEEK 1 .... WEEK 2 .... WEEK 3 .... WEEK 4 .... WEEK 5 .... WEEK 6 .... WEEK 7 .... WEEK 8

DAY 2

God wants to deliver both you and your husband from the bondage of shame. And ironically, one of the greatest ways He can bring that deliverance is through a healthy sexual relationship that is characterized by real intimacy. And what is real sexual intimacy? Based on our study today, here is how God defines it:

NO SHAME	ONE FLESH	FULFILLING
AFFECTIONATE	YIELDING	VULNERABLE
CONSENSUAL		

If your sex life isn't characterized by affectionate, selfless, shameless vulnerability, then it's time for a hard reset. Simply put, here are two questions you can ask about your sexual activity to help discern if it's healthy and holy:

Does this behavior bring us together?

Does this bring either of us shame?

The answer should be YES to question one and NO to question two. These two questions should serve as guideposts as you navigate how to have both healthy and fulfilling sexual encounters.

HEARTWORK

As we end today, spend some time in prayer and deep reflection. Do you believe that God desires for you to experience healthy and real intimacy? What is God speaking to your heart about things that need to stop in your marriage in order to experience true intimacy? What do you and your husband need to start doing instead? Write out your reflective responses below. Ask God to give you wisdom on how to communicate both your concerns and needs to your husband.

_____

_____

_____

_____

CHARGE

Real intimacy is critical for success. I will value my marriage enough to be vulnerable.

REAL BOUNDARIES

Ephesians 4:15 "Instead, speaking the truth in love, we will grow to become in every respect the mature body of Him who is the head, that is, Christ."

WEEK 7 DAY 3

KEY THOUGHT: Real intimacy brings wholeness, not harm. Boundaries create a safe framework that guides us to this kind of intimacy.

Yesterday, we outlined what real intimacy looks like. On the lines below, write out the seven words (found in all caps on the last day of yesterday's lesson) that God gives us to define a healthy sexual relationship.

_____

_____

_____

It may have been difficult as you took inventory of your sexual relationship at the end of yesterday's lesson. Perhaps you realized that your sexual experiences were far from God's plan. If your reflective prayer time revealed that your sex life is characterized by both fear and shame instead of vulnerability and affection, it's not a lost cause. God can redeem and heal what is broken, but it will require you to set some firm boundaries.

What thoughts come to mind when you hear the word "boundaries"?

_____

_____

_____

For me, the idea of setting boundaries is quite intimidating. In fact, I shy away from creating boundaries. As a people pleaser, the idea of creating a hard guideline for someone else to follow brings me a sense of fear. What if I set a boundary and they reject it and threaten to end the relationship? What if I set a boundary and don't have enough courage to enforce consequences? People without boundaries set themselves up for **manipulation**.

Or perhaps you have the opposite feeling about boundaries. You may love the idea of hard and fast guidelines because it gives you the opportunity to blame someone else or walk away if the boundary is crossed. Perhaps you prefer everything to be black and white because it shields you from the awkwardness of stumbling through life's "gray areas." People with too harsh or too many boundaries set themselves up for **isolation**.

So, where do we find the balance? Does God even talk about boundaries in the Bible? For a long time, I wondered if boundaries were actually biblical. Didn't Jesus serve people until He fell into an exhausted heap? For example, Matthew 4:23 says, "Jesus went throughout Galilee, teaching in their synagogues, proclaiming the good news of the kingdom, and healing **every** disease and sickness among the people." Matthew 9:35 reads very similarly: "Jesus went through **all** the towns and villages, teaching in their synagogues, proclaiming the good news of the kingdom and healing **every** disease and sickness."

At first glance, it may seem that Jesus had no boundaries when it came to His personal life, but the Gospels give us great examples of how He set clear guidelines for His ministry and His relationships. **Mark 1:35-39** is one illustration. Open your Bible and answer the questions below.

What kind of boundaries did Jesus establish in this passage? With both His personal time and His public ministry?

_____

_____

One of the most important things to be noted in this passage is how Jesus allowed His boundaries to be shaped. He knew His divine mission and purpose and created healthy boundaries accordingly. He came into this world to "seek and save the lost" (Luke 19:10). Because He knew His calling, He knew what things He could say "yes" and "no" to with the limited amount of time and energy He was given by His Father. When the disciples placed expectations on Him, Jesus did not allow their demands to dictate His decisions.

This passage shows us that it's OK to create firm boundaries with others. Just because someone has an expectation of us doesn't mean we have to meet it. Ephesians 2:10 says that you are "God's handiwork, created in Christ Jesus to do good works, which God prepared in advance" for you. God didn't create you to be a sexual doormat or an accomplice to sinful behavior. Your purpose and calling as His child, holy and loved, gives you the authority and permission to say "no" to anything that stands in opposition to your position in Christ (Colossians 3:12). It's OK to say "that's not OK with me."

Jesus also wasn't afraid to share His disappointment when the disciples failed to meet His needs. In Matthew 26:36-46, we read about Jesus' final hours before His gruesome death on the cross. He was overwhelmed with sorrow and grief at the thought of what He was about to face. He turned to His three closest companions with a clear and compelling request: "Keep watch with me."

WEEK 1 .... WEEK 2 .... WEEK 3 .... WEEK 4 .... WEEK 5 .... WEEK 6 ....  WEEK 7 .... WEEK 8

DAY 3

Jesus wanted to have His dearest friends' support during the most difficult hours of His life. They failed miserably. Read Matthew 26:36-46. What does it say the disciples did after Jesus left to pray? How many times did this happen?

_____

_____

_____

What was Jesus response to their actions?

_____

_____

_____

It's obvious from this passage that Jesus was upset. He was "overwhelmed with sorrow to the point of death," and His dearest friends failed Him at His moment of greatest need. Jesus expressed His deep frustration with them, stating, "Couldn't you men keep watch with me for one hour?"

Perhaps you have felt that same way. Your husband, the closest companion you have in this life, has betrayed you and neglected you at your hour of deepest need. He has left you alone to deal with deep emotional pain while tending to his own physical needs. This passage in Matthew 26 is a wonderful revelation that it's OK to express our hurt when we are disappointed by those we love! Again, Jesus shows us that it's OK to say, "that's not OK with me."

Boundaries are essential in a marriage that has been ravaged by lust. Without them, you essentially enable the unhealthy behavior by allowing it to continue. If you want to experience real and lasting intimacy with your husband, you must communicate clearly and specifically about your sexual noes and yeses. As financial guru Dave Ramsey says, "To be unclear is to be unkind."[51] You must create clear boundaries about what your husband must do or stop doing in order for you to resume a sexual relationship with him. Sexual addiction must be questioned and confronted. If your husband refuses to change, the painful consequences of continuing in the addiction must be allowed to run their course in his life (being discovered at work, potential loss of job, marital separation, etc.).

If you are still confused or unconvinced about boundaries, listen to these words from author Meg Wilson. She paints a beautiful word picture that was so helpful to me as I studied this idea:

WEEK 1 .... WEEK 2 .... WEEK 3 .... WEEK 4 .... WEEK 5 .... WEEK 6 .... WEEK 7 .... WEEK 8

DAY 3

Boundaries are limits or borders that outline a person's ownership and responsibility. Imagine a garden full of vegetables and flowers. The gardener works on her flower and vegetable beds—planting, weeding, watering, and harvesting. As she labors, visitors stop by. Some are welcome, some are unwelcome. The welcome visitors respect the garden bed—they're careful not to tread on plants, they ask relevant questions about the flowers and vegetables, they may even identify and pull out a weed or two while they chat. The unwelcome visitors are careless about where they step; they pluck flowers without asking; they point out that the tomatoes look small.

To keep unwelcome visitors outside the garden, the gardener needs to have a fence, a boundary. The fence needs a gate to let in the welcome visitors, and the gate needs to have a lock on the inside to keep out those who do not respect the garden and the crops. Notice that the gardener doesn't build a wall. Unwelcome visitors may stop by and look at the flowers and vegetables, but the boundary keeps the beds from being trampled and the flowers from being taken. The gardener decides who can join her in her garden, who must stay outside, and whom to share her flowers and vegetables with. With the boundary, her space is protected and she's in control of it. As she shares and chats with her welcome visitors, they both benefit.

A betrayal can be a wake-up call that we need to set up boundaries. By the time of our discovery, our gardens have already been trampled.[52]

Write down some of your initial thoughts after reading this excerpt. How does her illustration apply to boundaries within a marriage struggling under the weight of sexual addiction?

_____

_____

_____

_____

Has your garden been trampled? It's time to go to work and set up some fences and gates. So where and how do you even start? Our verse for today, Ephesians 4:15, reveals a very concise formula on how to set healthy boundaries: SPEAK THE TRUTH IN LOVE!

Boundaries are based on both truth and love. It's a combination of consequences and compassion. This very idea is at the very core of the gospel! We deserve death (the TRUTH) but God sent His Son to redeem our souls (His LOVE). Romans 6:23 states it beautifully: "For the wages of sin is death, but the gift of God is eternal life in Christ Jesus our Lord."

WEEK 1 . . . . WEEK 2 . . . . WEEK 3 . . . . WEEK 4 . . . . WEEK 5 . . . . WEEK 6 . . . . WEEK 7 . . . . WEEK 8

DAY 3

Read and write out these additional passages that talk about truth and love:

1 John 1:6

_____

_____

1 John 3:18

_____

_____

If your husband says he loves you but continues to pursue his addiction, he is living a lie. It's your responsibility and calling as his wife to speak the truth out of a heart of love. Avoiding conflict isn't extending grace, it's actually enabling him to avoid the truth.[53]

Which part of communication is harder for you, speaking the truth, or speaking in love? Why? Take a few moments to journal your thoughts.

_____

_____

_____

Boundaries aren't a form of punishment, they are a wake-up call. Your husband must feel the weight of his own sinful behavior instead of you carrying it for him. You must clearly define what is acceptable and unacceptable going forward, as well as the consequences that will be implemented if boundary lines are crossed. If he is allowed to continue on with his sexual addiction without taking responsibility for his actions (you are always available for him sexually, you let him guilt or blame you for his problem), then nothing will ever change. He has to experience "rock bottom."

In our marriage, we knew that home access to the internet was an issue. For a long time, we canceled our internet service, and I moved my home office to another location so the temptation was removed. We stopped watching certain movies and even changed some of our sexual behaviors that were fueled by pornography.

For Joel, the author of *Proven Men,* both he and his wife decided to get rid of the TV for a year. His wife also checked the mail daily to make sure there wasn't any inappropriate material coming into the house.

WEEK 1 .... WEEK 2 .... WEEK 3 .... WEEK 4 .... WEEK 5 .... WEEK 6 .... WEEK 7 .... WEEK 8

DAY 3

Those boundaries may seem simple and easy, but they still require direct and clear communication. They were established with love, coming from a heart that was willing to sacrifice comfort in order to create safe space at home free of lingering temptations. Other clear boundaries may include:

- Creating joint accounts for social media and email, or deleting social media all together

- Downloading software to block out inappropriate websites

- Finding a new place of employment if your spouse has developed an emotional or sexual attachment to a coworker

- Random phone and computer checks

- An accountability partner (not you) that checks in to ask the tough questions

WORST CASE SCENARIO

Perhaps your husband's addiction has progressed so far that it calls for extreme boundaries to be put into place. Is your husband continuing to pursue a sexual relationship with someone else? Has he solicited prostitutes, putting you in danger of a getting a sexually transmitted disease? Or maybe his addiction has drained all your savings because he spends it on his mistress. Is he physically aggressive, threatening to hurt you or your children if you don't meet his sexual demands?

These situations are dangerous and require very firm boundaries as well as outside intervention. A man who has no regard for his wife's safety needs intensive help to walk away from his addiction. In these kinds of cases, where the spouse is unrepentant and unwilling to change his sexual immoral behavior, God makes provision for a permanent boundary to be implemented—divorce.

In the Gospels, Jesus gives a clear boundary regarding divorce: The only valid reason that a marriage should end is sexual immorality (Matthew 5:31-32, Matthew 19:9, Mark 10:1-12, Luke 16:18). Making a decision like this is not one that should be taken lightly. You should seek wise, godly counsel and be in prayer daily. Sexual infidelity is not a marriage death sentence, and God can bring "beauty from ashes" (Isaiah 61:3) as "He makes all things new" (Isaiah 43:18-19). If your situation is one where you've pursued wholeness and healing with your husband and he refuses to change, I pray that God will give you wisdom on the right course of action to take. Marriage was designed to be for a lifetime, and divorce has long-reaching and devastating repercussions. Nothing is beyond hope with Christ, and He will guide you into His truth regarding your situation (John 16:13).

Remember the parable of the prodigal son that we looked at in week four? Reread Luke 15:11-24 to refresh your memory. That story of a father's love is a powerful example of boundaries at work.

Are you willing to let your husband go, just like the father did in the parable, even if it means he might never come back? Are you willing to stop carrying the weight of his sin and allow him to hit rock bottom?

WEEK 1 .... WEEK 2 .... WEEK 3 .... WEEK 4 .... WEEK 5 .... WEEK 6 .... WEEK 7 .... WEEK 8

DAY 3

If your husband comes running back with a heart of repentance, are you willing to embrace him with a heart of compassion?

HEARTWORK

Write out your reflective responses below. Include a prayer asking for God to give you wisdom on how to speak the truth in love to your husband. Ask Him to show you how to establish clear and healthy boundaries so that your marriage can be restored and whole.

_____

_____

_____

_____

_____

_____

_____

CHARGE

Real intimacy is critical for success. I will value my marriage enough to be vulnerable.

TRULY GENEROUS

Song of Solomon 7:10 "I belong to my beloved, and his desire is for me."

WEEK 7 DAY 4

KEY THOUGHT: As wives we are called to be both verbally and visually generous.

Hopefully at this point in the study, you are making some progress. You should have a better understanding of your husband's addiction and an appreciation for the unique calling God has placed on your life to help him find true healing. My prayer is that your heart has been both softened and guarded by the life-changing power of Christ's love and the truth of the gospel. I pray that you have been able to "speak the truth in love" so you can create healthy boundaries that will be beneficial for both you and your husband.

So, now what? There's still that tough area of resuming sexual activity. Some of the struggles I had about having sex with my husband again may be some of yours as well. What if he is thinking about pornography or another woman while we are having sex? What if he doesn't find me attractive enough to have sex with me after seeing all of those other images? Are his motivations pure when he is pursuing me sexually? If I agree to have sex with him again, isn't that just fueling the fire for his unhealthy sex drive?

It's important to understand what's going on inside your man's brain in order to appreciate why sex is so important to him. We've touched on it before in this study, but I want to boil it down to two very basic concepts that I hope will stay with you. Every man is wired to respond to two things: **how he is seen** and **what he sees**. In other words, your husband feels confident and validated in his "man-ness" when a beautiful woman **respects him** and **responds to him**. If you can learn to be verbally generous with your words to communicate respect and visually generous with your body to indicate your interest in him, you will truly be loving your husband well.

VERBAL GENEROSITY

Right now, we are going to take a deep dive into the Song of Solomon. It's a poetic song that shows the beauty and fulfillment that results from real intimacy in a marriage. Open up your Bible and take a few moments to read **Song of Solomon 5:10-16.**

When the wife describes her husband in chapter 5, what parts of his body does she focus on? Write down a few of the comparisons below that stand out to you most.

_____

_____

_____

_____

Notice that she starts at his head and moves down his body, then finishes by complimenting his mouth again. She also calls him both her love and her friend. She has a deep physical and emotional connection with this man. She uses her words to praise him and calls him "absolutely desirable."

The bride teaches us an important lesson here. She initiates and pursues her husband with her words and her actions. If you rewind to the beginning of the book of Song of Solomon, you will find that the first words are hers as well!

> Let him kiss me with the kisses of his mouth—for your love is more delightful than wine. Pleasing is the fragrance of your perfumes; your name is like perfume poured out. No wonder the young women love you!

She honors and compliments him. She talks about how just the mention of his name is pleasing. His reputation is sweet and has spread throughout their entire community to make him one of the most desirable men around! She's not afraid to tell him how she truly feels, and her words only encourage and build him up.

Do you take the time to encourage and build up your husband with your words? It may seem like there's nothing to compliment him for at this point in your marriage because you are so wounded, but that's not true. God has made your husband in His image and has given him special qualities that are a reflection of God's nature. Take some time to think about the things (physical, emotional, mental) that initially drew you to your husband. Were you captivated by his eyes? Were you drawn to his confidence? Is he a hard worker? Does he have a gentle spirit? Did you fall in love with the way he treated children? Take some time to write down the things that you appreciate about your husband.

_____

_____

_____

WEEK 1 .... WEEK 2 .... WEEK 3 .... WEEK 4 .... WEEK 5 .... WEEK 6 .... WEEK 7 .... WEEK 8

DAY 4

_____
_____
_____

Every man has a deep desire to be respected. Your words have so much power. Exercise VERBAL GENEROSITY toward your man. If you make a continued practice of lifting him up rather than tearing him down, he will take notice and respond! I have seen such a drastic change in the temperature of our home when I made a conscious effort to encourage and be thankful for my husband.

The same guy who wrote Song of Solomon also wrote most of the book of Proverbs, and he gives us some practical do's and don'ts on how to be a good wife:

Don't be like the wife in Proverbs 21:

Better to live on a corner of the roof than share a house with a quarrelsome wife (verse 9).

Better to live in a desert than with a quarrelsome and nagging wife (verse 19).

Instead, choose to be like the wife in Proverbs 31:

She brings him good, not harm, all the days of her life.

How do you think your husband would respond if you made a conscious effort to be verbally generous with him? Stop and write out a prayer to God asking Him to give you the words and the heart to lift your husband up.

_____
_____
_____
_____
_____

VISUAL GENEROSITY

Not only are we called to be verbally generous with our husband, we are also called to be visually generous. One of the obvious reasons that men look at pornography is the simple fact that they are visual creatures. In Matthew 5:28, we are warned that sexual temptation begins with a longing glance: "But I tell you that anyone

who looks at a woman lustfully has already committed adultery with her in his heart." Proverbs 6:25 also shows that women are well aware of the power of a longing glance: "Do not lust in your heart after her beauty or let her captivate you with her eyes."

The idea that your husband can be easily aroused by what he sees may be disheartening for you as a wife; but, in fact, it can be an advantage in your sexual relationship with your husband. Just like Eve was to Adam, you are God's gift to your husband, designed to bring him companionship as well as physical pleasure. It is your exclusive responsibility to meet his sexual desires. Rather than bemoan his inclination towards visual stimulation, you can use it in your favor to create inviting and exciting sexual encounters that will leave your husband wanting more.

This idea is called VISUAL GENEROSITY. Pastor Mark Driscoll explains the concept in a book he co-authored with his wife called *Real Marriage: the Truth About Sex, Friendship, and Life Together*. Although the book is somewhat controversial, there's a lot of great information that I think is helpful for this study. Here's a portion of the book that I think is very "revealing":

> Nearly all men are visual, to varying degrees. Men derive physical pleasure from the simple act of seeing a beautiful woman, which explains why companies put beautiful women in ads with their products.
>
> The fact that your husband is visual may be discouraging, but it can also be a great ally to your marriage if you learn to be a visually generous wife. Being a visually generous spouse means using your spouse's visual propensity to your advantage and your spouse's pleasure. Make love with the lights on, or by candlelight. Sleep together naked. Undress in front of your spouse. Bathe in front of your spouse.
>
> Some will ask, is this something the Bible teaches? Yes. The Song of Solomon records the 'dance of Mahanaim' in which a young wife entices her husband by using all her beauty and charm to allure him. Her boldness may have come from him constantly verbalizing his attraction to her.[54]

Driscoll mentions the Song of Solomon. Fast-forward a chapter in your Bible and read the portion he is talking about, found in **Song of Solomon 7.**

The husband takes the opportunity to compliment his wife's appearance as she stands before him naked. He starts from the feet and moves his way up, taking the time to intimately describe what he loves about each body part. It's almost enough to make you blush as you read it! The words sound like lyrics from a John Mayer or Marvin Gaye song instead of a portion of the Bible!

Driscoll gives us insight into what the husband is really saying with each compliment.

WEEK 1 .... WEEK 2 .... WEEK 3 .... WEEK 4 .... WEEK 5 .... WEEK 6 .... WEEK 7 .... WEEK 8

DAY 4

Fill in the blanks below from Song of Solomon 7:1-10, then read the corresponding commentary.

How beautiful your _____.

> Open-toed sandals were regarded as very erotic. He recognizes her beautiful and graceful feet as he watches her dance.

Your graceful _____ are like _____, the work of an artist's hands.

> He speaks of the beauty of her inner thighs as crafted works of art.

Your _____ is a rounded goblet that never lacks blended wine. Your _____ is a mound of wheat encircled by lilies.

> Commentators note that this is actually not the navel, but the vagina, especially considering the husband is talking about his wife's body from bottom to top. This may be a subtle and tasteful allusion to the intimacies of oral sex.

Your breasts are like _____, like twin fawns of a gazelle.

> Twin fawns conjures images of playfulness and fun that prompt a desire to pet, much like two baby deer.

Your _____ is like an ivory tower. Your _____ are the pools of Heshbon by the gate of Bath Rabbim.

> This city was known for its calm and beautiful pools, indicating the peace and stillness in her eyes.

Your _____ is like the tower of Lebanon looking toward Damascus. Your _____ crowns you like Mount Carmel. Your hair is like _____; the king is _____ by its tresses.

> He found her hair to be beautiful and alluring. As the Bible says, a woman's hair is her "crown" and "glory," which helps explain why it is important to many husbands.

How _____ you are and how _____, my love, with your delights!

> He delights in his wife's sexual abilities and body.

Your stature is like that of the palm and your _____ like clusters of fruit. I said, "I will climb the palm tree; I will take hold of its fruit."

> To fertilize a female palm tree, someone would need to climb the male palm tree to get some of its pollen-bearing flowers. He would then climb the female tree and tie the pollen-bearing flowers to the female tree. To "climb a palm tree" literally meant to fertilize it; likewise, the husband is clearly saying that he desires to make love to his wife.

WEEK 1 .... WEEK 2 .... WEEK 3 .... WEEK 4 .... WEEK 5 .... WEEK 6 .... WEEK 7 .... WEEK 8

DAY 4

May your breasts be like _____ on the vine, the fragrance of your breath like _____, and your mouth like the _____. May the wine go straight to my beloved, flowing gently over lips and teeth.

> Grapes swell and become increasingly round and full when ripe, like a woman's breasts when sexually aroused. Then he refers to the sweet smell of her breath. Her kisses are his favorite flavor. Like wine, her lovemaking is strong, smooth, savory, and satisfying.[55]

I think by now you get the point. The husband is entranced by his wife, and she knows it. His romantic expressions all lead up to our key verse for today, Song of Songs 7:10.

I _____ to my _____, and his _____ is for me.

This woman is sexually free, ready to be both admired and desired by her husband. She doesn't cover up or turn away when he admires her naked body, but savors every glance and basks in his poetic praise. She is VISUALLY GENEROUS.

Driscoll sums it all up perfectly for us:

> This nice God-fearing woman who married as a virgin speaks first in the series of love songs that comprise the Song of Songs. She also speaks last, and she speaks most. She initiates sex frequently, she talks about sex frankly, and she enjoys sex freely.

> Consider for a moment how radically free she is. Not only is the account of her stripping for her husband three thousand years old, but it is written in a conservative Eastern cultural context for devout Jews. Many wives wonder if they would be tramps to act in such a way. If it is with their husbands, then they are simply being wives to God's glory and their joy. The issue is not what is done, but with whom it is done. And we see from the husband's words that being verbally generous, encouraging and thankful creates a zone in which a spouse can safely risk being a visually generous servant lover.[56]

How do you think your husband would respond if you made a conscious effort to be visually generous with him?

_____

_____

_____

_____

_____

HEARTWORK

Stop and write out a prayer to God asking him to give you the ability to release your fears and insecurities so that you can love your spouse in this way.

_____

_____

_____

_____

_____

_____

_____

_____

_____

_____

__Become a Proven Wives partner today.__ Is your heart changing? Do you want to help other wives heal from the betrayal of learning about their husband's sexual sin? You can help by joining the sisterhood of Proven Wives by praying for the ministry, making a tax-deductible donation, and volunteering to lead or be a resource for other women who need support. Visit our website to learn more about how you can partner with us to advance this important work: *www.ProvenMen.org* or *www.ProvenWomen.org*

CHARGE

Real intimacy is critical for success. I will value my marriage enough to be vulnerable.

SELFLESS AND HUMBLE

Philippians 2:3-4 "Do nothing out of selfish ambition or vain conceit. Rather, in humility value others above yourselves, not looking to your own interests but each of you to the interests of the others."

WEEK 7 DAY 5

KEY THOUGHT: Is your desire to love stronger than your desire to be loved?

Recently a couple at our church shared their story about God's faithfulness through some difficult seasons of marriage. I was both encouraged and inspired as I heard them proclaim the miraculous power of God's love that saved their relationship. It's the same power that transformed my marriage as well, and it was refreshing to hear the hope in their voices. Something the wife said really stood out to me: "What if your marriage isn't about you?"

I think most of us would say that on our wedding day we were in love with our spouse and we were committed to love them without fail "until death do us part." As the weeks turn into months and years, we soon find that it's not easy to love at all times. Our good but fleshly intentions soon fail and the truth begins to surface: We got married because we wanted someone to fulfill our deepest longings and desires. It really wasn't about loving someone else, it was about loving ourselves.

When marriage gets tough and you aren't "feeling the love," that's where the rubber meets the road. Your good intentions on the day you got married won't be enough to carry you through the difficult seasons. When reality hits, you have a decision to make: Am I going to turn and run? Or am I going to lean in to the struggle and ask God to transform my selfish and proud heart so I can love like He does? God wants to use you in a way that no other person can to show His love and grace to your husband.

Mark Driscoll says it this way: "Marriage is for our holiness before our happiness. Your spouse is the most sanctifying, and often most frustrating, relationship you will have. God will use our spouses to expose our selfishness and make us to be increasingly more humble servants like Jesus Christ."[57]

Have you ever thought about that idea, that your marriage isn't about you? We've danced around that idea throughout this study, but putting it bluntly like that can really make you stop and think. So, what if your marriage isn't about you? How would your marriage change if you looked at it that way?

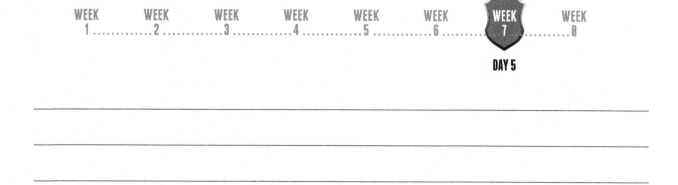

_____

_____

_____

Schaumburg also does a beautiful job of challenging our preconceived notions about love and marriage in *False Intimacy*. I've bolded a few phrases that are so challenging to my heart!

As you read, <u>underline</u> the portions that stick out to you and really make you think.

> All of us want better relationships. **But do we really want humility? Are we willing to develop it?** I think everyone who has come to faith in Christ as Savior has wanted the will of God for his or her life and prays to know it. However, I'm convinced we have no idea what we're asking. We tend to think about the **will of God only in terms of blessing or protection; in reality, being in the will of God costs us everything.** Let me explain.
>
> Broadly speaking, there are only two directions we can take in any relationship. One direction is to pursue meaningful relationship with the objective of self-centered fulfillment. When we go in this direction, our primary goal is relational fulfillment through a good friendship or a good marriage. While the desire for a good friendship is God-given and legitimate, in a fallen world real intimacy is unpredictable. When we head in this direction we may be directly limited in reaching our destination of a good relationship by the very person we seek intimacy with. We can't fulfill our desire for a good relationship on our own, so our natural tendency is to move in this direction cautiously. As we begin to walk in the muck and mire that accompanies real intimacy, we desire, we anticipate, and we are eventually disappointed at some level. In frustration we lower our expectations. We want meaningful intimacy, but the disappointment begins to lead to substantial pain. Further anticipation is unacceptable, so we numb our desires.
>
> We can courageously choose another direction. It does not come naturally; in fact, it is against our instincts. On this path we keep our desire for meaningful relationship alive; the passion for relationship is never lowered or numbed. In this direction there is a **passion to love that is stronger than the desire to be loved.** We can reach our destination without the other person's cooperation because the objective is other-centered fulfillment.
>
> Such an objective can **only come from God. The nature of God's love is always to give, never just to receive.** Anything less is a perversion. Deviation from God's love is the nature of sin. Sin always occurs when our natural desire has selfish intent, and selfish intent always springs from misgivings about God.

Humility is a willingness to surrender our right to our rights. If we are sorrowful and grateful and admit our utter dependence on God, then we become broken. Out of that weakness flows a humility of spirit that voluntarily gives up all the rights we have to ourselves.[58]

What are the two different objectives Schaumburg is saying we can have in our relationships? Which objective do you tend toward?

_____

_____

_____

_____

How does Schaumburg define humility? What does that mean to you?

_____

_____

_____

I love how Schaumburg reveals that our desire for healthy relationships does not have to be squelched by someone else's behavior. If we choose to love like God loves, then we won't become bitter when our fleshly expectations are disappointed. Yes, we will experience hurt, pain and frustration, but "we can reach our destination without the other person's cooperation because the objective is other-centered fulfillment."

It may be infuriating to you to think about loving your husband with selflessness and humility when he is being so selfish and proud. Our human nature wants to retaliate against or resent those who hurt us. But think about Christ's love for us.

Read Philippians 2:3-8. What does this passage say about Christ? About selflessness and humility?

_____

_____

_____

_____

WEEK 1 .... WEEK 2 .... WEEK 3 .... WEEK 4 .... WEEK 5 .... WEEK 6 .... **WEEK 7** .... WEEK 8

DAY 5

We love, humbly and selflessly, because we have been loved so greatly by Jesus Christ. There aren't any clauses or exceptions, just to love as he loved. "Love one another. As I have loved you, so you must love one another. By this, everyone will know that you are my disciples, if you love one another" (John 13:34-35).

On the lines below, write out the definition of love as found in 1 Corinthians 13:4-8a.

Love is _____, love is _____. It does not _____, it does not
_____, it is not _____. It does not _____ _____, it is not ____-_____,
it is not _____ _____, it keeps no _____ of _____. Love does not _____
in _____ but _____ with the _____. It always _____, always _____, always
_____, always _____. Love _____ _____.

It's hard to love someone like this! I get stuck right away with the patient part. I also falter at the "keeps no record of wrongs." Which parts of the definition are hardest for you? Go back and circle them.

Fortunately, God continues to work in and through us to learn how to love like He does (Philippians 1:6). He has stretched me and placed a desire to persevere and protect, two qualities that I believe are gifts from Him. Go back through again and put a heart next to the areas that you find easier or have grown in over the years.

Love encompasses all the words listed in the blanks above. Just mastering one or two is not enough. But when we learn to love this way, it stands the test of time, along with faith and hope (1 Corinthians 13:13). If you have faith in Christ, you can stand with hope in His promises and begin to love the way He does through the power of the Holy Spirit (Galatians 5:22-23). Real love pours out of a heart that is being changed from the inside out through the same mighty power that raised Jesus from the grave (Ephesians 1:15-23).

The main point today is to have the mind-set of Christ (Philippians 2:3-4) when it comes to your marriage by being selfless and humble (love does not boast, it is not proud. It does not dishonor others, it is not self-seeking). So how does selflessness and humility tie in to sexual intimacy?

If you approach intimacy with a humble and selfless mind-set, it brings clarity. You can filter every decision through these questions: "Am I being selfless? Am I being humble?" The answer to those questions is usually pretty apparent. If you find yourself responding with statements like, "Why should I do that for him when he has done so much to hurt me?" or "He doesn't deserve my forgiveness," then you aren't responding in love.

That doesn't mean you are a sexual doormat. Remember the concept of "speak the truth in love?" When you are pursuing humility and selflessness, it actually makes it easier to say a clear "no." If your husband is asking something that you know is unhealthy or unholy, you can say no because you are humbly and selflessly seeking his best. Your desire to help him grow closer to Christ enables you to speak the truth in love so that as a couple you can forge a new path to a healthy sex life. It's not the easy path, but it's the loving path.

A servant mind-set also elevates your "yes" when you choose to pursue intimacy even when your emotions are warring against you. When you are able to put aside your fleshly desires and insecurities to love your husband intimately within God's guidelines, your "yes" is an act of love. By meeting his sexual needs, you are "not looking to your own interests" but "to the interests of others."

Think about it. Knowing that your husband wants to be both respected and desired, what message do you think comes across when you constantly reject his sexual requests? How do you think it makes him feel?

_____

_____

_____

_____

_____

Likewise, what do you think gets communicated when you respond to his advances, or even pursue him sexually?

_____

_____

_____

_____

_____

Like you, I have a great list of reasons why I just don't want to have sex some nights. I have had a headache or been too exhausted to even think about sex. There are plenty of times I haven't been in the mood, or am preoccupied with stress from home or work, or am hurting inside from something my husband said or did. But that doesn't preclude me from walking in love. Yes, there's sensitivity that needs to be present on his part, but also selflessness on mine. If you truly are not in the right frame of mind or physically are not well enough to have sex, it's important to communicate that you want to find time in the future for it. A "rain check," if you will. That allows your husband know that you see his desires and needs and that you aren't rejecting him.

Driscoll boils it down like this:

> "Husbands and wives live on a continuum from selfish to servant both in and out of the bedroom.
> If a marriage is between two selfish people, it will be cold and functional. If a marriage is between

WEEK 1 .... WEEK 2 .... WEEK 3 .... WEEK 4 .... WEEK 5 .... WEEK 6 .... WEEK 7 .... WEEK 8

DAY 5

a selfish person and a servant, the marriage will be selfish and abusive. If a marriage is between two servants, it will be increasingly uniting and satisfying both in and out of the bedroom."[59]

The healthiest marriages are the ones where both the husband and wife learn to serve one another, to put their spouse's needs above their own. It's difficult to do when it feels one-sided, but you are called to love and obey Christ regardless of your husband's actions. Pray for him as you serve him. Your tenderness and love have the power to soften his heart and call him into something greater than his own selfish desires.

Jesus modeled this for us as He approached His final moments here on earth. As we end today, open your Bible and read John 13:1-17.

I love what John's Gospel says at the end of verse 1, "having loved his own who were in the world, he **loved them to the end**" (emphasis added). Jesus never stopped loving His disciples. Even when they fell asleep in the Garden of Gethsemane (Matthew 26:36-46). Even when they betrayed Him to the Jewish authorities (verse 2) and denied that they even knew Him (Luke 22:54-62).

Jesus displayed his humble and selfless servant's heart by wrapping a towel around his waist and washing their filthy, smelly feet. Jesus was about to die, yet He spends His last few moments serving those He loved. He wasn't looking to His own interests, but to the interests of others. Read Philippians 2:3-4, our key verse for today. He continued loving that way until that love was displayed on the cross for all to see. He could have defended and protected Himself but chose not to so that we could have eternal life. He is our Servant Savior. And He calls us to follow His lead.

Write out verse 16 below.

_____

_____

_____

HEARTWORK

End today with prayer, thanking Jesus Christ for His selfless and sacrificial love. Ask God to give you a selfless and humble heart, a heart that loves even when it is betrayed and wounded and abandoned. A heart that desires to love more than it desires to be loved. Ask Him to show you practical ways that He is calling you to grab a basin and towel and wash your husband's feet. Maybe it includes actually washing his feet. He will show you.

Ask Him to "give you a new heart and put a new spirit in you"; to "remove from you your heart of stone and give you a heart of flesh" (Ezekiel 36:26). And then pray for God to do the same for your husband. Commit the next ten minutes to prayer.

HOMEWORK

1. Read through Appendix I. It's an honest and candid look at how your body functions sexually. It will be helpful to you as you learn how to enjoy marital sex.

    Record your honest thoughts.

2. Also read through Appendix K. Do you relate to the story in any way? How does reading this story give you hope as you pursue healing?

CHARGE

Real intimacy is critical for success. I will value my marriage enough to be vulnerable.

PW

WEEK EIGHT

LOVE GOD, LOVE OTHERS

Luke 10:27 "Love the Lord your God with all your heart and with all your soul and with all your strength and with all your mind and love your neighbor as yourself.'"

WEEK 8 **DAY 1**

KEY THOUGHT: To truly live means to truly love.

Most of us spend our entire lives looking for love, believing it to be life's greatest happiness. It's reflected in these famous quotes:

> "There is only one happiness in life, to love and to be loved." George Sand, French novelist

> "The greatest thing you'll ever learn is just to love and be loved in return." Eden Ahbez, songwriter

> "The only reason to live is to love and the only reason to love is to live." Tonya Hurley, *NY Times* best-selling author

I bought into the idea of finding true love and happiness early on in life, dreaming about my future husband throughout childhood. I even wrote a poem about him and our wedding day while I was in elementary school. Like the raven-haired princess from *Snow White*, I was patiently waiting for someday when my prince would come. He would meet all my deepest desires and longings, and I would be "happy forever" like her:

> He was so romantic I could not resist
> Someday my prince will come
> Someday we'll meet again
> And away to his castle we'll go
> To be happy forever I know
> Someday when spring is here
> We'll find our love anew
> And the birds will sing and wedding bells will ring
> Someday when my dreams come true[60]

What about you? Does your idea of true happiness equal finding true love? Where did your ideas about true love and happiness come from?

_____

_____

_____

_____

If we are honest, most of us got married because we wanted someone to meet our heart's deep longing for love and companionship. It wasn't really about loving our spouse, it was about loving ourselves.

As we ended week seven, our key thought on day five was a difficult question: Is your desire to love stronger than your desire to be loved?

How would you answer that question if you thought back to your wedding day? What was stronger back then, your desire to love or to be loved? How would you answer it now?

_____

_____

_____

Jesus shows us that our mission in life is not to get love, but to give it. Open your Bible and **read Luke 10:25-37**. Write out what Jesus said in verse 27 on the lines below (our key verse for today).

_____

_____

_____

Perhaps this story is very familiar to you, and it's easy to miss some important details. Let's explore deeper to get to the heart of this parable.

THE VICTIM

The wounded man in this story was on his way from Jerusalem to Jericho. The road he was traveling was infamous for being dangerous. It was a seventeen-mile hike through desert country that included a 3,000-foot descent, making it a perfect place for robbers to hide. He was left for dead, naked, broke and severely injured.

WEEK 1 .... WEEK 2 .... WEEK 3 .... WEEK 4 .... WEEK 5 .... WEEK 6 .... WEEK 7 .... WEEK 8

DAY 1

THE PASSERSBY

The priest and the Levite refused to help the beaten man. Perhaps they were afraid that they, too, would be attacked if they stopped and helped. Or maybe their concern was that contact with his body would render them unclean according to Jewish law. They had made their trek to Jerusalem to show their love for God, but on their way back to Jericho they dismissed an opportunity to show love for their neighbor.

THE HERO

The hero in this story was of Samaritan descent. Samaritans were the enemies of the Jews, regarded as "lesser than" because they were half-breeds. Samaria was the capital of the Northern Kingdom of Israel, and the wicked Assyrians took it captive in the eighth century B.C. Some of the Jews stayed behind after the captivity ended and married the Assyrians, creating the mixed-breed subset known as Samaritans. No wonder the Jews hated the Samaritans; they intermarried with a wicked enemy instead of remaining loyal to their own people. In fact, the Samaritan woman at the well in John 4:9 reminds Jesus that they should not be speaking to one another because of the hatred between the two races: "The Samaritan woman said to him, 'You are a Jew and I am a Samaritan woman. How can you ask me for a drink?'" [for Jews do not associate with Samaritans.]

The Samaritan is an unlikely hero in this story. But the Samaritan wastes no time in showing mercy to the injured man, disregarding any concern for himself. In his sermon series, "In Earth as it is in Heaven," pastor J.D. Greear talks about the heart of the Samaritan when he approaches the wounded victim:

> The word that Jesus used for what the Samaritan felt toward the man on the side of the road is one of my favorite Greek words: *splagma*. We translate it as "compassion," but in Greek it means "pity from your deepest soul." Jesus is talking less about an action you choose and more about an emotion you can't control. The word even sounds like what it means—a love so deep-seated that it comes from your gut.
>
> God is not after rule-followers. He wants people who love like he loves, who respond like he responds. And that kind of change can't be produced by the law. *It can only be produced by a radical experience of grace.*
>
> It's when I experienced the loving grace of The Good Samaritan toward me that I became a loving person toward others. How can you experience that kind of grace and not become filled with grace?
>
> Those who have experienced the gospel develop an uncontrollable impulse to be generous and an insane ability to forgive.[61]

The Samaritan's actions reflected his grateful and grace-filled heart. His generosity led him to essentially write a blank check, willing to cover whatever medical costs the victim (who was a stranger to him) might incur. Jesus shows us through this parable that in order to find true life, which is eternal life, we must love the way the Samaritan did. First, we must love the Lord with all our heart, soul, mind and strength. The deep love that

WEEK 1 .... WEEK 2 .... WEEK 3 .... WEEK 4 .... WEEK 5 .... WEEK 6 .... WEEK 7 .... WEEK 8

DAY 1

we have for our Savior will spill out and overflow from a grateful heart for what He has done, compelling us to give lavishly to those who are in need.

Your sexually addicted spouse is your neighbor. He is the one that you will live next to for the rest of your life. His choice to walk in sin has left him battered and bruised by the enemy. Perhaps many have walked by and considered him already dead or an unworthy risk to take on. But God is calling you to stop, take the risk, and give without any expectations. You have the unique calling to care for your husband the way the Good Samaritan cared for the wounded man. God has called you to love your husband the way Christ has loved you (John 13:34-35). How has Christ demonstrated His love for you?

Read the verses below and then write them out in the space provided.

Psalm 86:15_____

_____

_____

_____

Romans 5:8_____

_____

_____

_____

Romans 8:37-39 _____

_____

_____

_____

_____

_____

WEEK 1 .... WEEK 2 .... WEEK 3 .... WEEK 4 .... WEEK 5 .... WEEK 6 .... WEEK 7 .... WEEK 8

DAY 1

_____

_____

1 John 3:1 _____

_____

_____

_____

_____

1 John 4:9-11_____

_____

_____

_____

_____

_____

_____

Perhaps you feel like you can't afford to love this way, the way God does. The idea of writing a blank "love check" is daunting and scary. It comes with a huge price tag, and you may never see the fruits of your labor. But true godly love doesn't run a cost-benefit analysis to see if it will be worth it in the end; it gives without regard for self (1 Corinthians 13:5). The parable doesn't end with the victim seeking out the Good Samaritan to thank him or repay him. We never find out if he gets completely healed or if they even speak again.

Loving your neighbor as yourself means responding to your husband with mercy and love because you have received those things from Jesus Christ. He exhibited the greatest form of love by paying the greatest price—laying down His life (John 15:13). And he calls us to do likewise: "This is how we know what love is: Jesus Christ laid down his life for us. And we ought to lay down our lives for our brothers and sisters" (1 John 3:16).

WEEK 1 .... WEEK 2 .... WEEK 3 .... WEEK 4 .... WEEK 5 .... WEEK 6 .... WEEK 7 .... **WEEK 8**

DAY 1

Again, loving like this doesn't mean you gloss over the sin or shield your husband from the consequences of his behavior. It means that you are willing to help your husband see where he is naked and bleeding, then point him in the direction of the Healer.

HEARTWORK

As we end the study today, I want you to think about what loving this way has already cost you and will cost you in the future. How far are you willing to go to love like Jesus does?

_____

_____

_____

_____

_____

_____

_____

_____

_____

_____

Love always protects, always trusts, always hopes, always perseveres. Love never fails (1 Corinthians 13:7-8a). Spend some time in prayer asking God, through the power of the Holy Spirit, to give you both the willingness and endurance to love this way.

CHARGE

I will take responsibility for what I can influence. I will prioritize my marriage only after Jesus and I will guard it.

ALL YOUR HEART

Proverbs 4:23 "Above all else, guard your heart, for everything you do flows from it."

WEEK 8 DAY 2

KEY THOUGHT: Trust God with all your heart, seek Him with all your heart, love Him with all your heart.

Yesterday we talked about the two greatest commands, to love God and love others. Find John 14:15 and write it out, then flip to John 15:12 and write it out next to John 14:15.

_____

_____

_____

Your love for God will overflow into a love for others. In order to love your neighbor (your husband) as you love yourself, you must first learn to love God with **ALL** YOUR HEART, MIND, SOUL and STRENGTH. The final few days of our study will narrow our focus on each one of these aspects. This final chapter will also emphasize the importance of finding trustworthy community to help encourage you as you learn to love holistically.

Today we will look at "love God with all your heart." The Bible mentions the heart numerous times. Let's take a closer look at what it says.

Read the passages below and write down what is revealed about the heart.

1 Samuel 16:7

_____

_____

_____

WEEK 1 .... WEEK 2 .... WEEK 3 .... WEEK 4 .... WEEK 5 .... WEEK 6 .... WEEK 7 .... WEEK 8

DAY 2

Psalm 51:10

Psalm 73:25-26

Jeremiah 17:9-10

Ezekiel 36:26

WEEK 1 .... WEEK 2 .... WEEK 3 .... WEEK 4 .... WEEK 5 .... WEEK 6 .... WEEK 7 ....

WEEK 1 .... WEEK 2 .... WEEK 3 .... WEEK 4 .... WEEK 5 .... WEEK 6 .... WEEK 7 ....

WEEK 8

DAY 2

In summary, what do these verses say about the human heart? How do we truly experience a "change of heart?"

_____

_____

_____

Truly, our hearts are wicked when left to their own devices. You only need to watch a few minutes of the evening news to know that's true. God sees our hearts, and despite the fact that they are dark with sinful intentions, He loves us anyway. He desires to dwell in our hearts through faith and strengthen us from within through the power of the Holy Spirit (Ephesians 3:16-17).

In this study's counterpart, *Proven Men*, author Joel Hesch describes the transformation that takes place when Christ dwells in our hearts through faith:

> When you trust in Jesus to be your Savior from sin and to be the Lord of your life, He immediately gives you a new nature and the Holy Spirit. The old nature, however, still remains; it still desires selfish pleasures. The new nature desires purity and holiness; therefore, a battle rages inside you between the dueling natures of self-centered and God-centered desires (1 Peter 2:11). Both compete for you.
>
> Your new nature, when yielded to the power of the Holy Spirit, will give you mastery over the old nature. The key to victory over the bondage of sin is developing an intimate, daily walk with the Lord Jesus Christ. It starts by flooding the new nature with healthy influences while at the same time starving the selfish nature by eliminating those influences that reinforce the old way of thinking and acting. These two things—eliminating self-centeredness and increasing God-centeredness—cannot be compartmentalized but must be simultaneously incorporated into your very way of life.
>
> Jesus said that the commands of God can be summed up into two commandments (Mark 12:30-31): 'Love the Lord your God with all your heart and with all your soul and with all your mind and with all your strength. Love your neighbor as yourself.' These should be guiding principles in life. If you follow them, you won't be permanently ensnared in sins flowing from selfishness and pride.

Our flesh competes with the Spirit and daily beckons us to live for self rather than God. It tempts us to place our trust in our own wants and needs. In order to love God with all our heart, we must daily submit our fleshly desires to Him. According to the reading above, what two things must we simultaneously incorporate into our lives to gain victory over sin?

_____

_____

WEEK 1 .... WEEK 2 .... WEEK 3 .... WEEK 4 .... WEEK 5 .... WEEK 6 .... WEEK 7 .... WEEK 8

DAY 2

Listen to these verses that echo the importance of placing total trust in God instead of ourselves:

> Psalm 28:7 "The LORD is my strength and my shield; my heart trusts in him, and he helps me. My heart leaps for joy, and with my song I praise him."

> Psalm 73:25-26 "Whom have I in heaven but you? And earth has nothing I desire besides you. My flesh and my heart may fail, but God is the strength of my heart and my portion forever."

> Proverbs 3:5-6 "Trust in the Lord with all your heart and lean not on your own understanding; in all your ways submit to him, and he will make your paths straight."

What happens in our lives when we trust in God with all our hearts? Look over all the verses listed in the section above and record your answers below.

_____

_____

_____

What are some of the things that you have been placing all your heart's trust in rather than God? Matthew 6:21 says, "Where your treasure is, there your heart will be also." What do your "treasures" (husband, money, dreams, children, job, friendships) communicate about what your heart truly loves?

_____

_____

_____

_____

When we place our trust in anything other than God alone, we will be constantly disappointed. Only God can strengthen and sustain our hearts. He knows that our hearts are easily lead astray, which is why he warns us through the words of Solomon to keep a careful watch over them.

Write out Proverbs 4:23 below. It's our key verse for today.

_____

_____

WEEK 1 .... WEEK 2 .... WEEK 3 .... WEEK 4 .... WEEK 5 .... WEEK 6 .... WEEK 7 .... **WEEK 8**

DAY 2

This Proverbs says that above everything else, we are to keep watch over our hearts. It reminds me of when my children were young, and we took trips to the playground. There were opportunities for great fun, but also for great danger. I had to carefully keep my eyes on them to keep them safe. I would stand at arms' length while they climbed the slide, then waited at the bottom to catch them before they hit the ground. I would carefully redirect them away from swings in motion so they wouldn't get knocked over. Knowing the potential for danger kept me on guard, ready to step in at a moment's notice if they had a misstep.

Our hearts are so often childish in nature, seeking out what they want without regard for the inherent danger or painful consequences. Paul describes the struggle in Romans 7:18-19, "I know that nothing good lives in me, that is, in my sinful nature. I want to do what is right, but I can't. I want to do what is good, but I don't. I don't want to do what is wrong, but I do it anyway." The flesh is in constant conflict with the Spirit, which is exactly why we need to guard our hearts.

So, how do we do this? Through daily submission to God and His authority in our lives. A trusting and obedient child looks to their parent first before climbing a ladder to make sure it's OK. A trusting child takes hold of a parent's hand and walks in step with them while crossing a busy street. Likewise, guarding your heart means looking to God with childlike trust, knowing that He has your best in mind and that His strength will not fail you. With childlike faith, we discover His guidelines and safeguards through prayer and reading His Word. Out of a trusting heart, we then obey His commands, even when it's not fun or when we don't understand why.

Another way to guard your heart is through godly friendships. The other day, I was sitting across the table at a coffee shop with one of my dear friends, and she asked me, "How's your heart?" We had a good laugh about it, joking about how funny it would be if men talked to each other the way women do. But her question sparked an honest conversation about what was going on deep down in my heart. In essence, she was asking, "How are you really?"

A godly friend is a woman who is willing to help actively guard your heart. She is the kind of friend who doesn't run when you honestly reveal what's going on deep inside your soul. She listens carefully and knows you well enough to recognize when your heart is wandering away from your first love (Revelation 2:2-4). She points you away from the dangers of sin and in the direction of safety.

It's challenging to be on guard all the time. We grow weary and faint, tired of fighting our flesh. We wonder if it's worth it. A godly friend is someone who is willing to come alongside to tag-team the devil. When two moms hang out at the park on a play date, there is an additional measure of safety for the children involved when there are two pairs of watchful eyes. There is power in numbers. An extra set of eyes will help catch something you may have glanced over or is hidden from your view.

Proverbs 27:9 says, "Ointments and perfume encourage the heart; in a similar way, a friend's advice is sweet to the soul." Like the familiar scent of a candle or your favorite perfume brings comfort to your heart, so do the wise and kind words of a dear friend. Do you have this kind of friend in your life that can encourage and challenge

WEEK 1 .... WEEK 2 .... WEEK 3 .... WEEK 4 .... WEEK 5 .... WEEK 6 .... WEEK 7 .... **WEEK 8**

DAY 2

your heart? The kind of friend that will point you back to God's Word and remind you not to lose heart because God is at work inside of you (2 Corinthians 4:16-17)?

In order to love God with all our hearts, we must guard them carefully from the poison of sin. Where is your heart weak? Where does it need some extra protection? Are you struggling with a bitter heart toward your husband? A sad heart that is wrestling with depression? A lonely heart that is aching for authentic love?

HEARTWORK

As we end today, reveal to God where you know your heart needs guarding. Confess where you have lost your first love and given your heart away to self-focused desires and attitudes.

_____

_____

_____

_____

_____

_____

If you have a friend that you safely trust, one that is godly and will point you back to the Scriptures and to prayer, schedule some time together. Reveal to her where your heart is weak and ask her to help keep guard over it. Pray together and commit to point one another back to Jesus, no matter what, so you can both truly love God with ALL YOUR HEART.

CHARGE

I will take responsibility for what I can influence. I will prioritize my marriage only after Jesus and I will guard it.

ALL YOUR SOUL

Psalm 42:1 "As the deer pants for streams of water, so my soul pants for you, my God."

WEEK 8 DAY 3

KEY THOUGHT: God has given us spiritual guides to shepherd our souls.

Yesterday we talked about loving God with all your heart; today we will talk about loving God with all your soul.

What's the difference between the heart and the soul? That's a great question for a deep theological debate, but to put it simply, think of the heart as your inner self and the soul as your eternal self. To love God with all your soul means to love Him with your very life.

Professor of Old Testament and Biblical Theology, Jason DeRouchie, says it like this:

> Along with our hearts, we are called to love Yahweh with all our soul. In the first five books of the Old Testament, the "soul" refers to one's whole being as a living person, which includes one's "heart," but is so much more. For example, in Genesis 2:7 we are told that "Yahweh God formed the man of dust from the ground and breathed into his nostrils the breath of life, and the man became a living [*soul*] creature" (Genesis 9:5).
>
> Elsewhere, corpses are called "dead souls," which simply means the person, once alive, is now dead (Leviticus 21:11), and Yahweh promises that his "soul [i.e., his being] shall not abhor" all who follow His lead (Leviticus 26:11). In light of these texts, it seems Moses starts with a call to love God from within and then moves one step larger saying that everything about us as a person is to declare Yahweh as Lord.
>
> So we are to love God with our passions, hungers, perceptions, and thoughts. But we are also to love him with how we talk, what we do with our hands, how we utilize our talents, and how we react to challenges—*our entire being is to display that we love God.*[62]

WEEK
1 .... 2 .... 3 .... 4 .... 5 .... 6 .... 7 ....

WEEK
8

DAY 3

Open your Bible and read Mark 8:34-37. Write out verse 36 below.

_____

_____

Nothing is more valuable than your soul. Your soul is what will last for all of eternity; it's worth more than anything this world can temporarily offer. Loving God with all your soul means to love Him with eternity in mind.

Matthew 10:28 also reminds us of the value of our souls: "Do not be afraid of those who kill the body but cannot kill the soul. Rather, be afraid of the One who can destroy both soul and body in hell." This verse sounds scary, but the context gives us a deeper appreciation for what Jesus is truly communicating.

In this passage, Jesus sends His disciples out "like sheep among wolves" to preach the gospel, drive out impure spirits, and heal the sick. He warns them of the danger and rejection they were going to face once they embarked on their journey. Matthew 10:28 is a reminder to His disciples that they shouldn't be afraid of humans, whose actions were only temporal. Their focus was to be on the One who carried the weight of their souls in His hands. Their love for Him was to supersede their fear of mere mortals.

Have you ever taken the time to evaluate the worth of your soul? Truly there is nothing that you have been given that carries more value. What areas of your life would be impacted most if you began to view them with an eternal perspective? Take some time to answer below.

_____

_____

_____

_____

During the difficult season of relapse in our marriage, both my husband and I had lost our eternal perspective. We were loving ourselves instead of loving God with all our souls. We had sacrificed the eternal on the altar of the immediate, choosing to pursue worldly comforts instead of God's presence. I am so grateful that God called us out of our sinful patterns so that we could rediscover His faithful and unending love.

God has given us individuals in our lives to be the voice to call us out of our sin and redirect our attention on to the Savior. In our marriage, the hard truth was spoken over us by our pastor and his wife. They have been dear friends to us, but more significantly they have been spiritual guides. Over the years, they have been willing to step in and say hard things, even at the risk of losing our relationship with them.

WEEK 1 .... WEEK 2 .... WEEK 3 .... WEEK 4 .... WEEK 5 .... WEEK 6 .... WEEK 7 .... WEEK 8

DAY 3

In chapter 2, I shared a little bit about their role in our story. They were a pivotal part of both the revelation and confession of my husband's decade-long struggle with pornography addiction. The words of wisdom they spoke in those moments stuck with me throughout our journey to wholeness and healing. When our pastor compared the lust to cancer, that word picture revealed how invasive the sin had become in his spiritual life.

One of the main verses our pastor referenced was John 10:10. He reminded us that God's desire for us is to "have life, and have it to the full." Take a few moments and read John 10:1-18 for context.

What does Jesus call Himself in verse 11?

_____

What does the shepherd do for His sheep in verses 3, 4, 9, 11 and 16?

_____

_____

It's evident in this passage how much the Shepherd cares for His sheep. When He talks about being the gate, it literally means that He lays across the front of the sheep pen with His body to protect His flock from harm. What a beautiful symbol of His care for us, made evident through His death on the cross!

God has given shepherds here on earth to help care and protect the flock. This person is a spiritual shepherd, or pastor. They are actually called shepherds in multiple passages of Scripture.

Read 1 Peter 5:1-4. What responsibilities does the shepherd have according to this passage?

_____

_____

_____

Now read Acts 20:28-31. What responsibilities do you find in these verses?

_____

_____

_____

WEEK 1 .... WEEK 2 .... WEEK 3 .... WEEK 4 .... WEEK 5 .... WEEK 6 .... WEEK 7 ....

WEEK 8

DAY 3

God has appointed these individuals to keep guard over your spiritual walk. Pastors have a calling to guide and guard their flock so that they will not be led astray by false teachers or sinful behaviors. They understand the natural condition of the human heart to wander: "We all, like sheep, have gone astray, each of us has turned to our own way; and the Lord has laid on Him the iniquity of us all" (Isaiah 53:6). Shepherds know that the only way for sheep to be rescued from selfish wanderings is through Christ's sacrifice on the cross.

To love God with all your soul, you must be willing to be led spiritually. Just like the sheep in John 10, you must listen and obey the Good Shepherd's voice. His voice can be heard in His Word and through prayer, but it is also heard through spiritual leaders that are seeking God with all their being. Like one of the first pastors, Paul, they are willing to stand up and say, "Follow my example, as I follow the example of Christ" (1 Corinthians 11:1).

Whose voice are you listening to when you get angry, discouraged, feel alone, or want revenge? Do you turn to friends that will bash your husband? Their voices may sound good at first, but their advice won't lead to wholeness and healing. It's important to have godly guides in your life to point you to the Good Shepherd. They will warn you about the thieves, robbers and wolves that are waiting to destroy you. They will redirect your attention to the One who is guarding you, guiding you, feeding you, and willing to die for you.

Do you have someone in your life that can do this for you? Are you part of a local church body that is preaching the Word of God faithfully? I am so glad that we had a pastor who was willing to step in and care for our souls so that our marriage wouldn't be destroyed by lust, selfishness and bitterness. I am so glad that he was a voice that gently but firmly reminded us that God had so much more in store for our relationship.

Take a few moments to think about the people in your life that you would call spiritual shepherds. Who are they?

_____

_____

_____

_____

Is it time to ask them for some words of wisdom and guidance? If you don't have someone, you need to find someone! The spiritual influences in my life have been the difference maker in my marriage. A sheep that is wandering all on its own is an easy target for a predator. Start looking for a local community that you can call your own.

Although the pointed words of our pastor were difficult to swallow during our moment of crisis, it marked the beginning of a spiritual awakening in our home. That pivotal moment ushered in one of the darkest seasons of

WEEK 1 .... WEEK 2 .... WEEK 3 .... WEEK 4 .... WEEK 5 .... WEEK 6 .... WEEK 7 ....  WEEK 8

DAY 3

my life, but it also caused me to seek after God with all of my being. The Good Shepherd was calling me back to His arms, and He used our pastor and his wife as a mouthpiece to get our attention.

Our rock-bottom moment forced us to look up to Christ and learn how to seek Him first and love Him most. One of my favorite Psalms reveals what it looks like to love God with all your soul. Open your Bible to Psalm 42 and read through it. On the lines below, write out every phrase from this passage that use the word "soul" in it.

_____

_____

_____

_____

What does this Psalm communicate about the writer's soul?

_____

_____

This Psalm is such a vivid picture of a person who loves God with all their soul. He compares his desire for God to the parched throat of a deer. Deer pant after running, and they run when they are being chased by an enemy. They come to the water in need of refreshment and sustainment. They can't continue on without its life-giving flow.

When I wake up in the morning, my deepest craving is for a glass of cold water. I'm unable to focus on anything else until I take a long, quenching gulp. God wants us to love Him with a thirst that drives us to seek Him before anything else, unable to function until we get a taste of Him. Just as our bodies will rapidly deteriorate without water, so, too, our souls will erode without communion with God.

One of the verses that stuck out to me in this passage was Psalm 42:8. I love it in the New Living Translation: "But each day, the Lord pours his unfailing love upon me, and through each night I sing his songs, praying to God who gives me life." Loving God with all your soul means recognizing that He is the author of your very life. Without Him, nothing would exist (John 1:3), including you. His love is unfailing, eternal, never changing. He is with you every moment of every day, loving you without fail.

How amazing! I pray that you will be able to fully comprehend the depths of His love for you (Ephesians 3:17-19). Understanding His sacrificial love creates in us a desire to love Him back with all of our souls. It allows us to look to Him for guidance just like a sheep follows the shepherd. It compels us to search after Him for refreshment as a deer pants for water.

HEARTWORK

As we end today, write out Psalm 23. Pray it out loud and ask God to give you a love for Him that engulfs your soul.

_____

_____

_____

_____

_____

_____

_____

_____

_____

_____

_____

_____

Begin a new rhythm in your life to declare your love for God. Every morning before you wake up and every night before you go to bed, take a few moments to pray. Prioritizing your relationship with Him is a practical way to express that you love Him with all your heart and soul. Challenge yourself to start and end every day with a few quiet moments in His presence.

CHARGE

I will take responsibility for what I can influence. I will prioritize my marriage only after Jesus and I will guard it.

ALL YOUR STRENGTH

Galatians 6:1-2 "Brothers and sisters, if someone is caught in a sin, you who live by the Spirit should restore that person gently. But watch yourselves, or you also may be tempted. Carry each other's burdens, and in this way you will fulfill the law of Christ."

WEEK 8 DAY 4

KEY THOUGHT: An accountability partner will help pull you up and push you through difficult times because they know where the source of true strength lies.

When my daughter turned thirteen, we took a surprise family road trip to commemorate her milestone birthday. She's a free-spirited adventure seeker, and her life will not be complete until she has gone parasailing, bungee jumping, and skydiving. The rest of us aren't as daring, so we settled on a happy medium—a high-ropes zip lining course.

Close to the end of our adventure, we came to our guide's favorite obstacle, the big Tarzan swing. From one of the highest platforms, we were instructed to hurl ourselves off the ledge and do a free-fall swing into a huge rope cargo net. Once we landed in the net, we had to climb up onto the next platform, which was quite a difficult task. At this point, we had been climbing, balancing, and pulling ourselves through obstacles for almost two hours, and our body strength was starting to fade.

As we got closer to the Tarzan swing, I noticed a teenage girl clinging to the cargo net for dear life. She was visibly exhausted, struggling to hang on to the net and muster the strength to pull herself up.

"Are you OK?" I called out to her.

"I don't have any upper body strength left," she replied breathlessly.

I encouraged her from my position directly below her, yelling out, "you can do it!" She made a few more feeble attempts to ascend the web of ropes but quickly got stuck again. "Do you want me to get some help?" I hollered. She was ready, and so I blew into the bright orange emergency whistle issued to every climber. Immediately a professional from the course ran to her aid. He hitched her tired body up to a cable system and hoisted her up to the platform so she could continue on with her journey.

WEEK 1 .... WEEK 2 .... WEEK 3 .... WEEK 4 .... WEEK 5 .... WEEK 6 .... WEEK 7 .... WEEK 8

DAY 4

At the end of our tour, I asked the guide a few questions about his training. He informed me that they practiced on the course daily, sometimes even navigating it backwards. They literally knew it backwards and forwards! As much as I wanted to be a help to the young woman, my limited experience only allowed for some encouragement until I recognized she needed special help and attention. The guide was able to use his expertise to help her move on and get past the obstacle.

Our experience on the ropes course reminded me of how important it is to have an accountability partner in life. Both husbands and wives need someone along the journey to come to your aid when you are tired and stuck. Like the teenage girl in the story, at times you will feel like you don't have the energy to keep going. An accountability partner has the important role of recognizing that you are in a rut and that you need some help to get back to a place of safety. They are willing to step in during a moment of crisis and give you the wisdom and advice that might be hard to hear, to "speak the truth in love." They are willing to go to great lengths to help move you forward in your spiritual journey, even if it's awkward and uncomfortable.

An accountability partner should be someone who knows you well enough to notice when your behavior isn't normal. They will pick up on cues and ask the tough questions, and then keep asking them until they get the truth. Acquaintances and friends may ask, "How are you doing?" and accept your answer at face value; but an accountability partner will know when you are lying and won't let you go until you answer honestly.

An accountability partner is someone who is willing to listen to you without judging you or your husband. An accountability partner is able to help you up because they know how it feels to be stuck as well. They have learned through experience that they must live by the power of the Holy Spirit, because they, too, have been overwhelmed by a sin cycle at some point.

Read Galatians 6:1-2, our key verse for today. Fill in the blanks below for each question.

What kind of person is called to help restore his brothers/sisters in Christ?

You who _____ _____ _____ _____.

How are they instructed to help restore them?

Restore that person _____.

An accountability partner is someone who is looking to the Holy Spirit to guide them daily. He/she has a humble, helpful heart that comes from an "I've been there too" mind-set. Galatians 6:3 says, "If anyone thinks they are something when they are not, they deceive themselves." I love the NLT version of Galatians 6:1-3 as well:

> Dear brothers and sisters, if another believer is overcome by some sin, you who are godly should gently and humbly help that person back onto the right path. And be careful not to fall into the same temptation yourself. Share each other's burdens, and in this way obey the law of Christ. If

WEEK 1 .... WEEK 2 .... WEEK 3 .... WEEK 4 .... WEEK 5 .... WEEK 6 .... WEEK 7 ....  WEEK 8

DAY 4

you think you are too important to help someone, you are only fooling yourself. You are not that important.

An accountability partner recognizes that his/her sin is just as ugly as yours. They understand Romans 3:10-12, "There is no one righteous, not even one; there is no one who understands; there is no one who seeks God. All have turned away." They will still love you and your husband in spite of your flaws, knowing that they too are "messed up" by sin.

It's important for you to have more than one accountability partner speaking into your marriage. You should have at least one for you and your husband should have one also. **You cannot be your husband's accountability partner.** Asking him the in-depth questions is a recipe for disaster. Your husband needs to have safe words that he can use to indicate that he is really struggling. That's when it's time to have an accountability partner step in and help assess the damage and point him in the right direction. When your marriage is in crisis, you also need a safe person to talk to that can understand your struggle without judging your husband.

How does this look practically? Your husband should have a godly male friend as an accountability partner. For my husband, it's a guy that he has known for almost two decades. They both share the same struggle with lust but are wise enough to know that their only strength to overcome temptation is in Christ alone. When they meet, they challenge one another to spend time in Scripture and prayer. They ask each other the tough questions.

This friend knows my husband well enough to recognize when something deeper is going on in his heart, and he's not afraid to ask about it. And my husband does the same for him. Sometimes my husband is the one stuck on the ropes course, needing a hand up. At other times, his friend has been in need of assistance.

When I am concerned with how things are going at home, it's time for an accountability check-in for my husband. If I know he is struggling hard with lust, I can gently recommend that he spend some time with his friend. His accountability partner provides a safe and gentle voice in his life that is challenging, yet non-threatening. This man also prays for my husband and genuinely cares about his well-being.

I also have a few friends that serve as accountability partners. All of them are married to men who have been open about their struggle with lust. Each one of these friends has a few special character traits that make them good accountability partners:

1. They don't allow me to throw my husband under the bus. When I am with them, I know that they will "call me out" if I begin to degrade or disrespect him. They won't view my husband as "lesser than" because of his struggle.

2. They are living by the Spirit, as instructed in Galatians 6:1. They know that they, too, are flawed by sin and must depend on God's power to have victory over it. They are faithful wives and moms who spend time with God every day, seeking Him through His Word and prayer.

WEEK 1 .... WEEK 2 .... WEEK 3 .... WEEK 4 .... WEEK 5 .... WEEK 6 .... WEEK 7 .... **WEEK 8**

DAY 4

3. They are trustworthy listeners. I know that my words are safe with them, that what is said will be kept between the two of us. If outside intervention is necessary (like professional counseling), they proceed with caution and grace to point me in the right direction.

If we are going to love the Lord with all our strength, we need to have a support system in place for when we are weak. Our spiritual growth is majorly affected by the people we surround ourselves with. Proverbs 12:26 says, "The righteous choose their friends carefully, but the way of the wicked leads them astray." Your friendship decisions will have a profound impact on your life's trajectory.

The passages below remind us of how important it is to have godly influences. Read each one and then list the character traits that are evidenced in someone who can be trusted as an accountability partner.

Proverbs 13:20

_____

_____

Proverbs 18:24

_____

_____

_____

Proverbs 19:20

_____

_____

Proverbs 27:5-6, 17

_____

_____

_____

_____

Ecclesiastes 4:9-12

_____
_____
_____
_____
_____
_____
_____
_____

1 Thessalonians 5:11

_____
_____

Hebrews 3:13

_____
_____

James 5:16

_____
_____
_____
_____

HEARTWORK

What are some areas where you find yourself constantly struggling? What sin patterns tend to get you "caught"? Write them down.

_____

_____

_____

Who could you ask to help keep you accountable? Pray specifically for those people by name. Ask God to give you the courage and humility to pursue this kind of relationship.

_____

_____

_____

What would accountability look like? Perhaps it would entail a regular meeting time with key questions being asked. Or maybe it's a phone call when you feel yourself slipping into unhealthy patterns. Write out a few ideas below.

_____

_____

_____

Within the next week, open up a conversation with the individual(s) that you have been praying for and ask them if they can be your accountability partner. Outline what that would look like together.

Who would be a safe person for your husband to ask? A great place to start is a Proven Men group. This ministry has been pioneering the path to sexual integrity for years and is the catalyst for this study. Proven Men provides a safe place for men to pursue wholeness and healing, and accountability is central to the process. I hope that he has been following the study already, but if not, you can find more information here:
www.provenmen.org

WEEK 1 .... WEEK 2 .... WEEK 3 .... WEEK 4 .... WEEK 5 .... WEEK 6 .... WEEK 7 .... WEEK 8

DAY 4

Pray for your husband, that he will have the courage and humility to be willing to take the first step toward sexual purity if he hasn't yet. God can use you to help him in this area, but your approach must be gentle, as mentioned in our key verse today. An accusing tone will only lead to withdrawal and/or anger.

NOT: "You need to get some help for your disgusting problem."

BUT RATHER: "I want to see you get healing. I want to have a relationship with you that is whole and healthy."

Ask God to give you the wisdom and the words to know how to broach the subject with him.

Accountability is CRUCIAL for both you and your husband. The application steps in this lesson aren't mere suggestions. Please take the time to thoughtfully and prayerfully seek out godly individuals to partner with both you and your husband. They will be a huge difference maker on your journey back to a healthy and thriving marriage. I speak from personal experience.

CHARGE

I will take responsibility for what I can influence. I will prioritize my marriage only after Jesus and I will guard it.

ALL YOUR MIND

2 Timothy 1:7 "For God has not given us a spirit of fear, but of power and of love and of a sound mind." (NKJV)

WEEK 8 DAY 5

KEY THOUGHT: Real love casts out fear.

At the very beginning of this study, I mentioned that I have sat across the table from countless women who have been devastated by their husbands' sexual addiction. I was on that side of the table at one point, wondering how my marriage would be able to survive the destruction of lust and pornography use. The pain in my own heart and the hearts of so many women was what compelled me to write this study.

God, in His faithful and loving kindness, brought individuals into my life to offer Spirit-filled wisdom and encouragement. Their words brought light into the darkest parts of my soul and helped transform me from a wounded woman into a hopeful warrior. This final chapter is a call for you to pursue a Holy Spirit-led community of believers that will always point you back to Jesus Christ and His Word.

So far, we've talked about the importance of three different relationships that encourage us to love God with totality, based on Luke 10:27: friend (your heart), pastor (your soul), and accountability partner (your strength). The last one I want to talk about is a counselor, who is an individual that will encourage you to love the Lord with all your mind.

I had a few older and wiser individuals speaking truth into my life during the darkest days of my marriage, which included Theresa Hesch (wife of Joel Hesch, author of *Proven Men*), a marriage counselor, as well as a few other godly women. They acted as lampposts along the way, illuminating a godly path to follow and helping me to see the "light at the end of the tunnel." All of these individuals shared a few things in common: a deep love for Jesus Christ and thriving marriages of twenty years or more.

My husband and I started our counseling journey by seeing a licensed marriage and family therapist over the course of a year and a half. At first, it was hard for my husband to go to counseling. A lot of men don't want to admit that they need help because they don't want to be perceived as weak. But we knew we needed major surgery to cut the cancer out of our relationship, and going to a counselor was the best thing we did for our marriage. It was an investment of time and money, but it was worth every second and penny.

WEEK 1 .... WEEK 2 .... WEEK 3 .... WEEK 4 .... WEEK 5 .... WEEK 6 .... WEEK 7 .... WEEK 8

DAY 5

A huge shift began to take place in our marriage as a result of intense counseling. We were able to verbalize our frustrations and concerns in a safe space with an unbiased third party. Our therapist cut through all the outer layers of our petty and cyclical arguments to expose the infectious lies and fears at the root. We learned powerful communication skills from him that we still use to this day.

I'll give you an example. One of the biggest fights we had during our "dark days" was about sharing meals when we went out to eat. I referenced it in my story in chapter 2. My husband and I got into a huge argument over sharing a meal, and our anniversary celebration turned into a disaster. We kept circling around the issue and it only escalated. During our counseling session, our therapist was able to boil it down to one important question that brought immense clarity: "Is your relationship with your husband worth $20?"

I was arguing with my husband to share a meal just so we could save $20. Sharing a meal triggered deep-seated fears for both of us, birthed out of our childhood poverty. My constant pushing to share a meal was perceived by him as an insult. It made him feel like I thought he couldn't take care of me financially. His constant pressure for both of us to get whatever we wanted off the menu triggered my fear of not having enough. As a child, I was always afraid we would run out of food, so I never liked eating out because I would think about how many grocery store meals could be purchased with that money.

Our responses to our childhood fears were competing with each other; one of us tried to control the fear by wanting to spend, the other by wanting to save. Once I realized that there was a deeper issue involved, and at the core of my husband's heart was a loving desire to care for me, I was willing to concede. I never thought about it that way. Of course, my marriage was worth an extra $20! The therapist helped me change my mind about something that I otherwise would have kept arguing about with my husband for years.

Our counselor pointed out that fear is at the root of every argument. Whenever we couldn't find a resolution on our own, he would ask the same question: "What fear button is being pushed?" That opened the door for us to discuss our fears and work together for a solution to avoid pushing each other's fear buttons.

Think about some of the arguments that you have over and over again with your spouse. The arguments that seem so petty, but you know that something deeper lies beneath the surface. Take a few moments to write out some specific details about a cyclical marital disagreement, the fight that you keep having over and over that never gets resolved. What fear button do you think is being pushed when you have that argument? What fear button do you think is being pushed for your husband?

_____

_____

_____

WEEK 1 .... WEEK 2 .... WEEK 3 .... WEEK 4 .... WEEK 5 .... WEEK 6 .... WEEK 7 .... WEEK 8

DAY 5

What do "fear buttons" have to do with loving God with all of your mind? Take a moment to consider where fear originates. In the mind, right? Fear starts with our thoughts, and then those fearful thoughts begin to consume us. The thoughts become actions, also known as "fight, flight, or freeze" responses.

If you truly love God with all your mind, there is no room for fear. 1 John 4:18 tells us that there is no fear in love; in fact, perfect love drives out fear. Loving God with all our minds means we choose to trust what we KNOW about His love. It's a deliberate decision to rest in His love instead of running with our fears.

Read through 1 John 4:7-21 below. As you read, circle every time you see the word "love." Underline every time you see the word "know."

> **7** Dear friends, let us continue to love one another, for love comes from God. Anyone who loves is a child of God and knows God. **8** But anyone who does not love does not know God, for God is love. **9** God showed how much he loved us by sending his one and only Son into the world so that we might have eternal life through him. **10** This is real love—not that we loved God, but that he loved us and sent his Son as a sacrifice to take away our sins. **11** Dear friends, since God loved us that much, we surely ought to love each other. **12** No one has ever seen God. But if we love each other, God lives in us, and his love is brought to full expression in us. **13** And God has given us his Spirit as proof that we live in him and he in us.
>
> **14** Furthermore, we have seen with our own eyes and now testify that the Father sent his Son to be the Savior of the world. **15** All who declare that Jesus is the Son of God have God living in them, and they live in God. **16** We know how much God loves us, and we have put our trust in his love. God is love, and all who live in love live in God, and God lives in them.
>
> **17** And as we live in God, our love grows more perfect. So we will not be afraid on the day of judgment, but we can face him with confidence because we live like Jesus here in this world. **18** Such love has no fear, because perfect love expels all fear. If we are afraid, it is for fear of punishment, and this shows that we have not fully experienced his perfect love. **19** We love each other because he loved us first. **20** If someone says, "I love God," but hates a fellow believer, that person is a liar; for if we don't love people we can see, how can we love God, whom we cannot see? **21** And he has given us this command: Those who love God must also love their fellow believers.

There's a lot of information to absorb here, but the main point is that if we KNOW God, then we will love God and, in turn, love others. The progression of knowing God to loving others looks like this:

1. We recognize God's deep love.
    "God showed how much he loved us by sending his one and only Son into the world so that we might have eternal life through him" (verse 10).

WEEK 1 .... WEEK 2 .... WEEK 3 .... WEEK 4 .... WEEK 5 .... WEEK 6 .... WEEK 7 .... WEEK 8

DAY 5

2. We put our trust in that love.
    "We know how much God loves us, and we have put our trust in his love" (verse 16).

3. Our love grows as we live and trust in Him.
    "As we live in God, our love grows more perfect" (verse 17).

4. The love we have received from God manifests itself through a deep love for others.
    "But if we love each other, God lives in us, and his love is brought to full expression in us" (verse 12).

Our love for others is proof that we both know and trust God. We come to know Him with our minds, we trust Him with our hearts (Proverbs 3:5-6), and then we love Him with our lives.

What do verses 9-11 say about how much God loves us? What happens when we recognize how deep His love is for us (verses 11, 16 and 19)?

_____

_____

_____

_____

God pursued you, loved you, died for you! The very things that you crave from your husband have already been given to you by God! He loved you first, and He loves you more than you can imagine. God has fulfilled the desire of every human heart to be known and loved. God knows you completely and loves you fully, and no one else in this world can even come close to caring for you in that way! In Him, we have more than our hearts could ever hope for or desire.

Take a few moments to journal about what this truth really means to you. In what ways do you want to better know God's love?

_____

_____

_____

WEEK 1 .... WEEK 2 .... WEEK 3 .... WEEK 4 .... WEEK 5 .... WEEK 6 .... WEEK 7 .... WEEK 8

DAY 5

_____

_____

_____

When we truly embrace God's love for us, when we acknowledge with our minds what that truly means, then we can walk through life without fear. What does verse 18 tell us that love does to fear?

_____

_____

_____

The word "perfect" in this verse may be intimidating. How can we learn to be perfect in love? Only God is perfect. Perfect in this verse doesn't mean without flaw, it just means to come to completion or to be fully grown. God's love was made perfect, or complete, by His death on the cross. As a result, we don't have to live in fear of punishment because He took on the weight of our sin at the cross.

His love gets perfected in us over time as we live in Him. As His children, we begin to learn that we don't have to be controlled by fear because our lives are in the hands of a God that loves without exception and without end. We can cast our fears and anxiety on Him because we know He cares for us (1 Peter 5:7).

Our verse for today, 2 Timothy 1:7, says that God has not given us a spirit of fear. What three things has He given?

_____

_____

_____

What fears are getting in the way of you experiencing God's power, His love, and a sound mind?

_____

_____

_____

_____

WEEK 1 .... WEEK 2 .... WEEK 3 .... WEEK 4 .... WEEK 5 .... WEEK 6 .... WEEK 7 ....  WEEK 8

DAY 5

One of my deepest fears when I found out about my husband's sexual addiction was that he was going to abandon me. In fact, it's a deep fear that has been in my psyche ever since I was a child. Both my parents were abandoned by their fathers, and I think deep down I had a fear that the same thing would happen to me. The nagging fear was that anyone I loved would eventually abandon me, leaving me alone and unloved.

The beauty of the gospel is that Jesus Christ's sacrifice means you are never alone or unloved. You don't have to walk in fear because He promised to never leave you or forsake you (Hebrews 13:5). Even if your husband never repents of his addiction, even if he cheats on you, even if he abandons you, even if your marriage ends... God's love never changes. He is with you to the end. God's unfailing love casts out every fear.

Loving God with all your mind means choosing to believe that He loved you first and loves you most. When you are in Christ, you don't have to walk in fear of judgment, punishment or abandonment. He pursued you in love and sacrificed Himself for you. That knowledge allows us to walk in freedom to love others without fear of how they can hurt us because we are secure in God's faithful love.

As we come to the end of this study, you still may have some deep and real fears. Sexual addiction thrives on fear. The fear of being judged, caught, condemned, and ashamed keeps the addict in hiding. The fear of being alone, unloved, and taken advantage of keeps the wife in hopelessness. KNOW that God loves you. KNOW that He doesn't want you to be held captive to fear. Choose to lay down your fears and anxieties at His feet, believing that His love is complete and that He is with you every step of the journey.

Who can you ask to help remind you of this truth? Who has God put in your life that will encourage you to love God with all your heart, soul, strength and mind? Do you need to spend a few hours with a trusted friend? Maybe you need some direction from a pastor or spiritual mentor. Or perhaps you need to confess some sinful thoughts and behaviors to an accountability partner. Or it might be necessary to have a counselor to step in so that you can see what fears are being pushed to the surface through this difficult season of marriage.

The journey doesn't end with this study. God wants to continue to reveal Himself to you and to your husband. He desires healing and wholeness and is perfecting His love in you through this difficult season.

As we end today, pray out loud to God. Confess to Him your fears. Ask Him to destroy your fears with His love. Pray something like this:

> God, I love you. I trust you. I choose to lay down my fears at your feet. I don't know what the future holds, but I know that you hold it in your hands. I choose to rest in your faithful love. I believe that you loved me enough to die for me, and that you love my husband too. Help me to love the way you do. I trust you, God.

WEEK 1 .... WEEK 2 .... WEEK 3 .... WEEK 4 .... WEEK 5 .... WEEK 6 .... WEEK 7 .... WEEK 8

DAY 5

CHARGE

I will take responsibility for what I can influence. I will prioritize my marriage only after Jesus and I will guard it.

*Congratulations! You have finished the study. Our experience has been that lasting healing comes when you regularly revisit this material and continue to do the important "heartwork" the study helps to facilitate. Therefore, we encourage you to consider making a plan to walk through the study again alongside a different woman or group of women this time. If you have a person in mind, reach out today and ask them if they'd be interested in doing the study with you. Also, please consider joining our ministry support team by financially supporting our ministry with a generous tax-deductible donation. You can learn more about partnership opportunities at our website: *www.ProvenMen.org* or *www.ProvenWomen.org*

AFTERWORD

I love the beach. I grew up in the Philadelphia area, so at least once a summer we would go "down the shore" for a day filled with sun, surf and sand. The New Jersey beaches were crowded, littered with cigarette butts, and you had to pay to get access, but I still loved it. The sounds and smells are so intoxicating to me... the steady crash of the waves on the shoreline, the salty smell of the air... it's like my life's story is immediately flipped back to the first few chapters every time I go to the beach.

While the ocean is terrifically beautiful and relaxing, it can also be terrifying. I shudder thinking about being stuck out in the middle of the ocean during a storm in the dark. I appreciate the strength of the waves and the power of the current. While on vacation this year as we were listening to the sounds of the ocean below our hotel room, my husband and I watched footage from the 2004 tsunami in Thailand. The devastation that came from one single wave is mind blowing. The ocean is an uncontrollable, unmanageable force.

Marriage is so often like the ocean. It's deceptively beautiful. Before we get married, we imagine our future will look like the beach on a perfect summer day. The postcard snapshot with the sun rising, hues of peaches and pinks splashed across the horizon as they meet the clear blue waves. But in reality, most days marriage is a struggle. We get sand in our bathing suit. We step on a jellyfish or a broken shell. We wait for hours to catch a great wave, but find ourselves bored and disinterested as the tiny swells roll in. Or the waves are perfect, but our timing isn't, and we watch others gleefully ride the tide, leaving us behind. We walk away from what we expected to be the best experience of our lives, burnt, sore, tired and sweaty. It looks nothing like the postcard image.

While on vacation, I was watching my two teenagers ride their boogie boards. I stood on the shore, smiling from ear to ear as they caught the waves. My favorite moment was when they caught a wave together and they both laughed out loud as they rode in tandem back to the shore, spontaneously high-fived, and then rushed back out to give it another try. It reminded me of a moment a few years ago when the same thing happened to my husband and I. We managed, after hours of trying, to ride the perfect wave in together. We laughed as we looked at each other glide to shore on our matching pink and blue boogie boards.

Why this long homage to the beach and boogie boarding? If I took the time to really think about it, boogie boarding seems to be more effort than it's worth. Experience has taught me that catching an awesome wave is a lot of work and takes a lot of time. You need the perfect combination of good weather, reliable equipment, physical ability, and a large amount of patience. Why even bother?

Because when you finally do catch the perfect wave, the euphoria in that moment is indescribable. And the struggle it took to get there makes it even more beautiful. Marriage is just like that. Because of the sinful world we live in, most days will be filled with struggles and distractions that will leave us tired and confused, ready to quit. Some days you will fail and will get knocked down repeatedly by the surf. Some days will just be mundane and tiresome. You'll get water up your nose and sand in your bathing suit.

But if you keep pressing on, willing to fight each day, you'll catch that perfect wave. You'll look over at your husband and recognize that the long hours, the struggles, and the exhaustion were all worth it.

My husband and I want to keep going out there. Every day is a new chance to grab our boards, put on some protective sunscreen and hit the waves. When we get lost or tired, we will find someone close by who can offer help. And when we see others struggling to stay afloat, we will lend a helping hand.

I hope to hear stories from you, as you push through the pain and struggle, when you finally "catch a wave" in tandem with your husband, riding it to shore. I think that God smiles when He sees us finally get it, when we finally grasp how much He loves us and how much He wants us to show that love to others. And He doesn't get mad when we fall... He watches and waits to celebrate with us when we succeed.

Your husband is a gift, and your relationship with him provides daily opportunities for you to learn what true love really looks like. It may not be the postcard version you had in mind, but it can actually be so much richer and truer than you could have ever imagined. Keep pressing in closer to Jesus, the true lover of your soul.

We began day one with a prayer from the book of Ephesians, and we end this study with another prayer from the same book. It's my prayer for you and for your husband.

> Ephesians 3:14-21
> For this reason, I kneel before the Father, from whom every family in heaven and on earth derives its name. I pray that out of his glorious riches he may **strengthen you with power through his Spirit in your inner being**, so that Christ may **dwell in your hearts** through faith. And I pray that you, being **rooted and established in love**, may have power, together with all the Lord's holy people, to grasp **how wide and long and high and deep is the love of Christ**, and to know this **love that surpasses knowledge**—that you may be filled to the measure of all the **fullness of God**. Now to him who is able to do **immeasurably more than all we ask or imagine**, according to his **power that is at work within us**, to him be glory in the church and in Christ Jesus throughout all generations, for ever and ever! Amen.

My Dear Sister,

As Proven Ministries continues to grow, we have been immensely blessed to hear of countless women who have discovered freedom and healing. This is no small feat, and such personal experiences of victory have the capability to inspire and offer hope to a great many. As God is the Master Storyteller, we believe that each child of His is made with a custom-tailored story in mind. There are no two alike, and with each story rests the potential for a triumphant testimony to be found. Such testimonies can be used to shine a light on all those who have been hiding in the dark for so long. I wanted to personally ask you if you would share your testimony with our team. Your testimony of how the Proven Wives Devotional has supported your journey toward restoration and freedom could be used to inspire thousands. If you feel led to share your story to help others, please email your testimony to *info@provenmen.org.*

Do not be anxious about anything, but in every situation, by prayer and petition, with thanksgiving, present your requests to God. And the peace of God, which transcends all understanding, will guard your hearts and minds in Christ Jesus.

Philippians 4:6-7

Whom have I in heaven but you? and earth has nothing I desire besides you. My flesh and my heart may fail, but God is the strength of my heart and my portion forever.

Psalm 73:25-26

For we do not have a high priest who is unable to empathize with our weaknesses, but we have one who has been tempted in every way, just as we are— yet He did not sin. Let us then approach God's throne of grace with confidence, so that we may receive mercy and find grace to help us in our time of need.

Hebrews 4:15-16

Each one of you must love his wife as he loves himself, & the wife must respect her husband.

Ephesians 5:33

APPENDIX A: WHY JESUS?

This study is intended to help you find joy and hope in the midst of what feels like a disaster. Healing can be found for both you and your spouse if you feel lost in the powerful grip of pornography. While there are countless self-help books available on forgiveness and marriage, none of the recommended techniques will bring the true healing that your soul craves without Christ's redemptive power.

This study is NOT intended to be a "how to get your husband to stop looking at porn in eight weeks." Ideally, your husband will be journeying through the Proven Men study, which emphasizes the only true path for healing through a relationship with Christ. But, if your spouse decides not to pursue wholeness through Jesus, there is still hope for you. This study will show you how you are complete in His love, whether or not your husband ever turns from his sin and toward Christ. Biblical truth is the cornerstone for the next seven weeks of this study, and the entire Proven series rests on the power of the gospel to transform lives.

In order to find lasting hope and healing that both you and your spouse long for, you need to:

1. Invite Jesus to be your Savior.

2. Give Him permission to be in control of your entire life.

JESUS AS SAVIOR
When God created man and woman, He had a divine purpose for an eternal relationship with each one of us. Unfortunately, Adam and Eve sinned, and that decision brought sin and death into the human narrative. All of us, like them, choose to sin on a daily basis. The consequence for our sin is death. But we have a God who was willing to sacrifice all to give us life.

Over two thousand years ago, God sent His Son, Jesus Christ, into the world. He led a selfless, sinless life, and then he gave Himself as the perfect sacrifice through death on a cross. He then rose again three days later, conquering death (Luke 24:1-7).

> 1 John 4:10—This is love: not that we loved God, but that he loved us and sent his Son as an atoning sacrifice for our sins.

> Romans 5:8—God demonstrates His love for us in this: While we were still sinners, Christ died for us.

> 2 Corinthians 5:21—God made him who had no sin to be sin for us, so that in him we might become the righteousness of God.

Each one of these verses shows how God pursues us, even though we are undeserving. We were helpless to fix the problem on our own, and He lovingly stepped in and rescued us.

> Ephesians 2:8-9—For it is by grace you have been saved, through faith—and this is not from yourselves, it is the gift of God— not by works, so that no one can boast.

God provides each one of us with the gift of salvation, and desires that none of us should die (2 Peter 3:9). His gift is unearned, given with love, and comes with no strings attached. We simply must choose to accept the gift.

> Romans 10:9-10—If you declare with your mouth, "Jesus is Lord," and believe in your heart that God raised him from the dead, you will be saved. For it is with your heart that you believe and are justified, and it is with your mouth that you profess your faith and are saved.

> John 3:16—For God so loved the world that He gave his one and only Son, that whoever believes in Him shall not perish but have eternal life.

When we choose to accept Jesus' sacrifice on the cross as the only way to receive forgiveness of sin, God doesn't just leave us there. He also adopts us as His sons and daughters and gives us the gift of the Holy Spirit to guide us through life.

> Romans 8:14-17—Those who are led by the Spirit of God are the children of God. The Spirit you received does not make you slaves, so that you live in fear again; rather, the Spirit you received brought about your adoption to sonship. And by him we cry, *"Abba,* Father." The Spirit himself testifies with our spirit that we are God's children. Now if we are children, then we are heirs— heirs of God and co-heirs with Christ, if indeed we share in his sufferings in order that we may also share in his glory.

His transforming power brings freedom and security. We can walk in confidence through life because we know the Creator of the world is also our Abba, or Daddy—the perfect Father who desires to work all things together for our good (Romans 8:28-29). His power is at work within us through the Holy Spirit, filling us with love and hope (Romans 5:5, 15:13).

If you have not yet decided to receive God's gift of salvation, don't wait another minute. He desires to have a relationship with you, one that is motivated out of a deep love unlike any we can ever experience here on earth.

Here is a suggested prayer to give words to your faith:

God, I recognize that I am a sinner and deserve death. I believe that you love me, so much that you sent your only Son to die on the cross to rescue me from the penalty of my sins. Please forgive me. I want to be your daughter, to walk with you through this life and forever. I ask you to change my heart through the power of your Holy Spirit. I believe in you today and trust you as my Savior. In the name of Jesus, Amen.

If you just prayed this prayer, you are now God's child, and have stepped from death into life! Right now, the angels are rejoicing over your decision to repent (Luke 15:10). You are equipped with the power of the Holy Spirit to guide you and comfort you every day.

This life-changing decision is the foundation for hope and healing within every aspect of your life, including your marriage. The Holy Spirit that is in you is greater than the powers of this world (1 John 4:4). If your husband is not a believer, don't despair. God can use you in his life, especially through your response to his addiction and your willingness to partner with him (1 Peter 3:1-2).

APPENDIX B

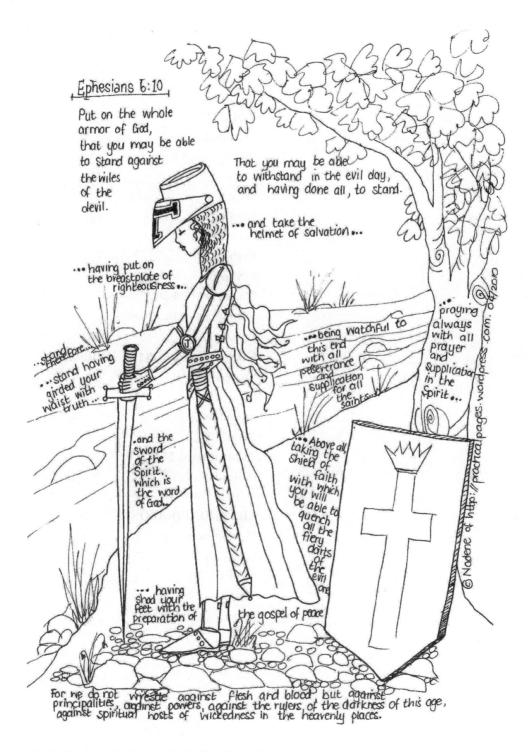

Used with permission from artist Nadene Esterhuizen.

GUILT

Psalm 103:12

2 Corinthians 5:17

Ephesians 1:7

Hebrews 8:12

1 John 1:9

FEAR/ANXIETY

Joshua 1:9

Isaiah 26:3

Psalm 4:8

Psalm 27:1

Psalm 56:3

2 Timothy 1:7

1 Peter 5:7

HOPELESS

Psalm 31:24

Psalm 62:5-7

Psalm 147:11

Romans 15:13

Hebrews 6:19

Lamentations 3:22-23

UNLOVED

Psalm 94:18-19

Jeremiah 31:3

John 3:16

Romans 5:8

1 John 3:1

DEPRESSION/SADNESS

Nehemiah 8:10

Psalm 40:1-3

Psalm 42:5

Psalm 147:3

John 16:33

Philippians 4:8

WEAK

Isaiah 40:31

Isaiah 41:10

Psalm 18:1

Psalm 28:7

Matthew 11:28-30

Philippians 4:13

CONFUSED/LACKING DIRECTION

Proverbs 3:5-6

Isaiah 55:8

Jeremiah 29:11

John 14:26

1 Corinthians 14:33

James 1:5

ABANDONED/ALONE

Deuteronomy 31:6

Isaiah 43:2

Psalm 27:10

Matthew 28:20

Romans 8:38-3

What are some of the things you struggle with? Here is a space for you to do your own research. Write down the lie you wrestle with and then a few corresponding verses to combat it.

_____

_____

_____

_____

_____

_____

_____

_____

_____

_____

_____

_____

_____

_____

TEN TIPS FOR MEMORIZING BIBLE VERSES

1. Choose a verse to memorize that speaks to something in your life right now.

A Bible verse that's relevant to what you're going through is easier to memorize than one that speaks to a topic that's abstract to you.

2. Start small.

Choose a short verse to start with... and make it even shorter by breaking it down into pieces. Memorize the first five words in the verse first, and when you've got them down, add the next five. As you become more confident, you can add more words, sentences, and even entire verses—but don't add anything new until you've got the previous words down pat.

3. Write it down.

A vast majority of Bible Gateway fans suggested this simple strategy: *Write the verse you're memorizing down on paper.* But don't just write it once; write it many times—five or ten times is a good start (and some people write out their memory verses up to fifty times!). Physically writing the words out is an extremely useful tactile memory aid.

4. Say it out loud.

Just as writing a verse out can help in memorizing it, so speaking the words aloud is an excellent way to burn them into your memory. One person suggested turning the radio off during your commute to work or school each day and reciting your memory verse out loud instead!

5. Incorporate the verse into your prayers.

When you pray, include elements of the verse in your words to God. Pray that God will help you understand and apply the verse to your life. Pray for God's help in fixing the verse in your heart and mind.

6. Put it everywhere.

Many people suggested writing your memory verse out on multiple index cards or sticky notes (combine this with tip #3 above!) and putting them all over the place, so that you'll see the verse many times throughout your day. Tape the verse to your bathroom mirror or computer monitor. Tuck it into your purse, lunch sack, car glove compartment, school textbook, pockets... anywhere you'll see it. One person suggested making the verse your computer desktop background, and another goes so far as to laminate the verse and hang it in the shower!

7. Use music to help.

Do you find it much easier to remember lyrics than spoken words? Try setting the Bible verse to a simple tune (perhaps repurposing a song you already know well) that you can sing to yourself. (If this sounds like a strange suggestion, consider that many famous hymns and worship songs use Bible verses as their lyrics and were written specifically as aids for Bible verse memorization.)

8. Make it a game.

Turn the act of memorizing into a personal challenge! You might write the verse out on flashcards, leaving keywords blank, and quiz yourself. Get some friends or family members to help quiz you, or even to memorize the verse along with you and encourage/challenge you.

9. Translate the verse into a different language.
This tip isn't for everyone, obviously, but several Bible Gateway fans suggested that if you're comfortable in more than one language, try translating your verse into a different language. Translation requires an intense focus on the meaning and language of a verse—an obvious help for memorization.

10. Repeat, repeat, repeat!
Whatever strategy you follow in memorizing a Bible verse, *do it repeatedly.* Write it down, speak it out loud, sing it out, pray it—but whatever you do, do it over and over until it's a natural, reflexive action. The goal isn't to reduce it to a mindless, repeated activity, but to slowly press the verse into your memory through repetition. Repeat your memorization activity over the course of several hours, days, or even weeks to pace yourself—there's no prize for memorizing a Bible verse fastest; the point is to internalize it over time. And that means you shouldn't be discouraged if it takes awhile for the verse to "stick"—keep at it, and it *will* take root!

If you've never tried memorizing a Bible verse before, it's much easier than you think! Pick one or two of the strategies above and give them a try, adapting your strategy as you figure out what does and doesn't work for you. One thing is certain: you'll never regret spending more time focusing intently on God's Word. And there's nothing quite so wonderful as an encouraging Bible verse springing forth from memory at just the time you need to hear it.

Adapted from Bible Gateway.

APPENDIX E

FOR THIS REASON I KNEEL BEFORE THE FATHER, FROM WHOM EVERY FAMILY IN HEAVEN AND ON EARTH DERIVES ITS NAME. I PRAY THAT OUT OF HIS GLORIOUS RICHES HE MAY **STRENGTHEN YOU WITH POWER** THROUGH HIS SPIRIT IN YOUR **INNER BEING,** SO THAT CHRIST MAY **DWELL IN YOUR HEARTS** THROUGH FAITH.

AND I PRAY THAT YOU, BEING **ROOTED AND ESTABLISHED IN LOVE,** MAY HAVE POWER, TOGETHER WITH ALL THE LORD'S HOLY PEOPLE, TO **GRASP HOW WIDE AND LONG AND HIGH AND DEEP IS THE LOVE OF CHRIST,** AND TO KNOW THIS LOVE THAT SURPASSES KNOWLEDGE-THAT YOU MAY BE **FILLED TO THE MEASURE OF ALL THE FULLNESS OF GOD.**

NOW TO **HIM WHO IS ABLE** TO DO **IMMEASURABLY MORE** THAN ALL WE **ASK OR IMAGINE,** ACCORDING TO **HIS POWER THAT IS AT WORK WITHIN US,** TO HIM BE GLORY IN THE CHURCH AND IN CHRIST JESUS THROUGHOUT ALL GENERATIONS, FOR EVER AND EVER!
AMEN.
Ephesians 3:14-21

APPENDIX F

What is sexual abuse?

Sexual abuse involves any contact or interaction whereby a vulnerable person is used for the sexual stimulation of an older, stronger, or more influential person.

Sexual abuse is much broader than forced, unforced, or simulated intercourse. It includes any touching, rubbing, or patting that is meant to arouse sexual pleasure in the offender. It may also involve visual, verbal, or psychological interaction where there is no physical contact.

Visual sexual abuse may involve exposing a victim to pornography or to any other sexually provocative scene (including exposure to showering, intercourse, or various states of undress).

Verbal sexual abuse involves an attempt to seduce or shame a child (or anyone) by the use of sexual or suggestive words.

Psychological sexual abuse includes interactions where a child is regularly used to play the role of an adult spouse, confidant, or counselor. For example, a mother who tells her twelve-year-old son her sexual frustrations with her father, and shares her deep thoughts and feelings with him in a way that invites him to a level of adult intimacy, has violated the young man's sexual identity.

As quoted from Dan Allender. The *Discovery Series*. Distributed by RBC ministries.[1]

APPENDIX G

Chart from Search for Significance

FALSE BELIEFS	CONSEQUENCES OF SPECIFIC BELIEFS	GOD'S SPECIFIC SOLUTION	RESULTS OF GOD'S SOLUTION
The Performance Trap **I must meet certain standards to feel good about myself.**	The fear of failure; perfectionism; drive to succeed; manipulation of others to achieve success; withdrawal from healthy risks	**Justification**—God not only has forgiven me of my sins, but also has granted me the righteousness of Christ. Because of justification, **I am completely forgiven and fully pleasing to God.** I no longer have to fear failure (Romans 5:1).	Increasing freedom from the fear of failure; desire to pursue the right things; Christ and His kingdom; love for Christ.
Approval Addict **I must be approved by certain others to feel good about myself.**	The fear of rejection; attempts to please others at any cost; overly sensitive to criticism; withdrawal from others to avoid disapproval.	**Reconciliation**— Although I was at one time hostile toward God and alienated from Him, I am now forgiven and have been brought into an intimate relationship with Him. **I am totally accepted by God** (Colossians 1:21-22).	Increasing freedom from the fear of rejection; willingness to be open and vulnerable; able to relax around others; willingness to take criticism; desire to please God no matter what others think.
Blame Game **Those who fail (including myself) are unworthy of love and deserve to be punished.**	The fear of punishment; punishing others; blaming others for personal failure; withdrawal from God and others; drive to avoid failure.	**Propitiation**— Christ satisfied God's wrath by His death on the cross. **I am deeply loved by God** (1 John 4:9-11).	Increasing freedom from the fear of punishment; patience and kindness toward others; being quick to apply forgiveness; deep love for Christ.
Shame **I am what I am. I cannot change. I am hopeless.**	Feelings of shame, hopelessness, and inferiority; passivity; loss of creativity; isolation; withdrawal from others.	**Regeneration**— I am a new creation in Christ. **I am absolutely complete in Christ** (John 3:3-6).	Christ-centered self-confidence; joy, courage, peace; desire to know Christ.

APPENDIX H–HOPE STUDY

I've mentioned before that I did a Bible study on the word "hope" that carried me through one of the toughest seasons of my life. These verses spoke life and truth into my depressed and desperate heart. This appendix includes the passages I studied from the book of Psalms. The writers of this book speak with true human emotion, which I found very comforting. This compilation would be a great place for you to go after you finish this study, as well as reading the book *Hope After Betrayal.*[1] Truly, our only lasting hope is in Christ alone. I pray that these Scriptures will both encourage and challenge your heart as you look to Jesus for hope.

You should grab a notebook or journal for your study and date each day. That will help you remember what God has spoken specifically to you through different seasons and how He has sustained and matured you.

If you've never studied Scripture on your own, or if you are looking for a method to help you dive deeper into the Word, I love the five P's that author and teacher Priscilla Shirer recommends[2]. It's been wonderful for me and perhaps will be beneficial for you.

POSITION: Get away from all the distractions, somewhere alone and quiet, so you can completely focus on what God wants to speak to you. Pray before you get started.

Psalm 25:4-5, "Show me your ways, Lord, teach me your paths. Guide me in your truth and teach me, for you are God my Savior, and my hope is in you all day long."

PARAPHRASE: Focus on quality, not quantity. Pore over the passage you are studying, carefully reading and considering what it says. Then put down briefly what the passage is saying, paraphrasing the major points.

PULL: Spiritualize the points that you just read. What do you think God is trying to teach? Is there a command to keep, a promise revealed, a character trait of God to discover?

POSE: Look at the spiritual principles and turn them into the form of a personally directed question. Am I heeding that command? Do I believe God is who He says He is in this passage of Scripture?

PLAN: Come up with a specific strategy on how you are going to apply and obey what you have learned.

I'll give an example of my own study at the end of the list, so you can see it in action.

As you go through these Psalms, make sure to read the entire chapter for context (so important when reading Scripture!). I've included the verses that specifically talk about hope in parentheses.

SCRIPTURES TO STUDY

Psalm 13 (verses 5–6)

Psalm 43 (verse 5)

Psalm 16 (verse 9)

Psalm 71 (verses 5, 14)

Psalm 31 (verse 24)

Psalm 119:49-56

Psalm 33 (verses 18, 22)

Psalm 119:105-120 (verses 114, 116)

Psalm 38 (verse 15)

Psalm 130 (verses 5, 7)

Psalm 39 (verse 7)

Psalm 146 (verse 5)

Psalm 42 (verse 5)

Psalm 147 (verse 11)

PSALM 71

POSITION: I usually do my Bible study in the morning, right after my kids are off to school. That way I don't get distracted by all the details of what I need to accomplish for the day. My favorite spot is in the living room, right next to our big window. I've got my Bible and journal sitting on the coffee table, waiting for me each morning.

PARAPHRASE: God, you are my safe place. Since my childhood, I have trusted in You. I praise you all day, for you are my strength. Remember me, even when I am old and gray. Prove my enemies wrong, show up for me so that they will shut up. I will constantly hope in You and will tell others what you have done to save me. My whole life you have been my guide, and I will tell of your awesomeness to those who follow after me. You are righteous and there is no one like You. Even though You have allowed difficulties to come my way, you have restored and comforted me. I will praise you all day, God, and tell others what you have done in my life.

PULL: God's faithful character is revealed in this Psalm. He allows us to experience struggles, but He is our strength in the midst of the pain. This Psalm challenges me to maintain hope, through my youth and old age, knowing that God will never stop guiding me. He has done amazing things, and He is what truly sustains me every day.

POSE: Do I "always have hope?" Do I "praise God more and more" like the Psalmist says in verse 14? Do I believe that He is my strength and that He will restore me after times of great struggle (verse 20)?

PLAN: Today I will take some time to "praise God more and more." I will praise Him for His faithfulness to me since my childhood. I will find someone to tell about God's mighty power in my life.

I encourage you to continue on through the rest of the Bible in your word study. There are SO MANY wonderful passages that talk about our hope in Christ. Grab your concordance in the back of your Bible; you'll find some of the more well-known passages there. Online concordances are helpful as well. I recommend organizations like Bible Study Tools and Learn The Bible.

APPENDIX I—GIRL TALK

We didn't talk about sex much while growing up. In a house filled with four girls, our "girl talk" never really included the "sex talk." My mom had some difficult experiences in her own childhood that made it difficult for her to talk about sex. In fact, we never even used the correct anatomical word when discussing our reproductive parts. We were told our vagina was called a "pee-she." According to urban legend, my husband was the one to finally convince me that it was actually called a vagina.

As a growing teenager with a lot of curiosity about my body and my own sexuality, I wasn't sure where to turn. I was nervous about intercourse but also knew that I had sexual desires that I hoped would be fulfilled one day by my husband.

Perhaps you have felt the same way or feel that way now. No one ever really explained to you how sex was supposed to work, or how you were supposed to feel sexually as a woman. Is it possible to experience pleasure during intercourse, and is that even OK? What if I've never had an orgasm? Is it OK to fake it? According to Meg Ryan in her famous scene from *When Harry Met Sally*[1], "most women at one time or another have faked it." But why? And when men discover the truth about fake orgasms, as Billy Crystal's character did, how damaging is it to their ego?

I want to address something that is truly important when it comes to a healthy sex life: communication. Because the male and female sexual organs are so very different, it's impossible for us to completely understand how to please our partner without talking about what makes us feel good sexually.

One of the most important things you need to know about your body is that you may not be able to achieve an orgasm through intercourse alone. This is a common misconception and part of the reason why, I believe, women fake orgasm. No man wants to think that he is incompetent in his lovemaking skills, and bringing a woman to orgasm is part of that success for him. After continual frustration, women eventually just begin to fake it so that they can "get it over with" and avoid making their significant other feel useless in the process.

According to the health professionals from Columbia University who make up the "Go Ask Alice!" panel, a simple anatomy lesson can unlock the answers to our questions and frustrations.

> "Many women experience frustration from their inability to feel sensation or sexual pleasure from vaginal-penile intercourse. It is common for women to feel closeness, and fullness, but not the intensity they believe that they 'should' be feeling.

> "A woman's sexual pleasure, and ultimately orgasm, is much more likely to occur from stimulation to the clitoris. The clitoris is highly sensitive and full of nerve endings. In fact, there are as many nerve endings in the tip of the clitoris as there are in a man's penis! Many of the clitoral nerve endings are subterranean, or below the surface; the visible part of the clitoris is just the

tip of the iceberg. However, even 'in hiding,' those 6,000 to 8,000 sensory nerve endings can be a mega source of incredible pleasure for many women.

"In contrast, the vaginal walls contain relatively few nerve endings. Only the lower third of the vagina has enough nerve endings to feel stimulation from a penis, finger, sex toy, or other penetrative object. This can make intense sexual stimulation, pleasure, and orgasm from vaginal-only penetration unlikely. In reality, the clitoris is perfectly placed. You might consider the clitoris to be "inaccessible" because in-and-out intercourse does not touch your button of joy. The challenge is for you and your partner to find and cultivate its potential."

It's important to know that your body isn't dysfunctional if you've never had an orgasm. It takes time and a willingness to learn and explore. Don't be afraid to try new things, to ask questions, to speak up when something feels great or not good at all. Ask him the same questions about his body, showing that you are interested in his satisfaction as well.

Sex is so much better when you are experiencing it to its fullest. I love that God created the female anatomy differently from the man's. It requires that the husband and wife take the time and effort to learn about one another and then fulfill each other's desires (in a respectful and selfless manner).

Go Ask Alice offers a few other practical tidbits:[2]

"Remember, if you are generally satisfied with your sexual activity, there is no need to be dismayed by your lack of vaginal sensation or feel pressured to feel pleasure or orgasm during intercourse. Instead, if you wish, you can view and use sex play as an opportunity for you and your partner to experiment with and learn from your bodies. Either way, it is important to verbally let your partner know what turns you on the most. And remember, it may take time to learn exactly what that is.

"The key is to have the confidence that your body is perfect, the courage to explore your individual responses on your own, the trust to share this information with a caring partner, and the humor to laugh as you learn together. You never know what the results could be!"

And, you may not believe it, but the Bible actually offers up some practical sex advice too! It even goes as far as to recommend a sexual position that may be something you want to try. Song of Solomon 2:6 says, "His left arm is under my head, and his right arm embraces me."

The husband and wife are laying next to each other in bed, and he has gently placed his left hand under her head. With his right arm he is embracing her, caressing her naked body. He has the ability to kiss and touch her at the same time, stimulating multiple parts of her body simultaneously. She feels cherished and honored as he takes the time to awaken her sexual desires. God cares enough about your sexuality that He included a "how-to" section about it in His Word!

If you are willing to take the time to unlock your body's sexual "code," you will find that your desire to have sex will increase and your husband will be affirmed in his masculinity. Deep down every man wants to know that he has what it takes to please his woman. You have to be willing to tell him, even if it's awkward and uncomfortable at first. It's so worth it! God desires for you to be fulfilled sexually. He created sex for a purpose and He wants you to enjoy it!

If you want to learn more about how your body works and how God designed for you to have a healthy and fulfilling sex life, here are three great books that are biblically based and very informative.

Intimate Issues by Linda Dilow and Lorraine Pintus

Intended for Pleasure by Ed and Gaye Wheat

Intimacy Ignited by Joseph and Linda Dillow, Peter and Lorraine Pintus

APPENDIX J (BY JOEL & THERESA HESCH)

Word for Wives—A Wife's Perspective

As a feeling-oriented woman, it's hard for me to put my feelings aside. In the face of this betrayal, I have to admit that a protective part of me was screaming, "Run! Give up on this marriage!"

As hard as it is not to run or give up in the face of such betrayal, we must never lose sight of the fact that the two greatest commands given by our precious Lord and Savior are to "love the Lord your God with all your heart, with all your soul, and with all your mind" and to "love your neighbor as yourself" (Matthew 22:36-40).

You might be wondering how you can love a husband who has betrayed you. It's important to remember that all marriages go through rough times. Marriage is a proving ground and perfecter of our faith. Whatever else happens, it is important to continually keep a God-focused life.

Remember that, as much as God loves you, you're just as depraved as the next human being (including your husband). We all are sinners. We all fall short in the eyes of a perfectly holy God.

As women, we tend to focus on the person causing us pain and lose sight of God in the process. When we focus on the sins of others, we cannot see what God is trying to show us about Himself. Therefore, we must commit to being passionate for the Lord, because to live at peace and have contentment in this world, regardless of circumstances, requires that we have an intimate, daily relationship with Jesus. He will enable you to love and even trust again.

Next, there is hope for restoration. God changes hearts and lives. But please know this: You cannot do it for your husband—nor are you expected to! If you try to take on too much responsibility, then you enable him to stay in the place where he is at, instead of him relying on God for the strength he needs. On the other hand, if you're too distant and see this as solely his problem, you won't be able to see what God can and wants to do in your life and in your husband's life through this struggle.

Certainly, you want a man who goes after God's heart … a PROVEN man. But don't expect or demand a PERFECT man. God wants to restore people, but He takes them at a pace they can handle. Your privilege as a wife is to be a helpmate. Help means just that—"help."

You're not to take care of it for him, nor are you to ignore or refuse any role in the healing process. This frees you up to let God work in your husband's life and in your marriage.

I know that your pain is real. But please guard against the fantasy that your marriage (or your life) should be pain-free or that this pain is worse than other trials and struggles you will have on earth. Yes, marriage is painful. Yes, marriage is hard work, but marriage also is a wonderful and purposeful institution sanctioned by God.

It's better to know the truth, as difficult as it may be to hear it. Beyond your husband's confession, there is another truth to face: There is no guarantee that—even if you do everything right—your husband will stop. Instead, your anchor of hope must be in God and the faithfulness of God—not your husband—and not based upon the outcome of this struggle.

With all of this in mind, there are some suggestions I would like to make. These are lessons I learned with God, the God who cares about the outcome, the God who says we have inherited his wisdom.

IT'S A "WE PROBLEM"

As for all issues in marriage, your husband's fight for sexual integrity is a "we problem," not a "he problem." You should be actively involved in the process. Consider reading books written by wives who have gone through the same struggles. One very practical book along those lines is *Living with Your Husband's Secret Wars* by Marsha Means. Another good book, one written by a wife of a former sex addict, is *Through Deep Waters: Letters to Hurting Wives* by Kathy Gallagher. In addition, read this book and other books your husband reads as he strives for purity so that you'll grow with him (not so you can point out his shortcomings).

Become a part of his healing process. Don't just focus on areas where he fails to live up to your expectations. But, please remember to encourage him when he succeeds. Be interested and active, but in a loving and gentle way. In addition, be patient during this process. It will take some time for the pain to subside and for full trust to be rebuilt. For instance, try not to be overly suspicious when your husband comes home a few minutes late.

Get together with other women; you're not alone, so don't isolate. If your husband reacts about telling others, ask him to read this book, including this chapter. At the same time, remember this is a matter of great shame to your husband. Be respectful and loving toward him and in your conversations with others. Generally, you should avoid telling your parents about it (at least not the full extent of his sins), because they may not welcome or forgive him even long after you forgive your husband and are doing better.

If you feel the need, it's okay to ask your husband to attend marriage counseling. It's important that you both are moving forward together, and sometimes a coach can be helpful in the process.

FOCUS ON YOUR OWN SPIRITUAL GROWTH

It's important that you use this time as an opportunity for reflection and spiritual growth. Ask the Lord what He is trying to teach you. Even if you feel like you are a victim of your husband's issues, you have issues too.

Begin by focusing on your own shortcomings and sins. For instance, have you been angry, bossy, bitter, or nit-picky? These things affect you and your husband spiritually. They should be acknowledged and confessed as sin. The natural tendency is to focus on the sins of your husband; i.e., if he were not selfish I would not have to complain. Make it your goal to restore your relationship with both Jesus and your husband, and don't let anger, bitterness or anything else stand in the way.

Always keep going to Jesus seeking His mercy, grace and strength to carry on. Get involved in a Bible-believing church where you are loved unconditionally. Attend a women's Bible study if it is available. Constantly strive for a closer relationship with Jesus Christ. In fact, make it your number one priority.

TWO TOUGH TOPICS

Now here are two difficult recommendations. First, don't withhold sex. Part of God's design for marriage is the oneness that comes from physical intimacy, when a husband and wife give themselves to each other. Withholding sex isn't just denying your husband the pleasure that comes from the physical act of sex. Withholding sex prevents unity physically, emotionally, and spiritually. Marriage thrives on intimate unity—something you need now, more than ever.

*(Of course, if your husband has had an affair, don't have any type of sexual contact that would put you at risk. Wait until after he gets tested.)

Second, don't threaten to leave. You may be tempted to tell your husband that if he looks at pornography one more time you will file for divorce. All this does is tell your husband that it is better for him to keep secrets and that you aren't willing to hear the truth or work through difficulties. Wouldn't you rather be a safe woman for your husband and value honesty? You've already discovered what secrets can do to you personally. God is honest with us, no matter how painful the truth can be. The truth can be dealt with. But lies never allow for healing and restoration.

It's better to know the difficult truth that your husband has trained his mind to lust and is in need of help in correcting his backward thinking. It won't just happen overnight, and he will fall. If you allow him to be open and honest with you about the struggle—including any setbacks or miscues—you will be able to work openly with him in moving forward down the healing path. This also helps build trust. The alternative is to have him believe the lie of Satan that it is better to keep a secret life from you and only tell you of victories. Therefore, plan on staying the course. Give the Lord time to usher in healing and change.

I am not saying that there is never a time or good reason for separation. Before you do, be sure to get guidance from your pastor and godly women. In addition, don't expect that he will never have a setback. This process takes time. A life of repentance is the key, not a life of perfection. Fight to keep an eternal perspective. For instance, focus upon the hope of a restored marriage, even knowing that it will require much effort, and fight against the desire to give up what occurs when you focus on how difficult and painful the process is.

ADDITIONAL REMARKS

Be mindful of avoiding things that may undermine his recovery. For instance, don't schedule events on nights he has a support group meeting. You can also assist in his recovery in many ways, such as monitoring together what TV shows you watch. Most shows contain sexually suggestive content. If he wants to give up TV for a season, be willing to sacrifice and play games or engage in other activities. Similarly, be aware of what magazines you leave around the house.

One more suggestion: If either you or your husband have had sexual abuse issues, I urge you to read together one of the following books: *Rid of My Disgrace* by Justin and Lindsey Holcomb (Crossway) or The *Wounded Heart* by Dr. Dan Allender (NavPress). If these issues are a hindrance to your marriage, I also urge you to seek Christian counseling.

And finally, I want to remind you that you are not alone. There is hope. My marriage is better today than when we first got married. It was hard to forgive and trust my husband again, but it was worth every tear and all of the effort. Besides, the Lord promises to use all our pain and struggles for His glory. Just as we hope our husbands will become needy, dependent servants of the Lord, we, too, must turn to and trust in the Lord during our darkest moments and strive to live out the same six elements of a PROVEN life necessary for a healthy marriage. Be patient and part of the process. Keep praying for your husband and looking for ways to build him up.

A NOTE FOR SIGNLE WOMEN

Because single women have not made wedding vows, which have longer-lasting repercussions to their lives, they have a different decision to make. What they need to wrestle with is whether they can deal with this particular life challenge. They still need to bear in mind that all men (and all women) will have some major issue in life. The question is whether they can live with this particular stronghold. It's better to know prior to marriage whether you can view this as a "we problem" and not a "he problem."

MY PERSPECTIVE AS A HUSBAND AND GROUP LEADER

As a group leader for many years, I am constantly aware that everyone has one issue in their life that they cannot win on their own. I believe God does this for our own good so that we don't try to live independently from Him. For some wives, it is also sexual sins, and for others it may be worry or gossip. Don't get me wrong, I am not saying that all forms of sin are as painful as betrayal in the form of sexual

sin. But my point is that humans are prone to sin and setbacks.

When I first began leading purity support groups ten years ago, I wished that every man in my groups would immediately stop looking at pornography or masturbating. But it didn't work out that way. In fact, even many of the small-group leaders that I handpicked and trained after they went through the twelve-week study had at least one setback while leading a group. I spent a lot of time trying to figure out if I was a poor trainer or if my study was not effective. What I have concluded is that none of us will remain sinless, but we can daily strive to be PROVEN Men. I am convinced that the Lord is very pleased by our striving to turn to and rely on Him. God loves a needy, dependent servant, even when there are setbacks; just read the life of David in the Bible.

I love leading weekly support groups. What excites me most is seeing spiritual growth. I am constantly amazed as I hear story after story of men sharing what they have learned and how they have grown spiritually after a setback. I certainly don't glorify setbacks, but I have tears of joy whenever I listen to a man describe the way he has experienced the Lord in new or deeper ways after he has repented and experienced forgiveness. I love listening to them share what they have learned from the Lord. Perhaps I view it as the harder the struggle, the sweeter the victory.

Men grow closer to the Lord through these trials than they do when they have had an easy week. God could simply take away every lustful thought or deed. I believe, however, that God gets glory when men recognize they're hopeless and helpless without Him, when men toil each day to fight for purity, and when men run to Him when they have setbacks. I love watching men grow in the Lord over twelve weeks of the support group. I constantly remind men that the twelve weeks is just the beginning of the process. This is just a time of learning the basic fundamentals, and that it will take a lifetime of effort to keep growing in their faith and the sanctification process on earth.

I privately tell men that I am glad that I had a sin I couldn't defeat on my own. What I really mean is that I am glad that God didn't just take away the sin. I am glad that it was the hardest battle of my life. I am glad I couldn't just give it up with one prayer or one meeting with another man. If God had simply taken it away, I wouldn't have learned to rely on Him. I would never have gotten to know God as a daily Lord and Savior. I would have kept relying on myself. I would never have learned to hug another man. I would never have experienced the freedom to raise my hands in praise to God. I would never have wanted to talk about my feelings or see the need to be open and honest in discussions with my wife. I would never have known a real marriage. In the end, I would be the same proud and selfish man, just without one particular sin I found disgusting.

The reality is that most men going through PROVEN Men support groups stumble. I don't use shame or guilt to try to get them to step in line because that is not how Jesus works. He uses unconditional love to draw us to Him. Thus, I have learned to tell men that victory is not absence of sin, but how they respond to it. Let me repeat that. The mark of a PROVEN Man is not whether he sins, but how he responds to a setback. In fact, a setback is an opportunity to learn from and lean upon God. I'd rather have a man who repents

than one who pretends he is setback free, and I am sure you do too.

As a former sex addict who sinned and deeply wounded his wife, but now leads support groups, I encourage all the wives reading this chapter to emulate Christ, who values openness, offers unconditional love, and is committed to being a helper.

Encourage your man to keep striving to be a PROVEN Man, knowing there is no perfect husband or wife. Both sexual healing and marriage are lifelong commitments. Be patient, courageous, and willing to join your husband as a partner fighting against the spiritual forces at work to destroy your husband and your marriage.

APPENDIX K—A SURVIVOR STORY (AS TOLD BY MY FRIEND)

The sexual abuse started when I was very young, only seven years old. My stepfather molested me. I immediately told my mom what had happened. We had a "family meeting," during which my stepdad denied his actions. His denial was painful, but even more so was my mother's response. She took my stepdad's side, believing his story rather than mine. Her refusal to believe me combined with her unwillingness to do anything about the abuse destroyed me. The rest of my childhood was clouded with fear, shame and confusion.

Although my stepdad never touched me again in a sexual way, I lived in perpetual fear of what he might do to me. He was with us for the next ten years, and I felt unsafe in my own home every day. When he entered my bedroom at night, he would rub my head, and I waited in fear for what he might do next. I remember sneaking in to my brother's room on many nights just to feel safe.

The abuse wasn't limited to my home life. One of my friend's brothers tried to rape me. I had multiple other encounters with people trying to take advantage of me sexually, including other women. I developed a deep fear of anyone touching me, even with a hug.

Internally, I was conflicted. I was told my entire childhood that sex is bad and dirty, but I enjoyed the way that sexual touch made me feel. I became sexually active at fourteen, exploring sexual behavior but drawing a strong boundary line with sexual intercourse. I was willing to do anything but have sex because I was told you had to be a virgin when you get married.

I carried my fear and confusion around with me for years. I didn't tell anyone my story—not in high school, college, or even when I got married. Unfortunately, my husband had to deal with all the consequences of my sexual abuse. I projected all my fear and mistrust on to him, and he had no idea why I was such a mess. I didn't want to be naked in front of him. My shame and insecurity made me hesitant to have sex, which in turn made him feel insecure, unattractive and angry.

In my mid-twenties, I went to see a counselor because my general doctor thought I was depressed. After finally opening up to someone almost two decades later, I felt like I could breathe again. A huge weight had been lifted off my chest. Through my counseling, I realized I needed to share my past with my husband.

I went crazy with fear right before I told him about my abuse. I was afraid that he would want to leave me. Rather than run, he listened to my story. He believed my story. He embraced me. He cried with me. His response was foundational for my healing journey.

I finally realized that I needed to surrender my fear. Sharing my story with the counselor and my husband opened the door to trust. I clung to 2 Timothy 1:7, "For God has not given us a spirit of fear, but of power and of love and of a sound mind."

God taught me that HE alone was my refuge. He had given me my husband to help me on the journey to healing, but he would certainly let me down at some point. In fact, he also struggled with looking at pornography. When I found out, my old fears and insecurities began to creep in. But God reminded me that my worth was in Him alone. Even if my husband failed me, God never would. He promised to never leave me (Hebrews 13:5).

I learned what it means to be truly loved. The same God that sent His only Son to die for me is the same God that also calls me His child, His own (1 John 3:1). My earthly stepdad was abusing his role as father for his own selfish desires, which brought fear and shame. But my Heavenly Father poured Himself out for me in selfless love, dying on the cross, so that we could share a relationship that brings wholeness and healing. I no longer needed to be a slave to fear, because "perfect love casts out fear" (1 John 4:18). That perfect love was not found in the arms of an earthly father or even my husband, but in the arms of my Savior.

 **APPENDIX L**

It all started with a rumor. It was a nasty rumor about MY husband. A friend of a friend of a friend told me there was reason to believe my husband, Scott, had been unfaithful to me. The source of this rumor was less than reliable, so mostly I tried to shrug it off. I had no apparent reason to suspect anything like this, but something in my gut wouldn't shake it. I took the rest of the day off work and went for a long walk in the nearby park to sort out my thoughts and pray. I knew I couldn't go to my husband with just a rumor—that would be way too easy to deny if it were true. I asked God to show me what to do and to lead me in the direction I should go. Hours went by and I still had no answers, and now I needed to get home to my two young children. I was minutes from my house when my phone rang.

I didn't recognize the voice on the other end at first. It was an ex-colleague of my husband's. She had moved away to a different state about a year ago. She called because she felt she needed to come clean about her affair with my husband. I was speechless. She was in tears. She said she had wanted to call for so long and tell me, but she didn't have the courage. She also told me she wasn't the only one. Now my head was spinning. How had I missed this? How did I have no idea? How had I been so completely fooled? As these thoughts raced through my mind, I couldn't help but also feel compassion toward this woman. You see, the Lord had been opening my eyes over the past few painful months to the depths of my own sin. The Holy Spirit had been lovingly showing me my desperate need for my Savior. It was wave after wave of ugly truth followed by His abounding grace to cover each and every offense. Now I knew why. He was preparing me for THIS moment. I remember telling this woman (who I knew to be a Christian): "I want you to know that I forgive you. I want you to know that God will completely cleanse you from this sin and you are holy and blameless as you stand before Him without a single fault (Col 1:22)." I knew God was speaking to this woman through me. This is what she most needed to hear, and strangely, I wasn't mad at her. Immediately after I said those words, I hung up.

It felt like I had been punched in the gut. While I felt an almost immediate release of anger and bitterness toward this woman, I did NOT feel that way toward my husband. That night, I confronted him with the information I knew. At first, he denied it; but eventually, he admitted that he had had several affairs over the course of our nearly ten-year marriage. He also admitted to using porn on a somewhat regular basis. I had never seen him so broken, and it was the first time I had ever seen him cry. I believed he was sorry, and he was willing to do whatever it took to repair our marriage. However, I asked him to move out of our home for a time, so I could sort through my emotions and decide if our relationship could be salvaged.

The next few months were a blur. I remember standing on the tile floor in my bathroom and feeling like my whole world had crashed around me. The only "solid ground" I felt I could stand on was the one square foot of tile under my feet. Everything else had fallen away. All that I thought was true of my marriage felt like a lie. During this tumultuous time, I sought out a counselor who helped me to see that Scott's decision to stray in our marriage was not ultimately about me at all. She gave a voice and validated my feelings without giving me license to necessarily act on them. Meanwhile, Scott was going through Proven Men, and God was using it to confront his pride and selfishness while revealing His grace and mercy at the same time. He wrote me letters every day, sharing what he was learning and how God was transforming his heart and mind.

I appreciated his efforts and I was encouraged to see the Holy Spirit at work in Scott's life, but my heart was so far from him. I felt insecure and unsure of myself around him. I wanted to hide and protect myself from any further hurt. He felt like the enemy. I was not sure I could forgive him; however, I had decided that I did not want to leave the marriage. I did not want to break up my family and split our home when Scott was clearly repentant and making himself accountable to godly men. I just didn't know what to do with my anger, sadness and broken heart.

It was about this time that God began to show me what my attitude was toward forgiveness and how much it differed from how He forgives. I had postured myself toward Scott like this:

"You need to make this better. I'm not going to tell you how. You just need to figure that out. IF you can do that *and* I FEEL like it, I will forgive you. BUT, you can NEVER do this again!"

Wow, that is *not* how God forgives.

"He does not treat us as our sins deserve or repay us according to our iniquities. For as high as the heavens are above the earth, so great is His love towards those who fear Him. As far as the east is from the west, so far has He removed our transgressions from us" (Psalm 103:10-12).

"I have swept away your sins like a cloud. I have scattered your offenses like the morning mist" (Isaiah 44:22).

"He is so rich in kindness and grace that He purchased our freedom with the blood of his son and forgave our sins" (Ephesians 1:7).

What if God forgave like I did? What if He was waiting for me to "pay my dues" and strive and strain to *earn* His forgiveness? I could never do it! And what if He was willing to forgive me so long as I never sinned again? I could never have His forgiveness. I would be lost in my sins.

But He forgives wholly and completely through Jesus. "He cancelled the record of the charges against us and took it away by nailing it to the cross" (Colossians 2:13-14). His forgiveness is "once for all" as the book of Hebrews recounts over and over again. And He asks me to "Be kind to one another tenderhearted, forgiving one another just as God, through Christ, has forgiven you" (Ephesians 4:32). I begged God to help me forgive like He does. He showed me it is an act of my *will* and not based on my feelings or circumstances.

I read once that "forgiveness is absorption." It is choosing to absorb the pain someone else has caused you without passing it along or continuing that pain in the world. This is what God had done for me. He had absorbed my sin in His own body, through Jesus, and clothed me with His righteousness.

"God made Him who had no sin to be sin for us so that in Him, we might become the righteousness of God" (2 Corinthians 5:21).

Before I could forgive Scott in this way, I first needed to "count the cost." I needed to list out all that his actions have cost me. I knew my list was not exhaustive, but it was necessary to see what I was actually forgiving him for. I wrote things like:

- You have broken my trust
- You have humiliated me
- You have wounded my sexuality and sense of worthiness
- You have told so many lies
- You have put my health at risk

I decided, with God's help, and as an act of my will, to forgive Scott. I made note of the day and time and circled it in my journal. I knew I would have to remind myself of this decision over and over as the feelings surfaced. I invited him over one night about four months after the initial discovery. I read the list I had written of all the damage done and the wounds inflicted. I told him that I was choosing to forgive him for each offense on the page. I was choosing not to hold his sin against him and to release him from anything that he owed me. I choked a bit on my words and it was very hard to do, but I knew God was leading me. *I told him that trust would have to be earned, but not my forgiveness.* I didn't know after that if God would restore our marriage, but I DID have peace knowing that God has plunged our sins so deep in the sea of His grace, that He was with me and that He would heal these wounds.

HEARTWORK

Based on what we have been studying this week, how does the wife in this story exemplify what it means to be a safe wife? How does she RESPOND to her husband in a safe way? What actions reveal her desire to show him RESPECT? What actions does she take to RESTORE their relationship? Consider the boundaries she put into place, the godly counsel she sought, and the forgiveness she extended. Write your responses in the space provided below.

_____

_____

_____

_____

_____

_____

_____

_____

_____

_____

 # Appendix M—It's A Big Deal

NOTE: The material in this appendix is quite heavy and may be hard to read with your heart in a such a raw state. It is not meant to discourage you, but more to give you an understanding that a sexual addiction causes so much pain and destruction. The physical, social, psychological, and spiritual damaging effects of this addiction are far reaching, but no sin has enough power to overcome the love and forgiveness of Jesus Christ through His death on the cross. Before you read further, take a moment to pray. Ask God to give you a heart of compassion just like His as you seek to understand your husband's addiction.

Is pornography really a big deal? Seriously, it's just pictures, right? According to our society, it's the norm for a man to look at pornography. A particular episode from the popular '90s sitcom *Friends* sheds great light on the mainstream perspective on this topic. Two of the main characters, Joey and Chandler, somehow get a free porn channel and refuse to turn off the TV for fear they would lose access. They create a "protective porn bubble" and don't want to be known as "the two guys who turned off free porn." The obvious message is that viewing pornography is intertwined with being a man. As the old saying goes, "Boys will be boys." After all, what harm can come from just a look?

Pornography is the biggest money maker on the internet. People spend billions of dollars each year on internet porn. Why is there such an insatiable thirst for these sexual images worldwide?

In his book *False Intimacy*, Dr. Harry W. Schaumburg explains the roots of sexual addiction in great detail. Schaumburg has over twenty years of counseling experience with individuals struggling with sexual sin. He explains that "sexual fantasy stems from a desire to **gain more in a relationship than is possible**. It's an attempt to **gorge ourselves with passion** and move into a state **free of any chance for disappointment**. Simply put, we want to enter the Garden of Eden again" (p. 88–89).

When a person chooses to look at pornography or escape into fantasy, they choose to ignore or withdraw from real relationships in an attempt to meet their relational needs in a safe and controlled environment. So, why is it so appealing to men (and yes, to women as well)? The truth is that Satan tricks us into swapping out real intimacy with false intimacy. He tempts us with the easy button.

Essentially, pornography is **lazy love. It promises a form of sex that doesn't require any effort.** The woman in the magazine or on the screen demands nothing but wants to provide everything you desire and imagine. She's always available at your convenience and requires no further commitment. You can look as long as you want, capture the image in your memory, and recall it later when you want it for your own personal pleasure. What is the result of this "lazy love"? Let's look at three major consequences of an addiction to porn or fantasy. Knowing how it harms relationships helps build a resolve to retrain our brains (and hearts) to seek true intimacy. It can help you, too, by knowing how your husband is being fooled and harmed by the master deceiver.

1. PORNOGRAPHY BREEDS GUILT AND SHAME

Porn and fantasy only provide a physical and sexual release. They don't fulfill any emotional needs. The initial momentary pleasure experienced after sexual release is immediately overshadowed by guilt and shame.

Genesis 2:24-25 says, "That is why a man leaves his father and mother and is united to his wife, and they become one flesh. Adam and his wife were both naked, and they felt no shame."

Notice a few things about the passage. Adam and Eve were naked and unashamed. Their relationship was unmarred by sin at this point in time, so they experienced complete freedom and acceptance within their marriage. They saw each other completely raw and unadorned in any fashion and were drawn to one another. They were giving 100 percent of themselves, unafraid and without any false pretense, resulting in unity and fulfillment.

A relationship with pornography reflects the exact opposite. The user comes to the table expecting something, wanting something to fulfill their own desires and wants, without any thought of how that desire will affect the other person. The object of their fantasy typically must live up to some kind of standard—a certain body size or shape, exhibiting specific kinds of behaviors (ex: overly aggressive or submissive), and must be willing to give all of themselves in order for the user to experience sexual pleasure. All take and no give. The result is guilt and shame.

David, known in the Bible as "a man after God's own heart" (1 Samuel 13:14, Acts 13:22), speaks of the guilt resulting from sexual sin. 2 Samuel 11 recounts a story that would rival any soap opera plot. David committed adultery with Bathsheba while her husband, Uriah, was off to war, and then successfully carried out a murder plot against him. Months later, when confronted by the prophet Nathan, David recognized the gravity of his sin.

Read Psalm 32:1-5, paying special attention to verse 3-4. How does David describe the guilt he felt in these verses?

_____

_____

_____

_____

_____

Have you ever felt that way? Do you think your husband has experienced these feelings as a result of his pornography addiction? Write down your thoughts.

_____

_____

_____

_____

_____

_____

At some point, sin will bring these intense feelings of conviction within your spouse if he is a believer (John 16:8). The Holy Spirit will convict him. Unfortunately, when the godly conviction designed to bring "repentance that leads to salvation" is ignored, Satan swoops in to bring condemnation and "worldly sorrow" that "brings death" (2 Corinthians 7:10). Satan's plot is to "steal, kill and destroy"; the guilt and shame that result from a pornography addiction are the fruits of his plan to annihilate God's design to bring abundant life (John 10:10).

Reflect on whether you are breathing life, God's word, or condemnation into your spouse.

_____

_____

_____

_____

_____

_____

_____

2. PORNOGRAPHY BRINGS ISOLATION

Shame results in isolation. Pornography is self-centered and anti-relational. Over time users train themselves to be selfishly served and instantly gratified. They also discipline themselves to withhold love and affection. A self-centered effort to control life and the effort of relationships ends up blocking perfect union with God. When an addict chases after the idols of selfish pleasure, they build a dividing wall. Every time they turn to pornography, they put on blinders to the Lord and to their spouse.

The user retreats into a fantasy world—alone and secluded behind closed doors. This stands in stark contrast to the marriage relationship found in Eden, where Adam and Eve shared a publicly open and free relationship with no guilt or shame.

Those with a pornography addiction live in fear of being discovered, convinced that rejection is certain to follow. This creates a dangerous cycle for a sex addict. Rather than coming to the light and sharing their struggle, they retreat again into their "safe" world of pornography where they feel accepted and desired.

Perhaps you have felt the result of the porn cycle in your marriage (guilt, shame and isolation). Before my husband confessed his addiction, I knew something was wrong with our relationship, but I just couldn't pin it down. What I was feeling was the third consequence of pornography.

3. PORNOGRAPHY HARMS REAL RELATIONSHIPS

Repeatedly turning to pornography and fantasy causes the addict to view women as sex objects. A woman is always viewed naked for the sole purpose of providing a sexual experience. Sex becomes an inward, self-pleasing form of a phantom relationship. Women become nothing more than objects of sexual desire.

Pornography creates a barrier to healthy sex. Inevitably, the addict will compare their wife to the airbrushed, perfect, naked images that are available at a moment's notice. Sex forums and stories create false ideas of what sex is like and how it should take place. The woman on the other side of the screen never says no and never has any needs to be met. The sexual encounter requires no effort on the addict's end.

When a wife learns about her husband's addiction, trust and respect are shattered. This damage to the foundation of a healthy marriage often results in her emotional and sexual withdrawal. Although it is a normal response, a wife reacting this way can bring additional guilt and isolation, which in turn perpetuates the unhealthy cycle of sin leading to shame.

For reflection:
How have you seen the three consequence of sexual addiction played out in your marriage?

Book Recommendations

Search for Significance by Robert McGee (Thomas Nelson, 1990)

False Intimacy by Harry Schaumburg (NavPress, 1992)

The Wounded Heart by Dan Allender (NavPress, 1990)

Love and Respect by Emerson Eggerichs (Thomas Nelson, 2004)

Intimate Issues by Linda Dillow (Waterbrook Press, 1999)

When Godly People Do Ungodly Things by Beth Moore (Broadman and Holman, 2003)

Living with Your Husband's Secret Wars by Marsha Means (Fleming H. Revel, 1999)

Through Deep Waters: Letters to Hurting Wives by Kathy Gallagher (Pure Life Ministries, 2001)

Hope After Betrayal by Meg Wilson (Kregel Publications, 2007)

Boundaries in Marriage by Henry Cloud and John Townsend (Zondervan, 1999)

Intimacy Ignited by Joseph and Linda Dillow and Peter and Lorraine Pintus (NavPress, 2014)

For your husband or significant other
Proven Men Study by Joel Hesch (2013)—www.provenmen.org

For women struggling with sexual integrity
Proven Women Workbook Study by Emily Woody and Joel Hesch (2019)—www.provenwomen.org

PW ENDNOTES

1. Harry Schaumburg, *False Intimacy*, p. 18–22

2. Harry Schuamburg, *False Intimacy*, p. 88

3. Mike Wilkerson, *Redemption*, p. 31–32

4. Wendy Alsup, blog entry, "Practical Theology for Women"

5. Mike Wilkerson, *Redemption*, p. 111–112

6. Mike Wilkerson, *Redemption*, p. 48

7. Mike Wilkerson, *Redemption*, p. 49

8. Mike Wilkerson, *Redemption*, p. 52

9. Tim Keller, *Counterfit Gods*

10. Douglas K. Stewart, *Exodus*, New American Commentary 2, p. 661

11. Robert McGee, *The Search for Significance*, p. 7

12. Robert McGee, *The Search for Significance*, p. 19-20

13. Robert McGee, *The Search for Significance*, p. 21

14. Robert McGee, *The Search for Significance*, p. 24

15. Robert McGee, *The Search for Significance*, p. 30

16. Robert McGee, *The Search for Significance*, p. 26

17. Robert McGee, *The Search for Significance*, p. 25

18. Robert McGee, *The Search for Significance*, p. 27

19. Robert McGee, *The Search for Significance*, p. 59

20. Robert McGee, *The Search for Significance*, p. 26

21. Robert McGee, *The Search for Significance*, p. 27

22. Robert McGee, *The Search for Significance*, p. 69

23. Chris Tomlin, "Enough"

24. Swindoll, *New Testament Insights*, p. 212

25. Swindoll, *New Testament Insights*, p. 214

26. Swindoll, *New Testament Insights*, p. 215

27. Pat Benatar, "Love Is A Battlefield"

28. Steven J. Cole, *God's Design—Marriage*

29. Linda Dillow, *What's It Like to Be Married to Me?*

30. Linda Dillow, *What's It Like to Be Married to Me?*, p. 98

31. Brené Brown, *Listening to Shame*

32. Harry Shaumburg, *False Intimacy*, p. 114–120

33. Charles of the Ritz, *Enjoli*, 1980

34. Brené Brown, *Listening to Shame*

35. Mike Wilkerson, *Redemption*, p. 80

36. Harry Shaumburg, *False Intimacy*, p. 211

37. Harry Shaumburg, *False Intimacy*, p. 211–212

38. Mike Wilkerson, *Redemption*, p. 134

39. Mike Wilkerson, *Redemption*, p. 83–84

40. Harry Schaumburg, *False Intimacy*, p.146

41. Harry Schaumburg, *False Intimacy*, p.146

42. Harry Shaumburg, *False Intimacy*, p. 124

43. Linda Dillow, *What's It Like to Be Married to Me?*, p. 102–103

44. Emmerson Eggrichs, *Love and Respect*, p. 57

45. Linda Dillow, *What's It Like to Be Married to Me?*, p. 104

46. Harry Shaumburg, *False Intimacy*, p. 18–22

47. Meg Wilson, *Hope After Betrayal*, p. 50

48. Meg Wilson, *Hope After Betrayal*, p. 50–51

49. David Guzik, *Bible Commentary*

50. Brené Brown, *Listening to Shame*

51. Dave Ramsey, "Ask Dave," To be unclear is to be unkind, https://www.daveramsey.com/askdave/relationships/to-be-unclear-is-to-be-unkind

52. Meg Wilson, *Hope After Betrayal*, p. 73–74

53. Meg Wilson, *Hope After Betrayal*, p. 87–88

54. Mark Driscoll, *Real Marriage*, p. 170–171

55. Mark Driscoll, *Real Marriage*, p. 171–174

56. Mark Driscoll, *Real Marriage*, p. 175–176

57. Mark Driscoll, *Real Marriage*, p. 159

58. Harry Schaumburg, *False Intimacy*, p. 145–146

59. Mark Driscoll, *Real Marriage*, p. 160

60. *Snow White and the Seven Dwarfs*. Directed by Larry Morey, David Hand, Ben Sharpsteen, Wilfred Jackson, Perce Pearce, and Wiliam Cottrell. 1937. The Walt Disney Company, Walt Disney Animation Studios, DVD.

61. JD Greear, "You Aren't the Good Samaritan" last modified April 24, 2017. https://jdgreear.com/blog/arent-good-samaritan/

62. Jason DeRouchie, "Love God with Your Everything" last modified October 10, 2013. https://www.desiringgod.org/articles/love-god-with-your-everything

Made in the USA
Middletown, DE
27 February 2023

25821866R00157